THE
PIRATE COAST

Author of:
Siwa, the Oasis of Jupiter Ammon (1923)
Personal Column (Autobiography) (1960)

THE
PIRATE COAST

BY

SIR CHARLES BELGRAVE

LONDON
G. BELL AND SONS LTD
1966

Printed in Great Britain by
ROBERT CUNNINGHAM & SONS LTD, ALVA

CONTENTS

PLATES

The first six plates are taken from the collection of sixteen, published in April 1813 by W. Haines, of 10 South Molton Street, London. They were drawn by Major R. Temple of H.M. 65th Regiment, and are described on the title page as 'Sixteen views in the Persian Gulf taken in the years 1809-10, illustrative of the Forces employed on the Expedition sent from Bombay under the command of Captain Wainwright of H.M.S. *Chiffone* and Lieut.-Colonel Smith of H.M. 65th Regiment against the Arabian Pirates', and the book is dedicated to Lieut.-Colonel L. Smith and the Officers of H.M. 65th Regiment.

INTRODUCTION

FRANCIS ERSKINE LOCH, whose diary covering the years 1818 to 1820 forms the basis of this book, was the fourth and youngest son of George Loch of Drylaw, near Edinburgh. He belonged to a family of great antiquity, which originated in the Forest of Dean, on the borders of Gloucestershire and Herefordshire. In very early times, the name of the family was Lacu, later it became Loch. The Lochs moved to Scotland, and were established there at the beginning of the 13th century.

Francis Loch's father died when his son was an infant, and at the age of eleven, Francis entered the Royal Navy as a midshipman. He served in the Mediterranean, in South America, and off the coast of Spain. He was thirty years old, when he came out to the Persian Gulf in command of H.M.S. *Eden*. He had relations in India; one of them was John Adam, a distinguished member of the Bengal Government, who was a cousin on his mother's side, she being Mary Adam of Blair Adam, a member of the family to which belonged the two famous architects, Robert and James Adam.

Loch's diary is in the possession of Mary Freda Loch, the widow of David Henry Loch, who was a grandson of Francis Loch, and it is owing to her kindness that I have been allowed to make use of it.

Having lived in the Persian Gulf for thirty one years, from 1926 to 1957, in the service of the grandfather, and then the father of the present Shaikh of Bahrain, I know the people and the locality. I have tried in this book to describe the historical background of the places in the Gulf which Loch visited. In some cases, I have continued the subsequent history of the leading people with whom he had dealings.

With the diary, there is a letter from Loch addressed to his children. It is dated June 6th 1835, and was written at Darnhall, a house near Eddleston in Peebles-shire, where Loch lived for some years—it was part of the property which the Loch family had owned for 600 years.

My Dear Children,

The following pages were compiled from various notes and Memoranda taken during the time that I had the Naval Command in the Persian Gulph and also while acting in concert with the Expedition which succeeded in the total overthrow and destruction of the Pirates of those Seas, likewise while in India.

I had long kept those notes and Memoranda by me without meaning to make the slightest use of them, but on casually showing them to some of my intimate friends and acquaintances they strenuously advised me to place them in such a shape that they might hereafter be an amusement, if not a utility, to you all. I so intended when, on again showing them to some more of my friends, they conceived that my manuscript ought to be published.

Loch gives the various reasons why his friends were in favour of his publishing the journal. 'One stated that, even partial as was the account which I had given of the mouths of the Indus, yet it is more than is generally known and contains a great deal of curious and interesting information. It cleared up many points between ancient and modern history, which must naturally interest The Reading Man and give knowledge about what he did not thoroughly understand before to the Geographer.'

This refers to Loch's lengthy dissertations on the course of the voyage of Nearchus, an Admiral of Alexander the Great, along the Indian and Persian coasts, and his theories about the Jewish settlements on the west coast of India. These I have not included in the extracts from his diary.

Loch continues: 'Again I was requested by a Gentleman to allow him, at some future date, when he had leisure, to make extracts for the purpose of printing them at his own expense. Lastly I was informed by another of my friends that the time – I thought my book would come out in the Spring of this year – was just when as I ought to publish, as there was an expedition on the point of starting, under Captain Chesney, to explore that part of Syria lying between the Mediterranean and the Euphrates, and from thence to India, for the purpose of establishing steam navigation by that route.'

Chesney's survey was successfully carried out in 1835-37 and in 1850 he published an account of the expedition in four large volumes. In one of them he devoted several chapters to the exploits of Alexander and Nearchus.

Encouraged by his friends, Loch determined to get his manuscript published; he was advised that 'London was the place where it should be brought out. So off we all went, I expecting that it would at once be placed in the hands of one of the great publishers, by them to be got up in the usual way, being placed in the hands of one of their "Hack Writers", who, as you must know, are the real book makers, frisking out such parts as meet his approbation, dressing it up for the sake of the public, adding what he thinks of advantage and cutting off what he thinks extraneous. In fact, a man's book is not his book but the mind from which it is compiled is all that belongs to him. While I buoyed myself up with the hope that there would soon be published "A Narrative of Transactions, written by Francis E. Loch, esqr, Captain R.N. while in command of the *Eden* in India", I received, to my chagrin, a letter saying that the papers had not been sent to a publisher but were to be read to some more of my friends in London.'

Some of Loch's friends thought that it was too late to publish a book because other people had written on the subject since he had been in the Gulf, and some suggested that 'the people of the Gulf had totally changed from what they were at the period of my having written about them. Another thought that it ought not to be published, but should be kept as a private Memorandum.' The suggestion that the Gulf Arabs had 'totally changed' in a period of fifteen years shows how little Loch's friends knew about the Gulf.

After these disappointments, Loch decided to place the manuscript in the hands of 'some entire stranger, on whose judgement I might depend'. But after six months, he received an unfavourable report from 'the entire stranger', who pointed out that much of Loch's scientific information had been anticipated by later publications.

At the end of Loch's long letter, he says:

... the time lost, the aspersions against the book appearing, the feelings of some of my nearest friends against it being brought forward, is the cause of its being as it now is, in its naked state, instead of being well and gaudily dressed, fit to enter into the best society, as I at one time expected the Darling Child of my brain would have been. But you, my dear children of my body, must have a kindly feeling for your brother in misfortune and look upon him with the affection which is naturally produced from knowing that you have sprung from the same sire.

Believe me, my dear children,

to be your most sincere and affectionate father,

Francis E. Loch.

I am glad to think that 130 years after Loch wrote this letter to his children 'the Darling Child' of his brain will see the light of day.

CHARLES BELGRAVE

CHAPTER I

'High on a throne of royal state, which far
Outshone the wealth of Ormus and of Ind,
Or where the gorgeous East with richest hand
Showers on her kings barbaric pearl and gold.'
Paradise Lost: John Milton – 1608-1674

THE Persian Gulf, which the Arabs now call the Arabian Gulf, is almost an inland sea. At its widest, it is 180 miles from the eastern coast of Arabia to the coast of Persia, and at the south-east end, the Straits of Hormuz, which divide the Persian Gulf from the Gulf of Oman, are only thirty-five miles wide. What used to be known as the 'Pirate Coast', reaching from the Qatar peninsula to the borders of Oman, has been named the 'Trucial Coast' since 1820, when a treaty was concluded between the British and the Shaikhs of the Coastal States. Though this designation is used by Europeans, it has not been adopted by the Arabs who live in the area.

The Pirate Coast was an ideal place for sea robbers. It is studded with little islands, indented with narrow, twisting creeks, protected by treacherous sand banks, and jagged coral reefs, which are often only a few feet below the water level. Even today, navigation along the coast is difficult and dangerous. Until the present century, the Gulf had not been thoroughly surveyed, and ships, when sailing inshore, had to move slowly and cautiously, taking soundings incessantly. Inland, beyond the bleak, low-lying beaches, a barren coastal plain extends to a range of low, rocky hills, or at some places, to where the sands of the great desert begin. At infrequent intervals, wretched villages of palm branch huts crouch on the shore near wells of brackish water. The coast is almost without vegetation, except around some of the wells where a few sparse date palms are, with difficulty, persuaded to grow. The Pirate Coast has always been a forbidding place, scorching hot in summer, whipped by savage sand storms and swept by sea gales when the shamaal wind rages down the Gulf from the north in the winter.

The Persian Gulf is one of the oldest sea routes in the world, and is probably the sea on which mankind first practised navigation. Danish archaeologists, who have been working in Bahrain, and elsewhere in the Gulf, for the last ten years, have now established the fact that the Bahrain islands are the ancient Dilmun, famous as a trading centre since the third millennium. In ancient times Dilmun traded with the cities of the Indus valley. Ships from Ur of the Chaldees, and later from Babylon, sailed down to Dilmun, and carried back to Mesopotamia cargoes of gold, precious stones, ivory, frankincense, teak wood, and copper from the mines of Makan in the mountains of Oman, where the ancient workings can still be seen.

These recent archaeological discoveries disprove the belief which used to be held by many historians that the Persian Gulf was the original home of the Phoenicians, and that it was they who built the vast necropolis in Bahrain. The thousands of sepulchral mounds, covering large areas of the islands, are now rapidly disappearing as the lorries of contractors remove the material from the tombs for building and road work.

As early as the 8th century B.C., there were pirates in the Gulf. Ships sailing in the Gulf in those days used to hug the coast, anchoring at nightfall, and continuing their voyage at dawn; the crews often slept on shore, and it was then that they were liable to be attacked. So serious was the danger from pirates that in about 690 B.C., Sennacherib, the Assyrian King, sent an expedition against them, and forced many of them to settle at Gerrha in Hasa, on the Arabian coast opposite Bahrain. Gerrha afterwards became an important port, whence caravan routes led northwards to Mesopotamia and westwards, skirting the Arabian desert. Gerrha is identified with either Oquair or Katif, most probably the latter.

In classical times more was known about the Persian Gulf. In 326 B.C., Alexander the Great was forced to abandon his project of advancing farther into India because his Macedonian troops refused to proceed. He decided to send part of his army back to Babylon by sea, while he and the rest of his troops returned by land, following the coast. He assembled a great fleet at Jhelum, in the Punjab, and after almost a year, the army and the fleet arrived at the mouth of the Indus. The command of the fleet was given to Nearchus, a man from Crete, who successfully navigated the unknown waters of the Arabian Sea and the Persian Gulf, arriving at Ahwaz after a voyage of 146 days. The voyage of Nearchus, the places which he visited, and the inhabitants of the coast – barbarians as he calls them – are fully described by Arrian. He mentions the tides, which were strange to the Greek sailors, accustomed only to the tideless Mediterranean Sea, and he remarks on the arrow-shaped fish traps, built of palm stick fences, which are still a curious feature of the seascape along the coasts of the Gulf, very conspicuous when seen from the air.

Other Greek and Roman writers refer to the Gulf, but they often repeat the statements which were made by Nearchus in his journal. There is frequent mention of the pirates who infested the seas, and Pliny describes the archers who were kept on the ships to defend them from piratical attacks. The people of the coast were, generally, said to be cruel and treacherous. In A.D. 45, the pilot Hippalus discovered the theory of the monsoons which till then had been known only to the mariners of the Eastern seas. The Periplus of the Erythrean Sea, a nautical directory of the Red Sea and Indian Ocean, written by a Greek towards the end of the first century, contains some remarks about the Gulf. He, too, mentions the pirates. In about A.D. 116, the Roman Emperor Trajan, in emulation of the exploits of Alexander, after defeating the Parthians, led a naval expedition into the Gulf, and ravaged the coast of Arabia, whence most of the pirates came. Again, in the reign of Shapur II, who was King of Persia from A.D. 310 until 379, a naval force was sent against the Arabs of Hajar, which is now called Hasa, in retaliation for their piratical raids on the Persian coast. The Arabs who were taken prisoners in this expedition had their shoulders pierced, and were strung together with ropes to prevent their escape. From his barbarous treatment of the prisoners, Shapur earned the name of 'Zulaklaf' – Lord of the Shoulders – by which he is known in Arab history.

In the period before the coming of Islam, while Persians and Byzantines were engaged in warring against each other, the Gulf Arabs continued their sea trade with India. Silk from China became one of the most valuable commodities in which they traded. They carried some of their merchandise from the ports of the Gulf by camel trains on the desert caravan routes leading northward and westward. Although it almost certainly existed, there is no mention of piracy at this period: it was always most

3

popular when the victims were of a foreign race and of a different religion.

Soon after Islam was established by Mohammed in the Hejaz, the tribes on the Arabian coast sent deputations to Mecca and subsequently embraced the new religion. Later, Oman which the King of Persia claimed as a vassal state, accepted Islam. But during the troublous times which followed the death of Mohammed, the Bahrain Arabs reverted to their old religion which in some cases was Christianity. In early Islamic times, the name Bahrain applied to the whole of the Arabian littoral, as well as to the islands, which were known as Awal. It was after Europeans came to the Gulf that only the islands were called by their present name of Bahrain. In the time of the first Caliph, Abu Bakr, and during the reign of his successor, Omar, the Gulf Arabs were once again converted to Islam, this time by force of arms. But Oman, in spite of attempts by subsequent Caliphs to subjugate the country, retained a certain independence, and for many centuries the Omanis elected their own religious leaders, who were known as Imams. At the beginning of the 9th century, pirates were again active in Oman waters and the Caliph despatched an expedition against them.

During the next two centuries the Arabs of the Gulf and the Bahrain islands supported two formidable insurrections against the authority of the Caliphs. The first rebellion was led by Ali bin Mohammed, a man of Persian origin, who claimed descent from the Prophet Mohammed. He raised a revolt among the negro slaves who worked in the saltpetre deposits in the marsh country south of Basra. He was joined by many of the Arab tribes from Iraq and Arabia, whose allegiance to the Orthodox faith was not strong. The slave rebellion lasted for some fifteen years, during which the Arab coast came under the control of the rebels, who in 871 had captured Basra.

At the beginning of the 10th century, Bahrain became the centre of another religious movement, whose fanatical followers were known as Carmathians, named after the founder of the sect, Hamdan Carmat, who came originally from Persia. Their belief was an extreme form of Shiism. For more than a century the Carmathians were in control of the whole of Arabia, and they extended their conquests into Iraq and Syria, plundering Basra and threatening Baghdad, the seat of the Abassid Caliphs. Their

4

1. The wall and beach near Ras al Khaima with the troops preparing to land, November 13th 1809

II. The troops landing at Ras al Khaima

influence spread to Egypt, whose Fatimid Caliph they acknowledged. In 928, a Carmathian army took Mecca, and after a
savage slaughter they removed the sacred black stone from the
Caaba, and set it up in Hasa, the Carmathian capital, where it
remained for twenty years. When the power of the Carmathians
waned, the Arabian peninsula was left in a state of anarchy, with
the tribes fighting against each other. Little is known about the
Arab coast of the Gulf from this time, until the first Europeans
made their appearance there.

In mediaeval times the city of Hormuz on the Persian coast
became the emporium of the Gulf trade, superseding the position
previously held by Kais, another port on the Persian coast. Hormuz was founded in the 3rd century by Ardeshir, the first of the
Sasanian Kings of Persia, whose dynasty reigned till the conquest
of Persia by the followers of Mohammed. The town was originally situated on the Persian coast opposite the island where it was
later moved for defensive reasons.

In 1271, Marco Polo, that famous Venetian traveller, visited
Hormuz. This was a few years before the city was transferred to
the island of Jerun, which then acquired the name of Hormuz.
He describes the opulence of the place, the trade in horses, and
'the finest asses in the world' which were famous in Bahrain many
centuries later. He saw ships bringing rich cargoes of spices,
pearls, cloth of silver and gold, and elephants' teeth from India
and the Far East. He had a poor opinion of the ships which had
no metal in their construction, the planks being bound together
with cord made from coconut fibre. The local wine, manufactured from fomented dates and spices, did not please him, nor did
he care for the diet of the people, which in spite of their wealth,
seems to have consisted mainly of dates, salt fish, onions and
lemons. Like all travellers who stayed at Hormuz, he complained
of the intense heat and the scorching wind which blew during
June and July. This is surprising, for the 'bara' wind which blows
in June higher up the Gulf is regarded as a cool wind. Marco
Polo mentioned the custom that if a merchant died without heirs,
the King took his property; another custom, referred to by a later
writer, was the 'droit de seigneur' exercised by the King of
Hormuz.

Hormuz was ruled by Arab princes from the beginning of the
10th century until 1262, when it came under Persian domination,

although the ruling dynasty remained as vassals of the King of Persia. At one time, the rulers of Hormuz controlled the other islands in the Gulf and the coast of Oman. The splendour and wealth of Hormuz has been glowingly described by many European travellers and writers, and a Persian proverb says: 'If the world were a ring, Hormuz would be the jewel of that ring.'

In 1498, Vasco da Gama made his historic voyage from Lisbon to India, rounding the Cape of Good Hope, which opened the way for the successful entry of his countrymen into the East. Some years before the voyage the King of Portugal had sent emissaries to discover the source of the spice trade which was in the hands of the Arabs. The King's men had visited Hormuz and Calicut, a port on the Indian Ocean, which was the focus of the Indian sea trade.

The Portuguese fleet anchored off Calicut where they met with opposition from Zamorin, the Hindu King. The city was bombarded and when it surrendered, the Portuguese Captain, Pedro Cabral, ordered it to be sacked. Within a few years the Portuguese established trading stations at Cochin and Calicut and, in 1510 they took Goa which became the Portuguese metropolis in India, and the seat of the Viceroy and Archbishop. In 1508, the famous Portuguese Admiral Afonso D'Albuquerque who later became the second Viceroy of India, decided to extend his conquests into the Persian Gulf.

At the end of the 15th century, Muscat was second in importance as a trading centre to Hormuz, to whose ruler she paid tribute. The Omanis were famous as merchants, sailors and pirates, and Dhofar, an Omani seaport on the Indian Ocean south of Muscat, was the starting point of one of the chief caravan routes from the Gulf. The first contact between Muscat and a European nation was when Albuquerque's fleet arrived at the port after having attacked and destroyed several towns on the coast, which refused to capitulate. The Muscatis must have been awed by the sight of the tall ships of the Portuguese.

There was a parley between the Portuguese and a deputation from Muscat, but negotiations broke down. The Portuguese ships began to bombard the town, which was taken after fierce fighting. Those of the defenders who were not killed or taken prisoners, both men and women, had their noses and ears chopped off. The city was plundered and wantonly destroyed by fire, and all the boats in the harbour were burned, after which the victorious fleet sailed along the coast taking several other ports, where the people, if they did not surrender, were treated with similar savagery. Muscat was held by the Portuguese for 144 years, during which 'only rare and feeble opposition told of deep resentment of their intrusion and brutality'. After taking Muscat, Albuquerque turned his attention to Hormuz, the key to the Persian Gulf.

When the fleet reached Hormuz, they found that preparations had been made to defend the island. The harbour was full of ships containing fighting men, troops were drawn up on the shore, foreign mercenaries had been called in to defend the island, and Bahrain had sent a fleet with 'relief of men and provisions' but the ships had been scattered by the Portuguese. But in spite of the military array, although heavily outnumbered, the Portuguese gained the day. The King of Hormuz agreed to pay tribute to Portugal instead of to the Shah of Persia. D'Albuquerque was unable to consolidate his conquest owing to dissension among his captains and, when his fleet left, the Hormuzian King resumed his allegiance to Persia, at the same time he adopted the faith of the Shia sect of Islam to which the Shah of Persia belonged.

Seven years later, a strong Portuguese force regained possession of Hormuz; this time, they firmly established themselves in the island, and completed the building of a fortress which had been begun when they first took the place. The fort was still standing in good order at the beginning of the present century. For the next 100 years Hormuz was the military and commercial centre of the Portuguese in the Gulf.

In 1521 the Bahrain islands were taken by the Portuguese; Bahrain was at this time a dependency of Hasa, whose ruler was tributary to Hormuz. Because the Hasa ruler failed to pay his tribute, the King of Hormuz asked the Portuguese to support him in an expedition against Bahrain. The islands were taken by a Portuguese and Hormuzian force and, after the fighting, the 'King' of Bahrain died from wounds. His body was being conveyed by ship to Hasa for burial when the Portuguese commander, Antonio Correa, intercepted it. He cut off the head of the dead man and carried it back to Hormuz in triumph, 'to make an agreeable present to the King of Hormuz'. A bilingual inscription was set up in the city commemorating the bold exploit of Antonio

7

Correa, and the King of Portugal granted him permission to add the title Baharem to his name and to display 'a Moorish King's head, decapitated, with blood, with turban and crown' on his escutcheon. The present descendant of the Correa family, the Count of Lousa, still bears this, quarterly, on his arms.

After Portuguese rule was established in the Gulf, piracy seems almost to have ceased. Muscat, Hormuz and Bahrain were under the domination of the Portuguese, and the seas were 'covered with a wood of ships, the product of the Government's great care'. There were occasional rebellions against the Portuguese garrisons, which were ruthlessly suppressed. In the middle of the 16th century a new opponent challenged the Portuguese. In 1534, Suliman the Magnificent took Baghdad from the Persians and began to extend his influence southwards. A Turkish fleet commanded by Piri Beg arrived in the Gulf. After attacking and taking Muscat, the Turks made an unsuccessful attempt to take Hormuz. Finally, the Turkish fleet retired to Basra with the Portuguese on their heels. Piri Beg had with him in his ship the Portuguese Governor of Muscat, who had been taken as a hostage. Acting on his advice the Turk left Basra with three galleons loaded with loot. He evaded the Portuguese fleet and sailed out of the Gulf, but he lost one of his ships off Bahrain. The sunken ship has never been found. Piri Beg was eventually tried, convicted and executed in Turkey, and his vast wealth, acquired by acts of piracy was confiscated by the Sultan. During the following years the Turks gained many successes.

They attacked Kishm and Katif and twice occupied Muscat, but were expelled from these places by the Portuguese. They attempted to land at Bahrain, but were ignominiously repulsed. By the middle of the 16th century, the Turks were vigorously challenging the Portuguese in the Gulf. The Portuguese ships were superior to those of the Turks and their men were better armed, but the religious sympathies of the Arabs were with the Turks, for the Portuguese were regarded as infidels. The Turks had the advantage of being nearer to their base; they were less affected by climate and disease, and they had not then acquired the reputation for cruelty and rapacity for which the Portuguese were notorious.

After 1580, the power of Portugal in the East began to wane, owing to the domination of Portugal by Spain, which lasted for sixty years. The Portuguese had difficulty in maintaining their garrisons and the quality of their reinforcements was not what it had been. The captains of their fleets, when they first arrived, were almost invincible, but they began to shirk encounters and paid more attention to enriching themselves by trade than to fighting. In the Gulf, Shah Abbas who ascended the Persian throne in 1587, soon sought means of ousting the Portuguese from Hormuz and recovering the trade which the Portuguese had taken from Persia.

In 1602, the Portuguese lost Bahrain. The islanders rebelled against the Governor, who was a relation of the King of Hormuz, overpowered the small Portuguese garrison, and seized the fort. The Prince of Shiraz sent a force to support the rebels and took control of the islands in the name of the Shah of Persia. Persia and Portugal were outwardly friendly, and when the King of Portugal complained to the Shah about his action in supporting the rebels in Bahrain, Shah Abbas made the flimsy excuse that he took Bahrain not from the Portuguese but from his vassal the King of Hormuz.

In 1559, Queen Elizabeth granted a charter to English merchants 'of their own adventures, costs and charges' to 'traffic and merchandise' in the East Indies. In 1608, the first English ship arrived off the coast of India, then for several years the English tried to obtain permission from the Mogul Emperor to have a factory at Surat. They had to contend with the opposition and intrigues of the Portuguese, who were long established at the Emperor's court and, with the apathy of the Emperor and his officials, in matters concerning trade. However, they were finally permitted to set up a factory at Surat, which became the main English establishment on the Indian coast.

Previously, several adventurous English gentlemen, the most famous being the Sherley brothers, had visited the court of the Shah, who showed favour to the English, while endeavouring to curb the power of the Portuguese by weakening their positions. Because there was no water supply in Hormuz, the inhabitants depended on some wells on the mainland near Bundar Abbas where the Portuguese had built a small fort. In 1607 the Khan of Fars seized the wells: he retired when paid to do so, but retained two forts in the vicinity. Eight years later, the Khan took the town and fort of Bundar Abbas from the Portuguese, thus depriving them of their last foothold on the Persian coast.

In 1616, an English vessel from Surat, the *James*, managed to elude the Portuguese navy and reached Jask on the Persian coast. The captain of the *James* travelled inland to the court of the Shah, and obtained a firman from him, which was followed a year or two later by the establishment at Jask of the first English factory in Persia.

The Portuguese strongly resented the intrusion of the English in India, Persia and the Gulf, where they had established a monopoly of trade for over a century, and in the Spice Islands in the Far East the Dutch were equally resentful of their new rivals. The Dutch and Portuguese regarded the English as sea poachers, preying on the rich commerce which was in their hands.

In 1619 the King of Portugal despatched a large naval expedition to the Gulf to strengthen the garrison of Hormuz and to suppress the activities of the English 'corsairs'. It was commanded by Captain-Major Ruy Freire de Andrada, a gallant and distinguished soldier. Ruy Freire reached Hormuz in June 1620 and on December 28th he attacked the English fleet off Jask, suffering a heavy defeat. In Europe, Portugal and England were at peace, yet in Eastern waters they were fighting. There had been times when European forces in distant parts of the world were unaware whether their governments at home were on friendly terms or at war. But at this time, in the Gulf, both the Portuguese and the English knew that their countries were at peace.

Back in Hormuz, Ruy Freire began to make preparations for a possible attack by the Persians. He had orders from his King to build a fort on Kishm island, about twelve miles distant from Hormuz, where there were fresh water wells. As Kishm belonged to Persia, this was an unwise move, certain to cause retaliation. The capture of Kishm and the building of the fort took many months during which Ruy Freire was besieged by the Persians for eight months. Meanwhile the Portuguese navy, which was still in control of the sea, harried the Persian coast, sacking ports and villages and slaughtering men, women and children, earning the intense hatred of the Persians. The object of this operation was to prevent the Persians sending reinforcements to oppose the Portuguese in Kishm. This was the situation when the Persians applied to the English for help against the Portuguese.

At the end of 1621, when the Khan of Shiraz made his request for military help, there was an English fleet at Jask, which had lately arrived from Surat. The Khan made it plain that if the English did not come to the assistance of the Persians they would lose the trading facilities which they had obtained with so much difficulty. It was the granting by Persia of these facilities to the English which had provoked the hostilities with the Portuguese. The idea of supporting the Moslem Persians against the Christian Portuguese was repugnant to some of the English captains, they were afraid, too, that they might incur punishment from King James of England for fighting against Portugal with whom he was at peace. But, after long deliberations, the English decided to throw their lot in with the Persians. An agreement was drawn up under which all Portuguese prisoners were to be handed over to the English, and Moslem prisoners would be taken by the Persians.

The siege and taking of Kishm and Hormuz by the combined Persian and English forces are graphically described in the commentaries of Ruy Freire de Andrada, published in Lisbon in 1647. The English went first to Kishm where Ruy Freire was holding out in the castle against a large Persian force. There was a parley at which Ruy Freire refused to surrender unless all prisoners were handed over to the English. To this, the English could not agree, so the attack on the fortress began. It was occupied on February 11th 1622 without much resistance, as some of the Portuguese troops mutinied, being urged to surrender by their priests. Ruy Freire and two of his captains were sent to Surat as hostages, later Ruy Freire escaped from the English and played a distinguished part in the hostilities between the Portuguese and the English in the Gulf until his death in Muscat in 1632. He was buried in the Church at Muscat on the foundations of which the present Sultan's palace stands. The Moslem prisoners were handed over to the Persian Khan who, contrary to his promise, murdered them most inhumanly.

On February 19th, the English and the Persians' combined force moved to Hormuz, the Persians landed without opposition and took the town: the Portuguese retired into the fortress. The siege of the fortress lasted for over two months. The English used the guns on their ships to destroy the Portuguese fleet, and with their shore guns they bombarded the fortress. The Portuguese defended themselves bravely, but the walls of the fortress were successfully mined by the Persians with gunpowder, provided by the English. Finally, after a two-days' truce the Portuguese surrendered to the English rather than wait for the final assault by the Persians, which would certainly have led to the massacre of the defenders. There is a description by an English sailor of the appalling conditions inside the fort at the time of surrender. The small amount of water left in the cisterns had been contaminated, and the dead were lying unburied in the intense heat, being devoured by dogs and cats.

The surrender of Hormuz gave rise to bitter disagreements about the spoil. Both Persians and English seem to have behaved badly. The Persians got away with enormous quantities of booty which they did not share with the English, as had been agreed, and the English captains and crews seized as much plunder as they could and took it away in their ships. For the English Company the affair was not a material success though, in a wider sense, it was of the utmost value. The Portuguese failed in their many attempts to recover Hormuz and, with its loss their influence in the Gulf decreased.

CHAPTER II

'For I shall sing of battles, blood and rage
Which princes and their people did engage,
And haughty souls that moved with mutual hate,
In fighting fields pursued and found their fate.'
Aenius VIII Trans: Dryden

THE expulsion of the Portuguese from Hormuz was the beginning of the end of their domination in the Gulf, though they still held Muscat which was strongly fortified, and they possessed a powerful fleet which harried the Persian and Arab coasts. They made several unsuccessful attempts to recover Hormuz, very nearly succeeding in 1625 when they were beaten off by a combined English and Dutch Fleet. At Hormuz the Persians destroyed all that they could, concentrating on the development of Gombroon, a port on the mainland, which was named Bundar Abbas in honour of Shah Abbas. Sir Thomas Herbert who accompanied an embassy to Persia and visited Hormuz in about 1627, writes: 'This poore citie is now disrobed of all her braverie': a city which, according to Herbert, was 'the only stately citie in the Orient'. Dr. Fryer, about fifty years later, described Hormuz as famous only for its salt cliffs, 'a cure for the most burning fever, the only known remedy for such cases in this climate'. The English were allowed to open a factory in the new port which they retained for almost a century and a half.

The gratitude of the Persians for the help given to them by the English in taking Hormuz soon evaporated. The Persians were displeased when the English declined to give them further assistance in a projected expedition against Muscat. The action of the English Company at Hormuz had met with the strong disapproval of the Government, which was only allayed by substantial payments by the Company to King James, and to the Duke of Buckingham in his capacity as Lord High Admiral. A few years later, the Portuguese had established themselves at Basra, in the realm of the Ottoman Sultan, and had built a factory at Kung on the Persian coast, having come to terms with the Persians in 1625.

From these ports they competed vigorously with the English. Peace was made between England and Portugal in 1634, a peace which has lasted for over 330 years. But besides competition from the Portuguese, the English had to deal with competition from the Dutch and, to a lesser degree, from the French.

The Dutch East India Company was founded in 1602 after several voyages had been made to the East Indies by Dutch ships. Within a short time, the Dutch Company had acquired a monopoly of the lucrative spice trade which was wrested from the hands of the Portuguese. The Dutch Company enjoyed the full support of its Government, it was wealthy and it had a strong fleet manned by Europeans, not, as was the case with the Portuguese, by crews of Portuguese, Indians and half breeds. Chardin who was in Persia in 1666, writes: 'the Indians are by no means proper to navigate European vessels, they are the worst thieves and murtherers. The Holland Company would never make use of them.' Although on one or two occasions the Dutch combined with the English against the Portuguese, they soon presented a formidable threat to the commercial and political position of the English. The situation worsened after the death of Shah Abbas. His successor showed preference for the Dutch and skilfully played off the European competitors in his domain, one against the other.

In 1660, the Portuguese lost Muscat, their last stronghold in the Gulf, to the Arabs of Oman. Captain Alexander Hamilton who was in Muscat some twenty years later, tells the story of how the Portuguese were expelled. The Imam, which was the title then held by the rulers of Oman, was preparing an expedition against the Persian coast. His army was in the neighbourhood of Muscat and his fleet was lying off Matra, a port on the coast a few miles from Muscat. The Imam sent a civil message to the Governor of Muscat, asking permission to buy provisions in the town. The Governor, in reply, sent a piece of pork wrapped in paper, with a rude message, saying that if the Imam wanted such provisions he could furnish them. The messenger, unaware of what the parcel contained, handed it to the Imam and delivered the message. The Imam, besides being the temporal ruler, was the religious head of the Omanis, and it was a gross insult to send him pork. However, although shocked at the Governor's ill manners, 'he dissembled his resentment'.

But news of the insult reached the army, and the Imam's wife, who was in her tent. Enraged by so gross an affront, she swore by her ancestor the Prophet Mohammed that she would not set foot outside her tent till Muscat was taken. She chided her husband for taking the insult so calmly and urged him to action. The army then threatened to mutiny unless they were allowed to take their revenge, so the Imam gave way and ordered an attack on the town. Muscat was besieged, the Omanis broke through the defences, and great loss of life on both sides ensued: the small forts were attacked and finally surrendered. Another writer suggests that the Arabs were enabled to make an entry owing to the treachery of an Indian merchant, whose daughter had been carried off by the Portuguese. The big fort on the cliffs above the town, into which the Governor had retired, held out for some months. The Portuguese would have surrendered, but they could not agree to the terms offered by the Arabs. The Governor, when the situation became desperate, rather than fall into the hands of the enemy, hurled himself down from the fortress on to the rocks below, after which the garrison capitulated.

At the time of his visit, Hamilton says that the cathedral which the Portuguese had built 'still retains some marks of ancient grandeur' although it had been converted into a palace which the Imam occupied for two or three months every year, spending the rest of the year in the more salubrious parts of his territory. This is still the custom of the Sultans of Muscat.

In 1652, a strong Portuguese fleet from Goa arrived off Muscat, but retired without a fight in the face of a large Arab fleet. One or two more ineffective attempts were made to retake Muscat, but most of the Portuguese activities at sea consisted of piratical attacks on vessels. A French Abbé describes how, on one occasion, the Viceroy sent a fleet from Goa up the Gulf with strict orders to the captain of the fleet that he should on no account return unless he had retaken Muscat, an enterprise for which his fleet was totally inadequate. He knew that the Viceroy was jealous of him, and had, therefore, despatched him on a hopeless mission. After the loss of Muscat, the only place held by the Portuguese on the Persian coast was Kung. The Imam, not content with taking Muscat and encouraged by the apparent pusillanimity of the Portuguese, followed up his victory by attacking the Portuguese at Diu and Daman on the coast of India, carrying

15

off many prisoners into slavery and taking great quantities of treasure.

The departure of the Portuguese from Muscat gave an impetus to piracy which was mainly carried on by the Arabs of Oman. They were such a formidable threat both to trade and to the security of the Persian ports, that the Shah offered privileges to the English if they would reduce the pirate strongholds, but the English were in no position to do so. Not only were there Arab pirates, but the seas were infested with 'outlawed Portugals and a mixture of that race, the most accursidly base of all mankind, who are known for their bastard brood as Buccaneers'. These, according to Fryer, 'wreak their malice on the unarmed Merchants, who, not long able to resist their unbounded Lust, become tame Slaves to their lawless Rage'.

In 1652, England and Holland were at war, and the position of the English Company in Persia and the Gulf was very precarious. Trade had diminished and everywhere the Dutch, who were more popular at the Court of the Shah than the English, were gaining ground. The inability of the English to suppress the pirates was held against them by the Persians who, themselves, had no effective sea power. Throughout its history Persia has been at a disadvantage from lack of a navy. Persians as a race have a strong disinclination for the sea, although the tribes on the coast are seafaring people, but they, in many cases, are the descendants of Arabs who crossed the Gulf and settled on the Persian coast. Although the Dutch took no conspicuous action against the pirates, yet the Persians were impressed by their evident strength and wealth. Then, as today, nothing impressed the Arabs and Persians more than strength and wealth. In 1672, John Fryer was at Bundar Abbas, where the English, the Dutch and the French, who had recently appeared on the scene, had factories, each one surmounted by their national flag. He found in the harbour two large Dutch ships, two large Arab vessels, and one little English ship. He says: 'The English Company's trade is but small here, only carrying off some few drugs, wool, dates, goats and horses.' It was the interest of the English in exporting horses which caused a Persian to enquire whether any horses existed in Europe. The French had even less trade and, according to another traveller, only remained at Bundar Abbas because their interpreter was making a profit out of wine, 'lounging his time away', paying and receiving many calls. The Dutch had established themselves at Muscat, and the Dutchman in charge had the ear of the Imam, constantly trying to make trouble between him and the other European nations and so deprive them of trade. Fryer sums up the position of the English by saying 'the Persians allow us little more than a name'.

In 1673 a curious French mission had obtained some concessions from the Shah. Sir John Chardin, himself originally a Frenchman, gives an amusing description of this bogus embassy in his *Travels in Persia*, published in 1720. It consisted of some members of the French East India Company, who had no diplomatic standing. A ship's captain 'made himself an Ambassador', and when he and several of the party died on their way to Isfahan, the interpreter, a French merchant born in Persia, after much thought about whether he should dress in European or Persian style, assumed the role of Ambassador. He was encouraged by the Capuchin monks who were anxious that a French mission should appear and, according to Chardin, the monks composed and wrote the letters which were delivered to the Shah. The letters were palpable forgeries in Chardin's opinion, 'Pieces too ill contriv'd to bear being made Publick'. However, the 'Embassy' was accepted by the Shah, possibly the 'King', as Chardin calls him, 'was in his wine as usual', for Chardin describes him as being constantly drunk.

In 1688, England and Holland were again at peace, but the Dutch were now beginning to lose credit in Persia and the Gulf. Their arrogance and the aggressive measures which they adopted, made them unpopular with those people with whom they wished to trade. At the beginning of the 18th century, the French were making some progress, but they were never in as strong a position as the other European competitors. In about 1708 the Shah ceded to them the island of Kharak, but they made no use of it and, towards the end of the century, it was held for a short time by the Dutch. Perhaps the most important development in the Gulf in the 18th century was the remarkable rise to power of the ruling dynasty of Muscat and Oman.

No state in the Gulf has had such a turbulent past as Oman, whose history goes back to early times when some of the coast towns were important trading centres. The original inhabitants consisted mainly of Yemeni tribes, who settled in Oman; their early history is based on tradition. Oman has always been an isolated country; the remote interior was almost unknown to the Arabs of the Gulf, who were only familiar with Muscat and the coastal towns. The Omanis have clung to their independence up to the present day. Although the country was at various times invaded by the Persians, the Caliphs of Baghdad, the Mongols, the Portuguese and the Wahabis, none of these invaders subjugated the inland regions and, in most cases, they only had nominal control of Oman. In some ways Oman resembled the Yemen which has frequently been invaded, but never wholly conquered. The Omanis retained their own way of life, electing their own Imams, often engrossed in tribal wars, but keeping apart from their Arab neighbours. Only the people of the coast had contact with the outside world, and as they were 'the best mariners in all Arabia', according to Niebuhr, piracy became their principal occupation.

Early in the 17th century, the rule of the Yariba dynasty a tribe of Yemeni origin, was established in Oman. It was they who were in control when the Portuguese were expelled from Muscat. A few years later, the Omanis took Bahrain from the Persians, and threatened Bundar Abbas. The Persians, having no ships of war, endeavoured to obtain the help of the Portuguese to transport their troops to Bahrain. The negotiations broke down because the two parties were unable to come to terms about payment. Shortly afterwards, a Portuguese fleet which had been despatched from Goa was defeated at sea by the Imam's navy.

During the first three decades of the 18th century, there was a rapid decline in the power of Persia, whose rulers were feeble, indolent and effeminate, concerned more with palace plots and intrigues than with maintaining a strong army. The few outstanding men who held commands were usually removed, or murdered, owing to jealousy in the court. In 1722, Persia was invaded by the Afghans. Though the Persian army greatly outnumbered the Afghans, it put up feeble resistance. Isfahan, the capital, was besieged, and Shah Husayn, after trying unsuccessfully to buy off the enemy, surrendered himself and the city to Mahmud the Afghan chief. So ended the rule of the Safavi dynasty which had produced one or two notable men and several of mediocre calibre. It was during these years of chaos and wars in Persia that the rulers of Oman strengthened their position in the Gulf. After taking Shiraz the Afghans made a descent on Bundar Abbas, but the Europeans in their factories put up such stout resistance that the Afghans retired, after obtaining some supplies. In the years following the Afghan conquest, Persia was devastated by wars and terrible massacres.

In 1730, after a war between the Turks and the Persians, which lasted for several years, the Afghans were routed by a Persian army under the command of an outstanding man, Nadir Kuli. He started life as a shepherd, at one time he was a brigand, then he became a military leader. He came to the support of the young surviving son of the Shah Husayn, but after some time, he deposed and imprisoned the Shah and, in 1736, usurped the crown of Persia and became known as Nadir Shah. He was a man with great ambitions and one of his designs was to control the Persian Gulf.

To control the Gulf, it was necessary for Persia to hold Oman and Bahrain, the latter was in the possession of the Hawala Arabs who had migrated from Arabia to the Persian coast. There are in Bahrain many of these Arabs at the present time. The conquest of Bahrain and Oman could not be achieved without a fleet. For several years Latif Khan who had been appointed Admiral of the non-existent fleet by Nadir, and Taqi Khan, the Governor of the province of Fars, tried by persuasion and sometimes by threats to obtain ships from the Dutch and English companies at Bundar Abbas. Persia was at the same time engaged in hostilities with the Turks and the English did not wish to endanger their position with the Turkish authorities at Basra or with the ruler of Oman at Muscat by providing ships for operations against them. The Dutch and English, very reluctantly, did lend four ships for a Persian expedition against the island of Kais in 1733 and, after much bargaining and threats from the Persians, they arranged for two vessels to be provided from Surat. At one time, owing to the attitude of the Persians, the English considered evacuating Bundar Abbas, but it was not until 1761 that Bundar Abbas factory was closed, and two years later, the English opened a factory in Bushire.

Bushire was chosen by the Persians as their naval base. By 1736, they had collected a number of vessels, some they purchased, some they commandeered. In this year, they took Bahrain during the absence of the Shaikh who was making the Pilgrimage.

In the following year the Persian fleet, manned mainly by Hawala Arabs, arrived at Bundar Abbas. Two of the ships were commanded by Englishmen, one of whom, a sea-captain, had sold his ship to the Persians.

The Imam of Oman, Saif bin Sultan, who was engaged in a civil war – a very usual state of things in Oman – had asked Nadir for help against his rebellious subjects. This gave Nadir the opportunity of getting a foothold in Oman. Latif Khan, with a strong force, landed in Oman; in a very short time the rebellion was suppressed but, as has so frequently happened in the Gulf, the force which was called in to help the ruler, became the master of the country. Then followed a period of confusion, sometimes the Imam was on good terms with the Persians, at other times, he opposed them.

The Persian occupation of Oman, which lasted for about eight years, was in some respects a tragi-comedy. The sailors and many of the troops were mercenaries, badly fed and often unpaid, with no feelings of loyalty to Persia. The seamen, most of whom were Hawala Arabs, were tough and independent and of a different religious sect from the Persians, for whom they had no liking. They were resentful of the Persians for having dispossessed them of Bahrain. There were constant mutinies and frequent quarrels between the commanders of the forces, and between the commanders and the Imam, whom the Persians were supposed to be supporting. Latif Khan, who had been in command during the early part of the occupation, was poisoned by Taqi Khan, the Governor of Fars, who arrived in Oman in 1738. Having disposed of his rival, Taqi Khan assumed command.

In 1740, during one of the mutinies, the whole fleet was removed by the seamen after they had murdered most of their officers. A new 'Admiral', Mohammed Taqi Khan, who knew nothing about the sea, was appointed by Nadir. On arriving at Bundar Abbas, he borrowed two Dutch ships and set off in pursuit of the mutineers who were in possession of the fleet which he was supposed to command.

In the following year, having failed to subdue them, negotiations were opened between the mutineers and their Admiral. The mutineers were represented by an Englishman who was serving with the Persian navy, and the Persian Admiral was represented by the agent of the East India Company at Bundar

III. Ras al Khaima from the S.W. and the situation of the troops

IV The attack on the fort at Luft, November 27th 1809

Abbas, who had been asked to mediate.   The negotiations failed.

In 1742, the Imam, who was in control of Muscat, again asked the Persians for help against his opponents.   Nadir sent his brother-in-law, Kalb Ali, to Oman whither Taqi Khan had returned after taking part in an expedition against India.   According to Niebuhr, Taqi Khan, on arrival at Muscat, gave a banquet for the Imam and his officers.   He plied the Imam with Shiraz wine and made him so drunk that he had no difficulty in obtaining the keys of the forts and the Imam's seal, whereby the Persians once again established themselves in Muscat.   It is said that the Imam died soon afterwards, overcome with shame and remorse.   In 1743, Taqi Khan rebelled against the Shah and murdered Kalb Ali, but the rebellion failed.   Owing to the rebellion, and because Persia was engaged in a war with Turkey, the Persian grip on Oman was relaxed.   This provided an opportunity for Ahmed bin Said, the Governor of Sohar, to rally the Omanis against the Persian invaders, and finally to expel them.   Ahmed was elected Imam, and became the founder of the dynasty which rules Muscat today.

Ahmed died in 1783 and was succeeded by his son, Said.   He soon found himself involved in quarrels with relations, who contested his claim to be the Imam; of these, the most forcible was his brother Sultan bin Ahmed who made himself master of Muscat and soon became the *de facto* ruler.   During these years, Oman was constantly harassed by the Wahabis, who swooped down from the desert, while the Joasmi pirates ravaged the coast.

For some time, Saiyed Sultan, as he came to be called, showed a preference for the French who were at war with England.   He encouraged trade with Mauritius, and allowed the French to use Muscat as a base.   In 1798, Britain made her first treaty with Muscat, under which the Sultan agreed to deny facilities to the French and the Dutch, to dismiss the French commander of one of his ships, and to allow the English to open a factory at Bundar Abbas, which was leased from Persia by the Sultan.   Two years later, a further treaty was negotiated by Captain Malcolm, afterwards Sir John Malcolm, with the Sultan, who agreed that 'an English gentleman of respectability' should reside at Muscat as agent of the East India Company, in order that 'the friendship of the two states may remain unshook till the end of time, till the sun and moon have finished their revolving career'.   The first

'English gentleman of respectability' to be appointed to Muscat was a Surgeon Bogle, but a few years later British agents were withdrawn owing to the high rate of mortality, due to the unhealthy climate. Muscat was the first Arab state in the Gulf to have direct diplomatic dealings with Britain.

In 1803 the Sultan went on the Pilgrimage, leaving his two young sons, Salim and Said, in charge of a Regent Mohammed bin Nasr, their maternal relation. During his absence, his nephew Bedr, who had been living at Lamu on the East African coast, seized Muscat and imprisoned the boys and the Regent. He occupied the town of Muscat but failed to take the forts. The Sultan returned in time to relieve them and drove out Bedr. In the following year the Sultan was killed at sea in an engagement with pirates.

Once again, Oman was ravaged by civil war between claimants to the succession, and during the confusion which ensued the pirates made the most of their opportunity to attack the towns on the coast. The two boys, Salim aged fifteen, and Said aged thirteen, were in Muscat with Mohammed bin Nasr, their guardian, when the town was attacked by Qais, one of their uncles. The boys' aunt, Bibi Mooza, a lady of great character, who played a leading part in Muscat's history, suggested to the Regent that he should call in Bedr and his Wahabi friends to drive off Qais. This was done, and Bedr assumed the reins of government. At various times in the Gulf's history, ladies of the ruling families have wielded powerful influence behind their strict purdah; there have been instances of this in Bahrain and Dubai during the present century.

Bedr despatched the boys and the Regent to a distant part of the country and set off on an expedition against Bundar Abbas which had been occupied by Joasmi pirates. On his return, he found the pirates in possession of Muscat, but he was able to expel them and was soon well on the way to becoming ruler of Oman. Said, who had been sent to Barka by Bedr with Mohammed Nasr and the redoubtable Bibi Mooza, although only a boy, had distinguished himself in fighting against the pirates. He had with him a faithful body of Baluchis from Makran, who had served his father. Bedr was suspicious of these men and wished them to be disbanded. Until recently, Baluchis were employed by some of the Gulf Shaikhs in a sim ilarcapacity to the Swiss guards in Europe, being loyal and dependable fighters. In Bahrain the descendants of the Shaikhs' Baluchi bodyguards still hold position of trust in the households of the Khalifah. A dispute then broke out between Bedr and Said's brother, Salim. Salim had returned to Muscat without Bedr's permission and, when threatened by Bedr with death, fled back to Said at Barka. Bedr ordered Said to hand his brother over to him, which Said refused to do.

The story of Bedr's death is described fully by Maurizi, Said's doctor, who claims to have had it from the negro slave who was present at the time. Bedr, unwisely, went to Barka to deal with the two young men. Some writers suggest that it was Bedr's intention to kill both boys. He entered the fort near the town, where he was received by Said, and sat down in a room between Said and Mohammed – the negro slave stood at the door. There was a disagreement, probably about handing over Salim and disbanding the Baluchi bodyguard. Suddenly Said leaned forward, pulled Bedr's dagger from his waistbelt, and stabbed him on his left side. The slave slammed the door shut. Bedr, though wounded, made for the window, jumped out and fell on a heap of horse dung below. There were saddled horses close by, he leapt on to one of them, and galloped away towards a Wahabi camp near the town. Said, with his brother, Mohammed bin Nasr, and the negro slave, followed Bedr on their horses. They caught up with him, and Mohammed attacked him with his sword and unhorsed him. The slave finished him off with a spear.

According to Maurizi, Said then persuaded Mohammed bin Nasr to disappear for the time being. Meanwhile, he told his excited supporters that Bedr had been killed by Mohammed. It is unlikely that the people of Barka, or the Baluchi bodyguard, cared who had done the killing. Bedr, whom they all disliked because of his friendship with the Wahabis, was dead. That was all that mattered. They applauded the deed, and rallied round Said, who took ship to Muscat, and was hailed there as the deliverer of his country from one who had turned renegade and had been hand-in-glove with the invaders. Said was acclaimed as ruler and, as Sultan of Muscat and of Oman, became one of the most outstanding men in the Middle East for over half a century.

The only people who were thoroughly shocked were the English, who for some years refused to have anything to do with him. Considering the conciliatory attitude of the English towards the pirates and the Wahabis, who never ceased from murdering and plundering, Macaulay's remark: 'we know of no spectacle so ridiculous as the British public in one of its periodical fits of morality', might well apply in this case. Political assasinations, until quite recently, were of frequent occurrence in the Gulf, there was an instance of it at Kuwait at the end of the last century, and three predecessors of a Shaikh who now rules one of the Gulf states were 'eliminated' during a period of six years.

In 1808, Said's uncle, Qais, was killed in battle; his death removed the last possible rival to the Sultanate. In the following year, Said made representations to the British, urging them to take action against the pirates who were as much their enemies as his. This resulted in the expedition of 1809. It caused a temporary lull in the pirates' activities, but a few years later piracy was again rampant.

CHAPTER III

'It was by instigating the Quwaism (Joasmi) tribe
of Arabs to acts of piracy in the Persian Gulf that
the Wahabis first attracted the attention of the
British Government.'

Treaties and Engagements and Sennads.   Vol. XI.
Edited by C. U. Aitcheson.   Revised 1933

TOWARDS the end of the 18th century, the Wahabi movement became an important factor in the affairs of the Persian Gulf.   The founder of the sect, Mohammed bin Abdul Wahab, the son of a Kadhi, was born in about 1703 at Ayaina in Nejd.   He is said to have learned the Koran by heart at the age of ten, and he was married when he was twelve.   He travelled in Iraq, the Hejaz and Syria, becoming an authority on religious matters, it seems that much of his religious thinking was based on the precepts of Ibn Taymiya, a religious reformer who died in the 14th century.   In 1744, he returned to his home town where he started a religious campaign, his adherents becoming known as Wahabis.

He preached a doctrine of pure monotheism, a return to the fundamental tenets of Islam as laid down in the Koran.   He denounced the heresies and superstitions which had crept into the religion, such as intercessions to the Prophet Mohammed rather than to the Deity, the worship of saints, pilgrimages to mosques and places of burial, and the building of domes and monuments. He sternly condemned the laxity and depravity of the Arabs and admonished men for wearing silk and gold, and for smoking tobacco.   He told his followers that it was their religious duty to convert their fellow men with fire and sword, and to plunder and destroy all those who professed to be Moslems but did not accept Wahabism.   It was the prospect of authorised plunder which attracted the desert Bedouin and the pirates of the coast to align themselves under the green standard of the Wahabis.

At first, Abdul Wahab gained some support, and made converts in Ayaina, where he was accepted as a religious leader; then came a test case. He was asked to give judgement in the case of a woman who confessed to being an adultress. His verdict was that she should be stoned to death and the sentence was carried out. The easy-going inhabitants of Ayaina were shocked at Abdul Wahab's uncompromising attitude and complained to the Beni Khalid Shaikhs who ruled over Hasa, and so Abdul Wahab was ordered to leave Ayaina.

At this time, Arabia was split into small independent Shaikh-doms, whose rulers were constantly at war with each other and with the desert Bedouin. Finding himself 'not without honour, save in his own country', he went to Daraiya, where he was given friendship and support by the Amir Mohammed bin Saud, the ancestor of the kings of Saudi Arabia who belonged to a branch of the famous Anaiza tribe. From then onwards, the Saudi family became Abdul Wahab's strongest supporters; after his death in 1792, the Saudi Amir assumed the position of Imam of the Wahabis, holding religious as well as temporal authority.

For the next thirty years, after Abdul Wahab joined the Sauds, Arabia was the scene of endless fighting between the partisans of Wahabism and those who opposed the new religious doctrines. There was not a full scale war, but there was continuous raiding and attacking. When the Wahabis took a town or conquered a tribe, they sent out religious leaders to teach the people the new faith. Usually, after some time the Arabs reverted to their previous ways of thinking, then another expedition would be sent against them. However, very gradually, the Wahabis made progress.

By 1775, all Nejd was under the Wahabis, and ten years later they were in control of Hasa and the coast which, being a stronghold of Shiism, suffered severely from their religious zeal. Shias are members of the Islamic sect who regard Ali, the son-in-law of the Prophet Mohammed, as the rightful Caliph. At the top of the Gulf the Utub, a sub-tribe of the Anaiza, had come out from the desert and settled at Grane, on the coast, which became known as Kuwait; these Arabs were the ancestors of the ruling families of Bahrain and Kuwait. In 1783, the Khalifah branch of the Utub, who had moved down the coast to Zabara on the Qatar coast, invaded Bahrain and expelled the Persians, since when the Khalifah have ruled the islands.

In the Gulf, piracy was rife. After some preliminary resistance the Shaikhs and the people of the Pirate Coast embraced Wahabism with fanatical zeal, and 'the Wahabi faith paved the way for every subsequent atrocity'. Under the guise of religion, the Pirates slaughtered all captives whose religious views did not coincide with theirs. After the union of the pirates and the Wahabis, the Arabs in other parts of the Gulf were reduced to terrified, though unwilling, submission.

At the end of the 18th century, the Wahabis had begun to extend their warlike activities beyond the confines of Nejd and Hasa. They invaded Iraq and, in 1801, took Kerbala, the holy city of the Shias. They massacred great numbers of the inhabitants, plundered the city and desecrated the mosque containing the tomb of Husain. Two years later, the Saudi Amir, Abdul Aziz, was murdered in a mosque in Nejd by a Shia from Kerbala, whose family was said to have been slaughtered by Wahabis. The Wahabis then tried to conquer Oman, but neither at this nor at any other time did they succeed in subjugating the whole country. In 1803, the Wahabi Amir Saud invaded the Hejaz and took Mecca. The city and holy places were pillaged, tombs and domes levelled to the ground, and many religious leaders who were opposed to Wahabism were executed. The Wahabis then retired, leaving a garrison which was massacred by the people of Mecca. Three years later Mecca was reconquered by the Wahabis, and this ended the rule of the Sharifs of Mecca who had been nominally subject to the Ottoman Sultan.

The success of the fanatical Wahabis, whose very name spread terror in neighbouring countries, caused consternation in the courts of the Shah and the Sultan. Previously, the Turks had not paid much attention to the doings of the tribes in Arabia, but they now realised that they were in danger of losing Iraq and the Hejaz. Mohammed Ali, Viceroy of Egypt, was authorised to proceed against the Wahabis. In 1811, after two years of preparation, the Egyptian expedition arrived in the Hejaz. In Oman the Sultan was defending his country against invasion by the Wahabis from inland and against the Joasmi pirates who raided the coast. He had occasional support from the British and some aid from Persian mercenaries.

The sea wolves of the Pirate Coast did not only prey on the ships of their Arab neighbours, they captured vessels belonging to the East India Company, attacked British men-of-war, and threatened the shipping on the west coast of India almost as far as Bombay. In earlier times the pirates were the maritime Arabs of Oman but when the Bu Said dynasty expelled the Persians and gained control of Muscat, there began the long struggle between the rulers of Oman and the Joasmi pirates. Not all the pirates were Arabs: at the end of the 17th century, European pirates, whose base was Madagascar, appeared in the Gulf. Many of them were financed and supplied from America. There is a story – perhaps a legend – that one of the English pirate chiefs was a woman.

In 1683, the Company's ship *President* was attacked, but the pirates were beaten off. In 1696 a Company vessel, commanded by Captain Sawbridge, carrying horses to Surat, was captured. Sawbridge began to expostulate with the pirates on their way of life, they ordered him to hold his tongue, but he continued to address them. They evidently resented being preached at, though as the Captain probably spoke in English or Hindustani it is unlikely that they understood much of what he said. With a sail needle and twine they sewed his lips together, and after keeping him with his hands tied behind him for several hours, they took him and his men on board the pirate dhow while his ship, with the horses in it, was set on fire. Sawbridge and his crew were then put on shore, where soon afterwards he died. In 1698, the Company in India appealed to the home government for naval help against the pirates; a few years later, the English, French and Dutch, although commercial rivals, agreed to combine in resisting piracy in the Red Sea, the Indian Ocean and the Persian Gulf. It was from this time that the beginning of the Indian Navy came into being.

From the middle of the 18th century, the Joasmi tribe, whose chief town was Ras al Khaima, north of Muscat, were the leading pirates. They were firmly established in their fortified towns on the Pirate Coast, and they held Kishm Island and Linga on the Persian littoral, thus controlling both sides of the narrow straits at the entrance to the Gulf. The only place which they failed to dominate was Muscat, whose rulers steadfastly opposed them, first alone, then with British support. Even when piracy was at its height, those who suffered from it acknowledged that the pirates had 'some noble traits', and that, in spite of their 'unrelenting ferocity' they respected 'the persons and virtues of females'.

They were certainly fearless and expected only death if they were captured, 'utterly remorseless only when vengeance was excited by defence costing lives'. These, however, were the opinions of Europeans who were better treated than Indians and Arabs who were taken by pirates.

One morning in 1797, the *Viper*, a 10-gun cruiser of the East India Company, was anchored in Bushire roads. Her Captain was on shore, the crew were eating their breakfast on deck, and the officers were down below. There were several Joasmi dhows in the harbour, whose captains had asked the Company's agent to sell them some powder and shot, and this had been supplied to them, as it appeared that they had no hostile intention. Suddenly, two of the dhows opened fire on the *Viper* and prepared to board her. Lieutenant Carruthers called the crew to their quarters, the anchor cable was cut, and the ship moved into the open sea, pursued by four dhows full of armed men. There was a running fight during which Carruthers was shot in the groin: he tied up the wound, and carried on till he was killed by a shot in the head. A young midshipman took command, and after a fight in which there were many casualties, the pirates were driven off. It was expected that the Company would retaliate after this treacherous attack, but the incident was ignored by Bombay, and no steps were taken to punish the pirates.

Finding that they could attack British ships with impunity, the pirates became more audacious. In 1804, the Company's cruiser *Fly*, carrying dispatches and treasure to Bombay, ran aground near Kenn Island and sank in shallow water. The officers and men managed to get to Bushire, where they chartered a dhow to take them to Bombay. On their way to Bombay, they were captured by Joasmi pirates and taken to Ras al Khaima, and there exhibited to the people as curiosities. Buckingham says: 'the Joasmi ladies were so minute in their enquiries, that they were not satisfied without determining in what respect an uncircumcised infidel differed from a True Believer'. After some time, as no ransom was forthcoming, the pirates determined to kill their prisoners, but the Englishmen bought their lives by offering to show the pirates where the ship with the treasure had sunk.

The pirates took their prisoners to the shoal where the ship lay. As soon as they arrived, many of the pirates dived into the sea to find the treasure, leaving a few guards with the prisoners who attempted to escape but were caught. The pirates recovered the treasure as well as the despatches, these they gave to the Englishmen, having no use for them. They released the prisoners on the island, having first murdered most of the inhabitants of the only village. When the pirates sailed, the *Fly*'s crew found a boat and a raft on the shore, in which they put out to sea. One of these boats was lost, but the men in the other one reached the Persian coast. The survivors started walking through Persia to Bushire, a long and arduous journey, during which most of the party died. Finally, two Europeans, an officer and a seaman, arrived at Bushire with the despatches. They ultimately reached Bombay with the packet, 'for the preservation of which they were thought to be adequately rewarded by a mere letter of thanks from the Government, after these almost unexampled sufferings!'

Still the Bombay Government took no action. Not only was it inactive, but commanders of the Bombay Navy were ordered not on any account to attack or molest 'these innocent natives of the Gulf', and were threatened with 'the displeasure of the Government' if they failed to carry out their orders. This policy was due to the Government's fear of becoming involved with the Wahabis, although it was known that they were supporting and encouraging the pirates, and receiving a proportion of the spoil.

The pirates, assuming that there would be no reprisals, became more daring. In 1805 they captured two brigs belonging to Mr. Manesty, the Resident at Basra. Many of the crews were murdered and the Captain of one of the brigs had his arm cut off because he was seen to fire a musket. He put his severed arm into some hot ghee, which saved his life. The two brigs were added to the pirate fleet.

At this period, employment in the East was still regarded, even by high Government officials, as an opportunity to amass a fortune by trade. Manesty had lived for twenty-five years in 'fever-haunted and insalubrious' Basra when he retired. The Company's officials seemed almost to have forgotten that he was there. The irregularity in the payment of salaries of men stationed in distant places was perhaps an incentive to make money by trading. Claudius Rich had, at one time, to wait for over two years for his pay. Manesty had gradually acquired in his own hands much of the trade of Basra. He lived with an Armenian mistress by whom he had a number of children, but he married the lady shortly before young Claudius Rich, with his eighteen-year-old wife arrived in Basra in 1808. Rich, aged twenty-one, was on his way to Baghdad to assume the post of Resident. When Manesty suggested that Mrs. Rich should call on 'Mrs. Manesty', young Rich was most indignant, describing the lady in a letter to his father-in-law as a 'dirty Armenian drab'. When Manesty retired a few years later, he proceeded home by the overland route with a cavalcade like that of an Oriental monarch. But a few years after he retired to England as a Nabob, he lost his fortune and committed suicide, leaving the unfortunate Armenian lady and a large family to fend for themselves.

Shortly afterwards, the Company's ship *Fury* was attacked, but the pirates were driven off. On reaching Bombay, the Captain was severely reprimanded for having fired on the pirates. Captains had been ordered not to open fire until fired on, consequently by the time a British ship was surrounded by pirate dhows, she had little chance of defending herself. Two more ships, the *Mornington* of 24 guns, and the *Teignmouth* of 18 guns, were attacked but they managed to get away. There was a feeling of intense frustration among the officers and men of the Company's ships.

In 1806, the Bombay Government made a long overdue attempt to deal with the pirates, partly in response to appeals from the Sultan of Muscat, who had never ceased campaigning against them. When the news of the expedition was known to the Shaikhs of Bahrain and Kuwait, they asked the British to guarantee them protection against the Wahabis who had so much control in these places that the Shaikhs were afraid of being forced to take part with the pirates. Their requests were refused. It is interesting to consider what might have been the ultimate outcome in the Gulf if these two states had become British protectorates. Reluctantly, the Government despatched a naval force to combine with the Sultan's forces against the Joasmi pirates. Kishm Island was blockaded, and Sultan bin Seggar, Chief of the Joasmi, sued for peace. In February 1806, a treaty was concluded at Bundar Abbas, which laid down that the Joasmi Chief and his people 'would respect the British flag and the property of the Honorable East India Company', and it was also agreed that the pirates would restore the property which they had taken and would assist any British vessels which might be driven on to the Pirate Coast. This treaty was made without reference to the Wahabis. For some time, British ships patrolled the Gulf, and as long as they were on the scene the pirates kept quiet, but when the squadron returned to Bombay, the treaty became a dead letter.

In 1808, another of Mr. Manesty's ships was captured by pirates after a running fight lasting for several days. Most of the crew were massacred and the Captain was cut into pieces and dropped overboard. Mrs. Taylor, whose husband was in Bushire, was a passenger in the ship. She was taken to Ras al Khaima, as Buckingham says: 'reserved for perhaps greater sufferings', but, in fact, the lady was unharmed and eventually ransomed. In the same year, the *Sylph*, a Company cruiser of 8 guns, was captured. The Captain, Graham, obeyed his orders, and did not fire until it was too late; his ship was boarded and most of the crew were killed. Graham, badly wounded, fell down the hatchway. Some of the crew who were in hiding, dragged him into a cabin and barricaded the door. Meanwhile, the pirates set sail for Ras al Khaima. Fortunately, another British ship intercepted the vessel and gave chase. The pirates took to their boats, and Graham and the other survivors were rescued. Another ship, the *Nautilus*, was attacked off Kishm Island, but the Captain ignored his orders and opened fire; after an action in which there were many casualties, the British ship gained the day.

The *Sylph* was carrying members of the staff of Sir Harford Jones who was going on a mission to Persia. He had the unique experience of being one of two British Ambassadors who were sent to Persia at the same time on similar missions, the object being to counteract French influence in Persia. Jones was sent as Ambassador from the Court of St. James as Envoy to the Shah. At the same time, General John Malcolm (afterwards Sir John) was appointed Ambassador by the Government of Bengal. Malcolm was a distinguished man and had been twice before in Persia; it was he who negotiated the treaty with the Sultan of Muscat in 1799. Jones, on arrival, was delayed in Bombay, so Malcolm got ahead of him. After much unpleasantness, orders and counter-orders and angry correspondence between Lord Minto, the Governor-General of India who backed Malcolm, and the Foreign Office, both Ambassadors reached Persia. This curious affair, which was given much publicity, did not enhance the prestige of British diplomacy in the East.

After these, and many other incidents, as well as attacks on Arab and Indian ships, the Bombay Government realised that unless they took action, they would lose their trade in the Gulf. The pirate fleet was estimated at this time to consist of over sixty large ships and several hundred smaller vessels manned by about 20,000 men. Many of their ships were armed with guns taken from captured vessels, but the pirates were not very efficient in their use. The Government, though still determined to avoid conflict with the Wahabis, decided to send an expedition against the Pirate Coast to give support to the hard-pressed Sultan of Muscat. The orders to the commander of the expedition were carefully framed to ensure that only the Joasmi should be attacked, though they were acting in concert with the Wahabis.

The expedition sailed from Bombay in September 1809, under the command of Colonel Lionel Smith of the 65th Regiment, whose father was a director of the East India Company. He was a distinguished soldier, who afterwards became Governor-General of Jamaica, where he took a prominent part in the emancipation of the slaves: later he was made Governor of Mauritius. The force consisted of about 1,000 men of the 65th and 47th regiments, a detachment of Bombay Artillery, and 1,000 Indian troops. There were eight of the Company's ships, four transports, and two Royal Navy frigates. Their departure from Bombay was inauspicious for, outside the harbour, one of the ships which was loaded with 'bombs and shells', sank with the loss of many lives. According to Buckingham, the ship had been previously condemned as unfit for service.

In Muscat, the Sultan had been preparing his ships and forces to co-operate with the British, though no-one was told the reason for his preparations. When, after a long voyage, the squadron reached Muscat, 'the city was filled with joy'. Counting on the support of the British, the Sultan then declared himself against the Wahabis, and expelled their representative from Muscat. After some delay at Muscat, which gave the pirates time to put their defences in order, the squadron set sail, and the Sultan and his ship, the *Sally*, went down the coast to Barka where several thousand troops, and a number of ships were in readiness. Maurizi, his Italian doctor, who was with him, describes how, at Barka they had a meal in the room in the castle where, three years before, the Sultan had stabbed his cousin, Bedr, who was then his rival to the Sultanate.

Ras al Khaima was the first town to be attacked. Troops landed under the cover of the ships' guns and, after several bayonet charges, the town was taken. Some sixty pirate boats were burnt, and houses in the town were set on fire. Early on the following morning, the troops were withdrawn and re-embarked, as it was reported that a large body of Wahabis was coming to the help of the Joasmi, though none was seen. The expedition left Ras al Khaima without receiving any formal submission from the pirates who had retired inland. The squadron then crossed the Gulf to Linga on the Persian coast, which was taken without opposition.

From Linga, part of the expedition went to Luft, on Kishm Island, while the other part returned to Muscat. The Joasmi who held Luft refused to surrender and put up a strong opposition: from their fortifications they picked off the attackers with their muskets. In their red coats and conspicuous uniforms the British troops must have made good targets. A howitzer which had been taken ashore, had to be abandoned, and the troops were forced to retire under the fire of the enemy. The Joasmi were given an ultimatum to surrender within a certain time but, early in the morning, before the expiration of the truce, to the surprise of the whole squadron, a man was seen waving the Union Jack on the summit of the walls. Lieutenant Hall, who commanded the *Fury*, had gone ashore alone during the night, and made his way to the gate of the fort which had been abandoned by the garrison. The few Arabs who remained, fled on seeing him, believing that he was leading a party of troops. The town was then occupied, and handed back to the Sultan from whom it had been taken by the Joasmi. Several other ports were visited by the squadron, and pirate boats were destroyed.

The last place to be dealt with was Shinas, and here the operations ended disastrously for the Sultan. In January 1810, the combined force attacked what Maurizi describes as 'the obnoxious town' of Shinas. Negotiations for a surrender came to nothing, and parleys were drawn out by the pirates in order to gain time. The town was taken, after a bombardment, and the inhabitants, except for a few who were taken prisoner, having handed over their arms, were allowed to leave. To enable the British and Indian troops to distinguish the Sultan's men the Muscat troops had been issued with pieces of sailcloth to tie round their heads, but as most Arabs normally wear white headcloths, this method of identification was a poor one and, later in the day, it led to much confusion.

After the fall of the town, as at Ras al Khaima, information was received that a large force of Wahabis was approaching. Colonel Smith formed up the troops on the shore with the Sultan's men on one flank. While this was being done, the Muscat cavalry, who had pursued some of the pirates inland, returned in disorder, closely followed by the enemy. In the mêlée which ensued, many of the Sultan's troops were killed by shots from the British batteries which opened fire, believing them to be the enemy. Colonel Smith refused to advance inland when asked by the Sultan to do so, because he had no cavalry, and his orders were to confine his attacks to pirate towns. The British and Indian troops then embarked in their ships, which were lying off the town.

Soon the Wahabis appeared on the shore, led by Mutlaq al Mutairi, one of the most famous Wahabi generals. As Maurizi says: 'that brave, though ferocious chief no sooner perceived the departure of the British than, like a lion thirsting for its prey, he fell upon the affrighted Muscatis. The battle, or rather the massacre, which took place under our eyes, lasted for about two hours, at the end of which time, Saiyid Said saw his army completely ruined.'

Maurizi was in a gunboat off the shore, attempting to protect the troops, and he describes how the sea was full of drowning men, who were trying to escape from the Wahabis. So many of them climbed into his boat that he had to force them back into the water to prevent the overloaded gunboat from sinking. Probably many of the Sultan's troops were inland Arabs who, unlike the men from the coast, would not know how to swim. The English watched the rout from their ships and were 'astonished at the cowardice of their allies'. Maurizi's strictures are unfair, for the English were secure in their ships, and safe from the fate which befell the Muscatis. The Sultan and the survivors of his army succeeded in reaching their ships.

Next morning Mutlaq, bearing a white flag, mounted on a horse, appeared on the shore, and there was a discussion between him and the English about a treaty, but no agreement was made. Maurizi says that Mutlaq offered to refrain from molesting British ships if the British withdrew their support from the Sultan. Maurizi was 'much surprised at the civility with which Mutlaq conversed, and the gentleness of his deportment'. He had a 'handsome person, a warlike air, intrepid courage, and was an able politician and a skilful general'. He was killed in 1813, fighting against Muscat troops.

Having carried out the instructions to destroy the pirate fleet, the British squadron returned to Bombay, leaving Muscat in imminent danger of being overwhelmed by the Wahabis. The authorities in Bombay assumed that, by burning the pirates' boats, they had put an end to piracy. For a year or two it seemed that this object had been achieved, but the suppression of piracy by the British, until 1820, was a constant repetition of events. The pirates remained quiescent until they had built and acquired a new fleet, then, in spite of the Sultan's efforts to destroy them, they became as strong as they had been before the British expedition. By 1814, the Joasmi, with the support of the Wahabis, had once again embarked on a campaign of piracy, plundering ships, massacring crews, and attacking ships sailing under the British flag, although the power of their Wahabi allies was beginning to wane. This was due to the advance of the Egyptians into Arabia, and the death of the Wahabi Amir, Saud bin Saud, who was succeeded by his son Abdulla, 'to whom public opinion ascribed talents of a very inferior sort'. Several times during these years, both the Joasmi and the Wahabis professed a desire for a treaty with Britain, but nothing came of their advances except assurances to the Wahabis that Britain's intentions towards them were friendly.

In 1816, the East India Company's ship *Deriah Dowlat*, was attacked by pirates who killed most of the crew. This was followed by a badly managed demonstration by four British ships off Ras al Khaima. Bruce, the Resident in Bushire, who accompanied the expedition, demanded from the Joasmi Shaikh the restoration of plundered property and the delivery of some of the Shaikh's relations as hostages for good behaviour. The orders from Bombay were that, if the pirates complied with these demands, no further action was to be taken, but if they refused to do what was ordered, 'the squadron was to signify to the Chief that he might expect the displeasure of the British Government'. So vague a threat would have little effect on any Arab Shaikh, either in those days or today, and it is not surprising that it was ignored by the pirates.

Buckingham went on shore with the naval commander as interpreter, and describes the meeting with the pirate Chief. The talk was carried on in the open street, the Chief and the Englishmen sitting on the ground. The Joasmi Shaikh was 'a small man, apparently about forty years of age, with an expression of cunning and something particularly sarcastic in his smile'. Behind him stood his bodyguard of fifty men, armed with muskets, swords and shields. He was given until noon on that day to comply with the British demands.

Unfortunately, however, the weather was bad, and because the anchorage was dangerous, the squadron of four ships went out to sea before the ultimatum expired. They crossed the Gulf to Kishm Island and returned to Ras al Khaima some days later. A letter was then sent to the Shaikh, explaining why the British ships had so suddenly departed and extending the ultimatum for a further period. The Chief's reply was an insolent refusal to comply with the British demands and a suggestion that he would send his own representatives to treat with the Government in Bombay.

The ships then opened fire on some pirate dhows which were anchored near the shore, but the dhows were too far distant for the gunfire to be effective. Guns from the town replied with slightly more success, for one of the shots carried away part of the sail from a British ship. 'At least three hundred shots were discharged from the squadron, not one of them seemed to have done any execution.' The ships then set sail leaving the pirates performing jubilant war dances on the shore, 'and thus ended the wordy negotiation and the bloodless battle'. But there was one casualty. An unfortunate European in one of the ships, who was seriously ill, 'was so much agitated by the sound of the discharge of the first gun, that he fell back and expired'.

Emboldened by the fiasco at Ras al Khaima, the Joasmi engaged in piracy with renewed vigour. They had good reason to believe that the British, in spite of their superior ships and armaments, were incapable of resisting them. This was the position in the Persian Gulf when Captain Francis Loch, in command of H.M.S. *Eden*, sailed from Plymouth in the summer of 1818, bound for the Persian Gulf, to take part in the final expedition against the Pirate Coast, which once and for all put an end to piracy.

CHAPTER IV

FROM PLYMOUTH TO TRINCOMALEE

> 'The ship was cheered, the harbour cleared,
> Merrily did we drop
> Below the kirk, below the hill,
> Below the lighthouse top.'
>
> *The Ancient Mariner*: Samuel Coleridge – 1722-1834

ON June 9th 1818, at half past one in the afternoon, H.M.S. *Eden* weighed anchor in Plymouth Sound, and set sail for India and the Persian Gulf, in company with H.M.S. *Tees*, bound for St. Helena. It was delightful weather, and a firm breeze was blowing from the east. The *Eden* was commanded by Captain Francis E. Loch, who had been commissioned in March by Lord Melville, First Lord of the Admiralty, to fit her for India. She mounted 26 guns, and had a complement of 125 officers and men. All the officers and men were new to Loch with the exception of Lieutenant Moffath, an old friend of his who had served with him in H.M.S. *Minstrel*. Loch had a high opinion of Moffath's capabilities; he had been with Loch in Plymouth during the two months that it took to fit the ship for the voyage, and it was due to his 'amiability and excellence of temper, added to strong good sense' that everything had gone smoothly. He was always known as 'Old Moffath', not on account of his age, but because he had a very staid manner. In the *Eden*, Moffath was the junior lieutenant, rather to Loch's regret, because both the other two lieutenants who had joined the ship were senior to him.

Besides the Captain, there were three lieutenants, a marine officer, a master, two surgeons, a purser, two mates, seven midshipmen and a Captain's clerk. In addition to the ship's officer there were two passengers, Colonel John Mansel, C.B., and Colonel Dunkin, of the 34th Regiment. Mansel, who was in the 53rd Regiment also kept a diary, but unfortunately the only entries during his voyage in the *Eden* were notes giving the dates of arrival and departure at the ports which were visited. The two colonels were going to join their regiments in Madras: they were pleasant and congenial companions for Loch, with whom they messed on the long voyage out, and when they left him, on arrival at Trincomalee, he says of them: 'I shall ever remember the many happy days and hours they assisted to while away on the long, tedious, sameness of the passage from England.'

Because the crew were new, 'as it were all strangers to each other', Loch was 'rather uneasy as to carrying a heavy press of sail during the night', consequently in the morning all the 'light sails were taken in, and two reefs in the top sails.' Even for practised seamen, the first day or night in a new sailing ship must have been something of an experience. However, all went well, and the *Eden* 'slip'd merrily along, crossing the Bay of Biscay almost without a roll, and with no more motion than we had when lying at anchor in Plymouth Sound'. With a wind from the east, the *Eden* averaged 124 miles in twenty-four hours. On June 18th, she anchored in the Bay of Funchal, off the beautiful town of the same name, the capital of Madeira. On the day after their arrival, Loch and Rennie, the Captain of the *Tees*, were taken by the British Consul, Mr. Reid, to pay their respects to the Governor, who received them 'with great politeness and good breeding, contrary to what is generally stated of the Governors of Madeira, and evinced every desire to be kind'. For some years, until 1814, Madeira had been occupied by the British, but at the time of Loch's visit it was held by the Portuguese.

When sailors go ashore in foreign parts they seem to take every opportunity of riding either on horses, camels or donkeys. As far back as 1676, John Fryer describes how 'The Europe sailors go donkey riding and many are thrown off, both to the sport of the standers by and mirth of their companions'. In recent times, when British sloops called at Bahrain, one of the first questions which the officers used to ask was whether they could borrow horses, and go for a ride – and not all of them knew much about riding! Probably at the beginning of the 19th century, naval officers were more proficient riders than they are today. Having finished his official duties, Loch with the two colonels, and two of the 'youngsters' (midshipmen), started off on an expedition into the hills behind Funchal. Loch had been lent a horse by Mr. Reid, the others of the party were mounted on donkeys.

They followed a rough road across ravines, and stretches of open ground, covered with myrtle and wild geraniums, until they arrived at the heights of the south-eastern shoulder of the island. From there, they looked down on Funchal, and the broad, blue Atlantic. To the north, the high mountains of Madeira seemed to rise into the clouds. A road bordered with trees and prickly pear bushes led them to the gate of the garden which they had come to see; the sight inside the gate was a striking contrast to the rugged ground which they had traversed. A road through groves of lemon and orange trees led to a formal garden, laid out with good taste, and very well kept. The beds under the trees were gay with flowers and, along the paths, there were many kinds of flowering shrubs. There was a summer house in the centre of the garden, close to two ornamental pools 'which in England would have seemed out of place, but in that warm climate they were delightful'. A fountain played over beasts and birds carved in stone, into a pool below, and the rippling and dripping of the water added to the pleasure of the shade from the rows of tall trees on each side of the pools which formed a screen from the hot, noonday sun. From a terrace, covered in climbing geraniums, beyond the two pieces of water, there was a view across the sea to the distant, rocky islands known as the Desertas. Loch and his friends stayed in the garden until the evening, regaled with delicious oranges, and then they set off on their return journey, down the steep mountain paths to Funchal.

Almost at once the pony on which Loch was riding became troublesome. It began to kick and lash out with its hooves, which caused great amusement to Loch's companions. However, he kept his seat. When he arrived at the Consul's house, he discovered the cause of the trouble; one of the Consul's servants, who was with the party, thinking that he would have some fun at seeing a sailor unhorsed, stuck a pin in the front part of the saddle, so that, when going downhill it pricked the animal's back and irritated it. Loch does not say what happened to the man who played this trick. Although it was an age when practical jokes were fashionable, such things would not be smiled on, if they were perpetrated by social inferiors. That evening, Loch and his party dined with the Consul, who gave them some of each of the many different kinds of wine which were produced on the island. After this libation, they spent the night in the Consul's house.

Next day, the same party, with the Captain riding the pony,

but this time without any misadventures, went up the mountain again to visit the convent of Our Lady of the Mount. On the day before they sailed, they sauntered through the town, admiring the superb churches and convents, and buying dried fruits and sweetmeats from the nuns. In the evening, on their way back from the expedition, Loch and Dunkin lost their way. Seeing a man in a garden, they went in to ask him where the road was. He was a black slave, and when they spoke to him, he began to shout and holler, as though they were going to murder him: the more they tried to pacify him, the louder he shouted. They were close to the windows of a house in the garden, and they began to think that they were in a rather dangerous situation, 'as a stiletto or a shot might have been their reception'. At last, by means of a douceur and a few words of Portuguese mustered up by Dunkin, the slave was made to understand that they had lost their way, and all that they wanted was to find the road: this they did without any further incident.

One of the people whom Loch met at Madeira was a young Englishman, who had left England in a hurry, and was on his way to America. He seems to have been a 'confidence man', for he had cheated 'the very Highest Society in England' with his pretensions of wealth and his claims to a peerage; he was now 'cheating the good people of Madeira, as he had done in England'. He carried documents, which he had drawn up himself, proving his wealth and his title. However, 'the Young Adventurer' was exposed. He told Loch that he was shortly going to Madras to take over a valuable estate which had been left to him by his grandmother. When closely questioned, he said that the estate was a place outside Madras called the Mount. The Mount existed but it did not belong to anybody's grandmother, it was an artillery barracks, the property of the Government. 'Poor creature,' says Loch, 'he was exceedingly annoyed at the discovery made of him.'

The *Eden* and the *Tees* sailed from Madeira on June 21st, two days later, they parted company, when the *Tees* changed her course for St. Helena which was an important anchorage for ships of the East India Company and the chief victualling station for ships going to India and the Far East. After sailing for a few days, the *Eden* ran into shoals of flying fish, which were being hunted by albacores (tunny fish), and banattas. The flying fish hit the sides of the ship in the daytime and at night, many of them coming into the ports and on to the decks, where they were struck with harpoons by people stationed there for the purpose, the fish being served out to the ship's company. All through the diary, Loch refers to the crew as 'the people', which was the custom in the Navy at the time.

On July 11th, the *Eden* crossed the Line, and this was celebrated in the usual nautical fashion – a rough experience for the sailors who had never crossed the Line before. 'At two in the afternoon, Neptune thought that we were within his limits. One of the oldest seamen, who had often crossed the Line, was dressed (I was going to say) but, on the contrary, was stripped, with the exception of a cloth tied round his waist, and a swab made up in imitation of long hair whitened with flour, as Neptune. He made his first appearance at the bowsprit, hailing the ship with "Ship Ahoy!" which, being answered by me from the Quarter Deck, he came from the forecastle in a car, which was two arm chairs fitted on to a grating. By his side was seated Amphitrite. The car was dragged by a number of men dressed (or undressed) as attendants or inferior Gods and Goddesses. I, of course, met the Watery God with all due form, and received his salutations and congratulations on the ship's safe arrival in his dominions. Neptune now retired to hold his levee.'

'The person to be introduced to Neptune is now blindfolded and led forward to a large tub, which has been filled with water, across which a plank has been placed, on which he is seated. The barber now commences operations by taking a brush of tar, and rubbing it over the face of "Johnnie Newcome", and on answering some questions, which are asked on purpose, the barber stuffs the brush into the poor fellow's mouth. When he is sufficiently lathered, the shaving commences. It is done with a notched iron hoop, instead of a razor. The board is then slipped from under the man, who falls, souse! into the tub. This is a signal for all who can reach him to throw buckets of water over him. At the same time a rope is placed in his hands so that he can pull himself out, but it is left loose, so it does not help him.'

'You now see the poor wretch floundering, kicking, sprawling, and roaring, half choked with water, till the bandage is removed, when he, in his turn, enjoys and assists in the initiation of the next victim.'

'In the evening, the hilarity of the few hours before was sadly

42

damped by one of the seamen, John Dobson, falling overboard at 8.30 p.m. He was drowned, in spite of all the exertions of those in the cutter and the jolly-boat, which were immediately lowered to his assistance. It being dark, he was not observed after reaching the water, the chances are that he was immediately seized by some of the numerous sharks which frequent these latitudes.'

Loch describes the sharks in this area as 'not so large as those I have seen in the East or West Indies, but I have seen them caught from twelve to fourteen feet long. One, taken at the time that I am writing, had a pair of jaws which, when cleaned, were so wide as to be slipped over my shoulders, and down, without touching any part of my body.'

At daybreak on July 26th, the high Sugar Loaf mountain at the entrance to the harbour of Rio de Janeiro was sighted, and that evening, the *Eden* anchored off the town, close to the Portuguese Admiral's ship. Loch was full of admiration for the magnificent scenery and the mountains of fantastic shapes which surrounded the bay, 'of all the grand and beautiful places which I have ever beheld in any quarter of the Globe, Rio Janeiro is the foremost.' Some days later, Loch discovered that the Admiral had considered it an omission that the *Eden* had not saluted his flag, so this was done, on the understanding that the Admiral's ship would return an equal number of guns. The *Eden* remained at Rio until August 6th.

Loch, with his friends Mansel and Dunkin, paid the usual visits to the Minister of Marine, and other officers of state, and were entertained by the Consul-General, Mr. Chamberlain. An English merchant, Mr. Young, invited them to dinner in his house. Soon after they arrived, Mr. Young appeared, and begged to be excused, as he was obliged to dine with the Minister of Marine, but to the surprise of his guests, he told them that his daughter, who was only fourteen years old, and her governess, an Irish Catholic lady, would do the honours at dinner. They had an excellent meal, and after dinner, they were taken to the opera by the young lady and her governess.

Though filled with admiration for the beauty of the scenery, the imposing appearance of the palaces and churches, and the splendour of their interiors, Loch was not impressed by the habits of the people. 'Murder', he says, 'is a crime considered of little consequence in this part of the world. An assassin can be hired

43

as easily as you can hire a porter in England, the price to be paid, being according to the danger of being discovered and the importance of the person to suffer. The price which is placed on one of the church is more than on any other member of the community, so it is not often that any of the clergy suffer. Yet one was murdered while I was there. To secrete the deed, his head had been cut off and cast into the bay, but it was driven ashore not far from the house of Mr. Chamberlain.'

One evening, Loch watched the funeral procession of an old lady who, he was told, had left large sums to the church. 'First came the clergy with large wax candles in their hands, accompanying the Host, then the corpse, superbly and most gaudily dressed, then more clergy singing a beautiful Requiem, followed by hundreds of well-dressed people, mostly in cocked hats, all carrying the same sort of candles in their right hands, these candles were about five feet long, and one and a half inches in diameter. The whole street was illuminated by them. All the people were on foot, none being in carriages or on horseback.'

On another day, Loch met a gang of slaves from the interior, bringing bales of sugar to Rio. They marched four abreast, naked except for a white sash round the waist. A man led them, singing a song as he marched, which the others joined in, keeping in step to the tune. In the markets they found fish, fruit and vegetables of excellent quality, but very expensive. The beef and mutton were not good, having been 'improperly killed'. Among the fruit, were oranges, each of which contained at the opposite end to the stalk, under the same rind, little entire oranges, which could be divided into sections like the parent orange.

By August 5th, having refitted the rigging and taken on food, water and provisions, the *Eden* was ready to sail, but the date of sailing was delayed for a day at the request of Mr. Chamberlain. He asked Loch to allow the *Eden* to act as escort for a short distance to a Portuguese ship, bound for India, carrying a large quantity of treasure belonging to English merchants. There were a number of ships from Buenos Aires cruising off the coast, 'who were not very scrupulous as to what they could master'. At 6 p.m., the *Eden* weighed anchor, and made sail with a firm, light breeze from the north. The Portuguese ship did the same. But the wind died down so the *Eden's* boats were ordered to tow her from the harbour. When she had cleared the harbour a breeze sprang up, all sail was made, and the Portuguese ship, still anchored, was left to her fate, as she had not the courage to follow, and the *Eden* had no time to spare.

Twelve days later, about forty miles from Tristan da Cunha, the *Eden* ran into a heavy gale, and the weather became thick and hazy. It was here, for the first time on the voyage, that what sailors call 'the Flying Dutchman' was seen. Loch describes it as 'the perfect image of our own vessel on the horizon, which ever way you look'. He explains the phenomenon as being caused by the humidity, and the thickness of the atmosphere, which reflects the image of the ship: the darker the night, the more distinct being the reflection. Sailors, however, would not accept this explanation of a phenomenon which has been the subject of so many legends, and is regarded as a sign of coming disaster. In this case, no harm came to the ship.

On August 28th, the man at the mast suddenly called out 'rocks on the starboard bow!' The ship was steered to pass the rocks as near as was prudent. Within a few miles from the rocks, the water was seen to be washing over them, but no rocks were shown on any charts though passing ships reported that there were rocks in these latitudes. Loch turned his glasses on to the rocks, and saw what he supposed to be barnacles sticking to them. The ship drew nearer. Then, to his surprise and relief, Loch saw that what had appeared to be rocks were, in fact, a number of whales enjoying themselves by floating on the surface of the sea, with their fins and tails projecting from the water. A few days later, in the same parallel, the man at the masthead sighted a sandbank with breakers washing over it. When the ship approached, the sandbank turned out to be the carcase of an enormous whale, covered with thousands of sea birds which, when they were scared off their meal, rose in a cloud which darkened the horizon. The detestable smell of the huge dead whale stuck to the ship for several hours.

Whales in the Indian Ocean are common, and sometimes they are seen near the entrance of the Persian Gulf, but they very rarely venture to the top part of the Gulf, possibly because much of the Gulf is very shallow. Some years ago, a dead whale was washed ashore on one of the Bahrain islands. Few of the Arabs had seen a whale and, for many days, until very little was left of it except the smell, local buses did a thriving trade in carrying out hundreds of Arabs to the shore, where the whale had been cast up. The smell of the decomposing whale was carried for several miles.

On October 6th, at 11 a.m., the *Eden* anchored in the harbour of Trincomalee, alongside H.M.S. *Minden*, the flagship of Admiral Sir Richard King, the Naval Commander-in-Chief of the Indian Seas, who later died of cholera while he was Commander-in-Chief at Sheerness. As soon as the ship was secured at anchor, Loch went ashore to the Admiral's house, carrying the letters and despatches which he had brought from England. The voyage from Plymouth to Ceylon had taken three days less than four months, including three days spent at Madeira and ten days at Rio de Janeiro.

Trincomalee, which Nelson when he was a young man serving in H.M.S. *Sea Horse*, described as 'the finest harbour in the world', was taken by the British from the Dutch in 1795. It became an important naval centre and dockyard, and in modern times it was the headquarters of the Commander-in-Chief, East Indies Station, who used to visit the Gulf ports every year in his flagship. Latterly, it was one of the few naval stations where the Admiral was allowed to have his family with him on board his flagship.

Loch describes the 'neat, well-built, small town' on the shore of Back Bay, with large houses surrounded by gardens for the Governor, the Fort Major, and other officers and officials. On the summit of a high cliff above the bay was a flagstaff, from which signals were given to the Admiral's house down below, notifying the approach of ships. Loch was very critical of the defences of Trincomalee, which consisted of a fort on the isthmus near the dockyard, and another fort on Osnaburg Hill, overlooking the bay, but neither of these positions commanded the entrance to the harbour. Of Osnaburg fort he says: 'it does not in any way command the bay, indeed it might as well be placed in the sky for all its utility as a protection'. Over 1,000 men were employed in the dockyards, and their wages amounted to £25,000 a year, which Loch seems to have regarded as a very large sum. He considered it 'strange that so much money has been spent on forming a remarkably nice dockyard, well stocked with naval stores, yet there has not been one farthing laid out in protecting it'.

Loch mentions the heavy taxation at Trincomalee. On a later visit, he brought a basket containing about two dozen mangoes, from Bombay as a present to the Commander-in-Chief. The mangoes which were grown at Trincomalee tasted so strongly of turpentine that nobody could eat them. Loch gave his Bombay mangoes to the coxwain to carry when he went ashore. On looking round for the coxwain, 'I was much astonished to see him and a couple of natives in a scuffle, and I overheard him swearing that he would not give up the mangoes'. The two 'natives' were revenue officials, demanding customs duty. Loch went to the Resident and Collector, and told him what had happened, but the Resident said that 'he doubted very much that he could allow the mangoes to pass, so strict were their instructions'. However, eventually Loch was allowed to bring his mangoes ashore. The mango incident seems to have upset Loch, and his comments on the 'natives' of Trincomalee are not flattering. 'The people, like their kinsfolk in Malabar, are famous jugglers, they work beautifully in jewelry, but do not consider it necessary to adhere to the truth and are not altogether honest.'

On October 7th, Mansel and Dunkin left in a country craft for Madras, at the same time Loch lost two of his officers who had to be invalided home. For the next three weeks, the crew were busily employed in 'stripping the masts and yards of the rigging, and refitting it, repairing the sails, and caulking the ship throughout. By October 30th, we were again all ataut and ready for sea.' In their off-time, the seamen were allowed to go ashore on an island in the bay which was called Sober Island, apparently it was named thus because the authorities believed that there was little chance of the seamen being able to obtain spirits there. This was far from being the case for, as Loch says: 'where money is to be gained, the demand will be supplied by some means. I can only say it was anything but a sober island while I was there, and some very jovial days have I had with poor Sir Richard and his friends.' From this rather odd remark, it appears that the Commander-in-Chief used to have parties on this island, which was supposed to be 'dry'.

On November 2nd, Loch received orders from Sir Richard King to proceed to the Persian Gulf, calling at Bombay, where the *Eden* was to be provisioned. He was told that, provided that he did not take too much time, he could call at any of the ports which he wished to visit on the Ceylon and Malabar coasts. On November 3rd, the *Eden* was ready for sea, and Sir Richard King came on board to muster and inspect the ship's company, the yards being manned for him. At daylight three days later the *Eden* sailed out of the harbour, bound for Bombay and the Persian Gulf.

CHAPTER V

'We'd a long brass gun amidships, like a well-conducted ship,
We had each a brace of pistols and a cutlass at the hip;
It's a point that tells against us, and a fact to be deplored,
But we chased the goodly merchantmen and laid their ships aboard.
Then the dead men fouled the scuppers and the wounded filled the chains,
And the paint-work all was spatter-dashed with other people's brains,
She was boarded, she was looted, she was scuttled till she sank.
And the pale survivors left us by the medium of the plank.'
          A Ballad of John Silver – John Masefield

THE voyage up the west coast of India was uneventful. Loch did not go ashore at many of the places where the *Eden* touched, as he was suffering from 'bilious fever and a swelling of the ankles', which, he says, was a common complaint among Europeans on their first arrival in India.   When the ship anchored, natives came off in canoes and catamarans (rafts made of logs), selling fruits, coconuts and monkeys, the last 'which might have been taken for the children of the men from their manners and appearance and mode of sitting'.   Although Loch said that the men looked like monkeys, he expressed admiration for the women who were 'contrary to the men, having fine figures and good faces'.

On November 11th, the *Eden* anchored at Cochin, on the Malabar coast, where the officers were entertained by an elderly couple called Schuller.   The husband was a German, and his wife was a French woman from Mauritius, 'a great Bonapartiste'.   Schuller ran a boat yard, and had built several small frigates for the Admiralty.   His wife traded in fruit, vegetables and poultry, selling them to ships which visited the port.   Between them, this elderly couple had acquired a monopoly of all the trade in the place.

Cochin was one of the first Portuguese settlements on the Indian Coast, and was later taken by the Dutch, who were evicted by the English in 1795.   Since then, all the fortifications had been destroyed, though many of the original houses remained.   They reminded Loch of the tall houses in the old part of Edinburgh, different families occupying each floor. From outside, they were imposing buildings, 'but misery and filth prevailed within'. While he was in Cochin, Loch went to see a neighbouring village, inhabited entirely by Jews, of which there were several thousands. Tavanier, in 1678, described Cochin itself as 'in old times a Republic of Jews', of the tribe of Manasseh. Another traveller remarked on the striking similarity of the features of the inhabitants, who looked as if they all belonged to one family. Loch says that the Jews in this village retained the manners and customs of their race, never marrying out of the tribe, and having their own laws as far as was consistent with the government of the country. Loch produces a lengthy argument, by which he endeavours to prove that this Jewish settlement had been established on the Malabar coast since the time of Solomon, and that they used to trade with Hyram, King of Tyre.

When Loch went to the village, a wedding was being celebrated. 'I witnessed, on the evening previous to the marriage of one of the young ladies, the dance which is given on such occasions, which is performed by a number of young females, the bride, of course, being the principal. All were drest in Jewish fashion, and loaded with jewels. Each lady took the other by the hand, going round in a circle, every now and then making a spring, and a sort of cut with the feet. At times they threw their bodies and arms into attitudes far from inelegant. The muslin dresses which they wore were very beautiful, each had a long scarf, one end over the left shoulder, and the other end falling in graceful, natural folds over the body. The men were remarkably good looking, their complexions were no darker than European Jews, and the girls were very pretty.'

The next port of call was Goa, which was reached on November 20th. The *Eden* anchored inside the entrance of the harbour which was strikingly beautiful. On the high ground surrounding the water, there were forts, barracks, churches and country houses, the white buildings stood out against a background of green gardens and vegetation. Some Carmelite friars came on board the ship as soon as she had anchored, bringing presents of fruit and vegetables and asking for alms. Loch, who seems to have had a certain antipathy towards Roman Catholics, says, rather grudgingly that the friars, 'having received their gratuity, departed leaving us their prayers and blessings, which I really believe to have been sincere – at all events, were it otherwise, they did us no harm'.

Goa, when Loch saw it, was no longer that splendid city which it had been when the Portuguese Viceroy lived there, whose churches had given Popes and Cardinals to the Roman See. The only British subject in Goa was a Mr. Forbes, a Scot with a Portuguese wife. He accompanied Loch when he made his official call on the Viceroy, and then took him, in his barge, about ten miles up the wide, smooth inlet to the old city, once the capital of the great Portuguese Empire in the East. They were rowed past high cliffs, covered with vegetation, and wooded islands, where tall trees threw deep shadows over the glassy water, and the only sound was the splash of the oars. Then, suddenly, on rounding a point the old town came into view.

'Before us were the ruins of magnificent churches, palaces, the Inquisition and the dockyards, built at the top of, and at the foot of a hill; the city, overlooking the water, which was here two miles wide, was backed by blue, misty mountains.' But in the great dockyards which were built by the Portuguese when they were at the height of their power, there was only 'one miserable brig of war'. Most of the buildings, on closer inspection, were seen to be ruinous, and the gardens, which had once surrounded them, were overgrown and reverting to jungle. But some of the churches and monasteries were still in use, and in a good state of repair. The grandeur and richness of the decoration inside them was a contrast to the forlorn condition of many of the other buildings. It was owing to the unhealthiness of the old town and its bad climate, that most of the inhabitants of Goa had moved from the city to the new settlement near the harbour.

On their way back, Loch was shown a vessel under repair, which had been rammed by a sword fish. The crew described the incident. The ship was on her way from Coromandel when suddenly they felt a violent shock, as though the ship had struck a rock, which was impossible as they were in deep water. For some time, she was quite unmanageable. They were near the Maldive Islands, and from there they came to Goa. When the ship was examined in dock, it was found that the long, bony snout of a sword fish had entered eighteen inches into the wood, and had loosened the stern part of the vessel.

In the evening, Loch came ashore again to dine with Forbes and his wife, who lived in a house on the southern point of the harbour entrance. He was met on the shore by a palanquin, carried by four coolies, who conveyed him from the beach to the house where Mrs. Forbes 'a very nice person, who did all in her power to make us comfortable, procured for me an excellent dinner, drest in the Portuguese style'. It is not clear whether it was Mrs. Forbes or the dinner which was 'drest in the Portuguese style!' Perhaps Mrs. Forbes was a descendant of one of the female orphans who used to be sent to Goa every year. Pietro Della Valle, who was in Goa in 1523, described how the King of Portugal sent 'a small annual investment of female orphans to India for the especial use of the settlers on the western coast. They were poor, but well-descended orphans, which were sent from Portugal at the King's charge, with a dowry which the King gave them, to the end that they may be married in India in order to further the peopling of the Portuguese colonies in those parts.' On arrival, the brides-to-be were lodged in a Convent, where the suitor was allowed to call on the lady of his choice, chaperoned by the convent matron. Rings were exchanged, and solemn promises of marriage were made in the presence of the Archbishop who afterwards performed the ceremony. Fryer, in 1676, reported that the ladies of Goa were 'not of that coruscant beauty that our English ladies are', but in those days 'to ogle a lady in a balcony, if a Person of Quality, is revenged with a bocca mortis (blunderbuss)'. But William Francklin, a young ensign in the East India Company, a few years later describes meeting 'three really fine girls' at Goa.

Three days later, on November 22nd, the *Eden* reached Bombay where she stayed for eleven days, taking on stores and enlisting a few seamen to complete her compliment. There had been several deaths among the seamen during the voyage and, on reaching India, two of the officers had to be sent home owing to sickness. There was, at this time, a good deal of ill feeling between commanders of ships of war and captains of merchant vessels on the subject of enlistment. Naval commanders had orders to bring their crews up to full strength when in Bombay, but they were not supposed to press seamen in time of peace, nor were they allowed to enlist men from merchant ships if, by so doing, they would endanger such vessels. If, however, seamen from merchant ships volunteered for service in the Navy, and

V. The attack of the enemy's cavalry at Shinas, January 2nd 1810

VI. The storming of Shinas, January 3rd 1810

were required, the naval captains had no option, and had to enlist the men if they were fit for service. In this case, the man's captain had to pay him up to the date of his leaving his ship. There were many complaints made by captains of merchant ships, or 'free traders' as they were often called, about the hardships which they suffered through members of their crew being enlisted into the navy 'from the caprice of a commander of a ship of war'. While in Bombay, Loch enlisted five seamen from two free-traders, the *Liverpool* and the *Batavia*.

Loch had letters of introduction to the Governor of Bombay, Sir Evan Napean, and during his visit he stayed in the Governor's house. He met many of the leading people of Bombay, though he says very little about them, except that their attentions and kindness 'made my visit most agreeable and delightful'. He was surprised to find that Bombay was so like a Portuguese town in appearance. The streets and buildings retained the form and style 'as when Bombay was delivered to Charles II as the marriage dowry of the Infanta Catherine of Braganza in 1661'. The island of Bombay, not having come up to the King's expectations, was at one time made over by Royal Charter to the East India Company on payment of an annual rent of ten pounds in gold on September 30th each year. Later, after various disputes and quarrels among the directors of the Company, it reverted to the Crown.

The *Eden* left Bombay on 4th December, bound for Muscat. The Governor had told Loch about the serious depredations committed by the pirates on the Guzerat and Kutch coast, and had warned him to be on the look out for pirate vessels. There were estimated at this time to be about sixty large, well-armed pirate vessels in action, as well as a number of smaller craft. Their base was Ras al Khaima on the Arab coast, whence they attacked both native craft and ships flying the British flag.

On the evening of December 18th, the *Eden* was sailing up the coast when two dhows were sighted off the town of Ambah. It was almost dark and lights could be seen on the shore. The *Eden* pressed in as close as possible, and anchored in 3½ fathoms of water, by which time night had fallen. Moffath was then sent in the gig to reconnoitre. On his return, he reported that there were a number of vessels of the type used by pirates, anchored close to the town which was a typical coastal town, defended by walls and towers. Owing to the darkness, and because the Arabs were dancing and beating drums, Moffath had been able to approach close to the vessels without being seen. There were no means of distinguishing pirate ships from Arab traders. Both used vessels of the same type and most of the ships were armed; the traders, when they could, carried guns to defend themselves against the pirates. Only one man in the *Eden* had been in the Gulf before – he was Lieutenant Dent, who had served with Commander Brydges: nobody else had the slightest knowledge of what the pirates or their ships looked like. However, it was assumed that the ships which were assembled in the harbour at Ambah were probably pirates.

The anchor was 'tossed up'. Decks were cleared for action, and the ship was kept under 'easy sail'. At daybreak the weather was fine, with 'light airs off the land', and the *Eden* found herself drifting towards the coast. Dent, who was sent in the cutter to do some sounding (for no details of this coast were shown on the charts), reported that it was too shallow for the ship to move farther in.

Before midday, a small dhow of about 20 tons with a crew of ten men was intercepted and boarded. The men in the boat said that they were fishermen, but they were taken on board the *Eden* and held as hostages. No reliable information was obtained from them about the vessels which were congregated in the harbour. 'I could not be certain as to what the vessels were', says Loch. 'Had I known that these were pirate vessels there would have been but one question to solve, which was how to destroy them.' He had been told that it was the practice of peaceful vessels to collect together for protection against attacks by pirates or by hostile Arab tribes but, he knew too, that the pirates were in the habit of massing together when they contemplated a raid.

Eventually, Loch sent Dent with Adey, the interpreter, and some of the men from the fishing boat, in the cutter to parley with the crews of the ships. Dent was told to 'explain who and what we were, and our object, and to be satisfied as to what the vessels were'. It was a dangerous little expedition. Strict orders were given not on any account to commence hostilities, but if they were attacked, the rest of the *Eden's* boats, which were manned and ready to start immediately, would come to the rescue.

The cutter went alongside one of the ships and the interpreter began questioning the crew. Then someone on board saw one of the men from the fishing boat in the cutter and 'immediately a club was raised to knock down the nearest seaman'. But the blow was warded off. Adey then, in spite of orders, seized a musket and was in the act of presenting it, when Dent knocked it out of his hands, 'preventing what must have been terminated in much useless bloodshed, for the signal of a musket shot would have signified that the vessels were pirates, and the ship's boats would have been despatched, and not recalled until destruction had been completed'.

The cutter returned to the *Eden* without any attack having been made on her, and Dent reported that the vessels were not pirates. She was again despatched to the harbour, this time in charge of 'old Moffath', with Adey, carrying with them silver-handled knives and bales of cloth, gifts for the Shaikh of Ambah. These were presented to him, and at the same time, he again assured the officers that the ships which were sheltering in his harbour were trading vessels which had gathered together to defend themselves from an attack by pirates. As a parting gift, the Shaikh gave the officers some sheep and goats and thoughtfully provided a supply of fodder for the animals to feed on. The cutter returned, the boats were hoisted up, and the *Eden* sailed, both officers and men disappointed at the peaceful ending of what they had thought was to be their first brush with the pirates.

Four days later, the *Eden* anchored off a shoal consisting of a long spit of white sand frequented by turtles, which Loch names 'Astola'. Here she found the cruiser *Psyche*, who accompanied her to Muscat. Parties of men and officers went ashore to hunt turtles. The method employed was to creep up to a sleeping turtle, if possible without waking it, and to push a strong spar under one side of it, using the spar as a lever to turn it over. Once on its back, the turtle was helpless. To chase a turtle and to catch it before it reached the sea was less easy, for the great unwieldy creatures had quite a turn of speed and could move rapidly when pursued. As they scurried towards the water, they scattered stones and sand with their flippers in the faces of the men who chased them. Many of the seamen 'had their faces peppered with stones and sand, and afterwards suffered from the effects of this peppering'. During the day, the *Eden's* crew succeeded in catching eight turtles, each one weighing about 150 pounds. They sailed from the turtle island on Christmas Eve, 'feasting on turtles, and enjoying the good messes which we made of them'.

Loch's first encounter with pirates was early on Christmas morning. Three strange sails were sighted, one of them in tow, which was, in itself, a suspicious circumstance. Two of them were 'batils', big, graceful ships, famous for their speed, with enormous lug or shoulder-of-mutton sails. In the last thirty years, the batil has become extinct in the Persian Gulf, although one could occasionally see a batil laid up on shore, falling to pieces. Arab boat builders have no explanation as to why batils are no longer popular, possibly they are less easily adapted to oil engines which today are being used in many of the sailing ships.

'The superior manner in which the sails were cut and set, as well as the rig of the masts and the form of the hulls, bespoke them at once to be pirate vessels. All was now crowded in chase, they using every exertion to run across our bow, and get before the wind.' To increase her speed, the pirate vessel which had a dhow in tow, abandoned her prize by cutting the dhow adrift. Loch sent the cutter to take possession of the drifting dhow, a manoeuvre which was carried out without shortening sail. By ten o'clock the *Eden* was within gun range of the pirate ships, when she opened fire with her starboard guns, but without effect. Then the wind died down. The sails flapped uselessly against the rigging with every movement of the ship and the *Eden* could make no way. The pirates, with their great, light sails made of locally woven cotton, drew rapidly out of gunshot.

The pirate vessels had many advantages over the heavier, slower European built men-of-war and merchant ships. They were faster and more easily handled, and there was nothing about the weather or the sea which the men who sailed them did not know. The Arab-built ships were shallower, drawing less water, and their captains were familiar with all the uncharted islands and innumerable shoals and reefs which made navigation on both coasts of the Gulf so difficult and dangerous. Even when she was several miles from the shore, the *Eden* could only proceed slowly, constantly swinging the lead, and sometimes sending a boat ahead to take soundings.

Finding it impossible to overtake the pirates under sail, Loch ordered the boats to be lowered and manned by every available officer and man, with the object of chasing and boarding the pirate vessels. Almost as soon as the boats were lowered and ready to start, the wind came up again, so the boats were hoisted back and the chase continued. But by this time the pirates were so far away that only half of their sails were visible above the horizon, and by midnight sight of them was lost. The prize, which was being towed by the *Psyche*, then sprang a leak and had to be sunk.

Next day was spent anchored off the Makran coast, to give the officers and men an opportunity of celebrating Christmas 'which is customary in the Navy, they having been cheated of it, owing to the chase of the batils'. This part of the coast was under the control of Muscat whose Sultan, Sayyed Said, was at war with the pirates and had consistently supported the British in their efforts to suppress them. But in spite of this, the Makran coast was much frequented by pirates who obtained water and supplies from the coast villages and towns whose people were afraid of refusing to help them.

At daylight on the 28th, seven pirate ships were sighted, three of them being in tow. At first, the pirates mistook the *Eden* for a merchant vessel and they began to close in on her. They were soon undeceived and made all sail to escape, towing their captured dhows. The wind was light and baffling, so that, at one time, the pirates seemed to be getting away. They were using their oars, each one pulled by four men, as well as sails over which they threw water to fill the pores of the canvas so as to catch every breath of wind. The wind constantly changed, first blowing gently, then subsiding and rising again. Sometimes the pirates were able to take advantage of it, and sometimes it favoured the *Eden*.

The pursuit continued throughout the day, and it was not until sunset that the *Eden* closed with the sternmost pirate, a large 'baggalow'. She was towing a captured dhow which she promptly cut adrift. The *Eden* ran close past the abandoned dhow, and continued in chase of the next ship ahead. Baggalas were big ships, sometimes over 300 tons, with high, square tower-like poops, and elaborately carved sterns, with rows of square ports fancifully decorated. They had curved prows, and two tall masts raking forward, which carried their enormous sails. 'Booms' which were also used by pirates, were ships of a similar type, but their characteristic feature was their long, straight stemposts.

Both booms and baggalows are still used in the Persian Gulf.

Darkness fell, and the moon came up over the sea. It was so bright that Loch was able to watch from afar the manoeuvres of the enemy ships which were silhouetted against the moon, the *Eden* remaining out of sight. The pirates, believing that they had got away from the British ship, seemed to think that they were no longer in danger. They began to sing, and to beat their drums. Meanwhile the *Eden* crept silently towards them, slipping through the water with her sails just full on a sea which was so smooth that there was hardly a ripple. All was so still on board, that the steps of the officers' feet walking the quarter-deck was the only sound that could be heard, apart from the drumming and chanting of the pirates which came louder over the water as the *Eden* approached them. The ship went along as if she knew that she must exert herself.

The breeze strengthened. The *Eden* shot abreast of one of the pirate ships, which had a captured vessel in tow. She was within half a musket's shot distant, when she fired her starboard broadside of grape and round shot, with such effect that the pirate had hardly time to haul the dhow which she had in tow under her quarter. As the pirate ship sank, those who could, jumped on board the prize, cutting her adrift and leaving their comrades to their fate. Meanwhile the leading pirate vessel, with a dhow in tow, made all sail before the wind, crossing ahead of the *Eden*, and soon ran out of sight.

At daylight, Loch sent the cutter with Moffath and Adey to take possession of one of the vessels. When they went on board, they found that the pirates had hidden themselves down below, but by dint of threats and persuasion, they were induced to come out from their concealment. There were only thirteen of them, the rest of the crew must have been drowned. They were taken on board the *Eden* 'and most uncouth, athletic and almost naked wretches were they'.

'Never shall I forget the scene that took place when they were first assisted on to the quarter deck, for they could not themselves ascend from the boat. They crept, knelt, and prostrated themselves, seizing the feet of those who were near them, kissing and hugging them. They showed all the extravagant misery of people who expected a most cruel and protracted death. Their own love of cruelty was such that they considered it totally out of the question that they would meet with any other treatment than that which they themselves had inflicted on the crews of the vessels which they captured. The crews of the captured vessels had been most cruelly mangled and murdered, as was the fate of all who were so weak and unfortunate as to fall into the pirates' hands.

'Nothing will efface from my memory the grasp which one of the oldest of these people took of my legs, with an imploring look and gesture, as if I had it in my power to save his soul from perdition, far less his mind from his present agonising state. His face was distorted and his muscles were literally quivering. It was not for a considerable time, that these wretches could be made to understand that their lives were secure. But no sooner were they certain of this, than their extravagance of joy was equal to their former despondency.' After their successful engagement with the pirates, the *Eden* and the *Psyche* set sail for Muscat which they reached two days later.

CHAPTER VI

''Tis moonlight over Oman's sea: her banks of pearls and palmy isles
Bask in the night beam beautiously, and her blue waters sleep in smiles,
All's hushed, there's not a breeze in motion: the shore is silent as the ocean.
If zephyrs come, so light they come, nor leaf is stirred, nor wave is driven,
The wind tower on the Emir's dome can scarcely win a breath from Heaven.'
Lallah Rookh: Thomas Moore – 1779-1852

'At night we saw Muscat whose vast and horrid
mountains no shade but Heaven doth hide,
though they cover the city with a horrid one,
reflecting thence the heat, scorching us at sun
setting aboard the ship.'
A New Account of East-India and Persia: J. Fryer – 1698

IT was New Year's Eve, 1818, when the *Eden* with her prizes
in tow, cast anchor in Muscat Cove in $9\frac{3}{4}$ fathoms of water,
which was so clear that the sea bottom could easily be seen.
'A salute of 13 guns was fired, and returned from the forts, with
as great precision as any salute would have been fired in Europe.
The report of the guns reverberated from rock to rock in such a
manner that it might have been supposed that a gun was fired
from every rock. The sound died away as the echoes receded
among the mountains.'

The view of Muscat town, as seen from the harbour, has hardly
changed since Loch first saw it from the deck of the *Eden* nearly
a century and a half ago. In Muscat there are no large modern
buildings or blocks of European style flats like those which have
sprung up along the sea fronts of the oil-rich towns, completely
changing the appearance of the skylines. Loch's description of
the dramatically arresting view from the harbour could be used
today without any alteration.

'On first observing land, enormous black serrated mountains
present themselves to view. On nearing them, you perceive
smaller hills, thrown up in all possible shapes, as black as coal.
Drawing still nearer, you observe a number of islands, not far
from the beach. Continuing to sail along, close to the shore,

you see through an opening, between two islands, the town of Muscat. The mode I took of running into the cove was by keeping along in shore, until reaching the most northern island. Round the north of it, the ship was hauled so close as to be able to chuck a biscuit on to the rocks. Then, all at once, sail was shortened, and the ship was shut into the harbour in water as smooth as glass.'

As the ship moved in closer to the shore, the town could be seen more clearly. 'At the head of the inlet, on a low, white sandy beach, stands the town, having a beautiful appearance from the bay. It is built of white stone, or whitewashed. On the commanding rocks above the harbour, there are forts with square or round towers, connected, where they can be, by walls, all in the Moorish style with embrasures and loopholes for musketry. On one of the islands is a strong castle in which the present Imam's uncle is confined, a close prisoner, in consequence of his attempting to wrest the government out of the hands of his nephew. The white buildings and the coal black rocks form a strange contrast, which is most painful to the eyes when the sun is shining on the former.'

The front of the town was open to the sea, on the land side it was defended by a wall with towers at intervals and a dry ditch. Outside the walls was a large suburb, inhabited by the poorer people who lived in palm branch huts. Many of the Gulf Arabs still inhabit these 'barastis', as they are called, which are cooler than mud or stone houses in the summer and warm in winter when the walls are lined with finely woven matting. The ground inside the barastis is covered with masses of tiny shells, which make a good floor covering and over this are spread matting and carpets. At the back of the town is a narrow defile, hemmed in by towering barren cliffs, which leads towards the distant high inland country, where in fertile mountain valleys, vines, crops and fruit trees grew luxuriantly. About a mile beyond the walls, there were two or three wells with little gardens around them protected by a fort. A few miles from Muscat, on the shore of another bay, is the town of Matra, shut in by mountains. It used to be accessible only by sea, but it is now connected to Muscat by a road over the cliffs, and is a busy, thriving port.

During the 19th century, and during the first decade of this century, sheets of scenes and characters were sold for 'The Juvenile

Drama', which was the name given to toy theatres, immortalised by R. L. Stevenson in his essay *A Penny Plain and Twopence Coloured*. Muscat harbour vividly brings to mind one of these scenes, though it is difficult to recollect which of the plays it may have belonged to. Possibly it was a scene from *Black Eyed Susan*, which was played at the Surrey theatre in 1825, or it may have belonged to *Blackbeard the Pirate*. The resemblance of the Juvenile Drama scene to Muscat harbour suggests that the artist who painted it perhaps saw the set of sixteen aquatints, which are now very rare, published in 1813 from paintings by Major R. Temple of the 65th Regiment, illustrating the expedition against the Pirate Coast in 1809, in which he took part, including two views of Muscat harbour.

At eleven o'clock on the morning after they arrived, Loch with four of his officers and Adey, the Greek interpreter, went on shore to pay their respects to the Sultan. As they rowed across the bay, Loch remarked on the quantities of little fish in the sea, which he said were similar to anchovies. When larger fish appeared, they scattered in all directions, springing out of the water into the boat. These fish are called 'manchus', in Arabic, and are netted and dried by the Gulf Arabs for use as fodder for camels, cows and donkeys. Though the cows have a regular diet of fish, their milk has no fishy flavour, and when Loch was at Bahrain, he described the milk which he bought there, as the best he had tasted since leaving England. Sometimes the little bones of the fish stick in the cows' tongues and set up an irritation, the bones then have to be removed one by one by somebody who is an expert in this work, a tedious, painful operation.

The naval party landed at a wharf facing an open square in the centre of the town, surrounded by two-storied houses. Here in the evening, the merchants of Muscat used to sit and watch the activity in the harbour. In other Gulf ports, the merchants and shopkeepers would sit smoking their 'hubble-bubble' pipes while they surveyed the scene, but in Muscat, even today, smoking in public is forbidden, as it is in Saudi Arabia. Loch was met on the wharf by Gaulaub, the Hindu agent of the East India Company. Muscat was the most cosmopolitan port in the Gulf and there were many Indians trading there from Bombay and Guzerat, as well as Persians, Arabs from other parts of the Gulf, Baluchis, and a small community of Jews, all living and trading harmoniously together. The customs were farmed to a rich Hindu merchant. One of the characteristics of the Muscatis was their tolerance and friendliness towards strangers and people of different religions.

Preceded by Gaulaub, the party walked through the town; everybody went on foot in Muscat, for the congested little town, squeezed between the cliffs and the shore, was unsuitable for riding. During the time he spent there, Buckingham never saw a horse or a camel. They passed the slave market which was then a flourishing concern. About 4,000 slaves were sold every year and taken to other places in the Gulf and to Iraq. They were exposed for sale in groups in the open. Women from Dongola and Darfur in the Sudan, and copper-coloured beauties from Abyssinia, sold for about 150 dollars, negresses from Central Africa fetched about 80 dollars. It was not until 1822, when the Sultan made an agreement with the British, that the slave trade ceased in Muscat.

The bazaar streets were narrow and crowded, roofed with ragged matting, through which shafts of sunlight lit on the goods exposed for sale in front of the cavern-like shops. The passage between the shops was filled with boxes, bales and baskets of dates, so that Loch and his party had to walk in single file. The Muscatis whom they met were similar in appearance and dress to the inhabitants of Muscat today. The pure bred coast Arabs are small, light complexioned, sinewy men, with scanty beards and hawk-like features: those with negro blood are of heavier build. Their appearance is deceptive: they do not look as stalwart as in fact they are. The men wore white shirts and trousers, girdled round the waist, turbans of blue check cotton, with silk and cotton borders of red and yellow, which were woven in Sohar. Some of them had swords slung over their shoulders, and carried small round shields, like a Scottish targe, made of wood, leather or rhinoceros hide, decorated with silver bosses. Many of them had their eyes darkened with kohl (antimony) which is thought to preserve the sight, a habit to which Muscatis are still addicted. They met a few wild-looking Arabs from the interior, with great masses of hair, wearing only a loin cloth and carrying spears and shields, who spoke a different language and seemed to be almost as much strangers in Muscat as the Englishmen.

Buckingham comments on 'the equality of value between the

dresses of the wealthiest and the lowest classes of people . . . the garments of the Prince, without his arms, could not have cost more than an English guinea'. He sums up the Muscatis as 'the cleanest, neatest, best dressed, most gentlemanly of all the Arabs that I have seen, who inspire by their first appearance a feeling of confidence, good-will and respect'. How different from Fryer's opinion of them: 'Fierce and Treacherous People, gaining as much by Fraud as by Merchandise' – but that was written in 1672. Many men from the Pirate Coast are now working in the oil fields in different parts of the Gulf. They are not popular among the more sophisticated Arabs of the oil states, who speak contemptuously of them, and suggest that they are addicted to Black Magic and other peculiar practices. But they are good workers and when there is a shortage of labour, the urban Arabs are glad enough to employ them.

When the naval party arrived at the palace which was at the end of the main bazaar street, the ponderous gates were opened by the guards who kept the visitors waiting for some time outside the gates, while they announced their arrival – so different to present day procedure in the Gulf, when official visits are timed to the minute, and important guests are received with guards of honour. Loch and his officers were then ushered into a court-yard, along a passage to the audience chamber where, to their great surprise, they found Saiyid Said seated on a chair with a table in front of him, and chairs on either side for his guests. Loch evidently expected to find him sitting on a carpet on the floor. He was told afterwards by Adey, his interpreter, that the chairs were specially provided in his honour, because he was the Captain of a man-of war. This was probably untrue, but typical of the type of remark made by interpreters to Europeans, who always suggest to visitors that the personage on whom they are calling is showing them some special favour.

One side of the room in which Loch was received was open to the sea and, between the pillars which carried the roof, there was a beautiful view of the harbour where vessels of every type and size were passing to and fro. In common with other Europeans who met the Sultan, Loch was very favourably impressed by the young Imam, by which title Loch always referred to him. He described him as 'extremely good looking, with a fair complexion, dark, handsome mustachios and beard, and an aquiline nose. His stature about five feet ten inches in height. He is well made and well proportioned, with the most agreeable and polite manner of any Arabian or Persian I have ever met with. His dress was a white turban, plain, without ornament, a white camel hair robe, not open in front, made in the form of a long shift. The robe was bound round the waist with a sash of fine white muslin, in which was stuck his yatagan (dagger), with a silver sheath and a handle mounted with precious stones. His large, wide, white trousers were of the same stuff. He had no covering on his feet or ankles, but his toes were stuffed into a slight pair of brown slippers.' Said at this time was about twenty-seven years old, and had been ruler for eleven or twelve years.

When Loch and his officers entered the room, 'the Imam advanced a few steps, touching the points of the fingers of his right hand with those of his left, raising his hand to his head, then placing it on his left breast, stooping forward and uttering the usual greeting: "salaam aleikum" and other salutations. After some conversation concerning the pirates captured by the *Eden*, he agreed to take charge of the prisoners, and to send them to Bombay on board one of his ships. Just as we were about to depart, a quantity of fruits, sweetmeats and sherbets were placed on the table, and we were invited to partake. The grapes and melons were most delicious, as excellent as those of Smyrna, the pomegranates, like those of the Mediterranean, were hard, dry and tasteless. Of the preserved fruits, the dates were the best, the sherbets were delightfully cool and refreshing in that more than oppressively hot place.'

After the visit, Loch and his party, escorted by a member of the Sultan's bodyguard, made a tour of the town and the bazaars and looked at the ships in the bay. The Sultan's navy, together with the ships of his merchants, numbered between four and five hundred vessels, ranging from 100 to 300 tons burden. He had 'three remarkably fine frigates, and seven other armed ships'. These, too, were used for trading on the infrequent occasions when Muscat was not engaged in war. Much of Muscat's trade was with Mozambique and Zanzibar, whence her ships brought slaves, ivory, gold dust and ambergris, which was exported to Persia, to be mixed with tobacco as an aphrodisiac. Very occasionally, ambergris was found off the coast of Muscat. Smaller ships carried slaves, opium and cowry shells, which were reshipped to 'the Eastern Islands' for which 'spiceries' and the produce of China were received in return. Some of the Abyssinian slaves who were brought to Muscat, after being given their freedom, set up as shopkeepers, and many of them became important merchants. Buckingham tells the story of an Abyssinian who was a slave and, when given his freedom, became a wealthy merchant and ship-owner: he transferred his business to Bombay where he lived for some time, but eventually returned to Muscat, which he regarded as his home. Intermarriage between Arabs and Abyssinian women was not infrequent. Maurizi mentions: 'the richer classes of courtesans from Persia and other countries who swarm in the capital'.

The *Eden* stayed for three days in Muscat, during which time two of the crew died and several others were put on the sick list. Loch describes Muscat as the most unhealthy place in or near the Persian Gulf, 'and no great wonder, for the surrounding hills, absorbing the rays of a tropical sun during the day, emit at night the absorbed heat, raising the temperature even higher than it is in the shade at midday, this continues until the refreshing sea breeze sets in on the following afternoon'. James Fraser, in his *Journey to Khorasan*, written in 1825, enlarges on Muscat's climate, saying that in one day, three lieutenants of H.M.S. *Liverpool* died of sunstroke at Muscat, and the men who dropped giddy and unconscious on the decks were given blood-letting, and bathing in tepid water. This was in the month of August, the hottest time of the year.

The climate of Muscat is more trying for Europeans than any other place in the Gulf, for there is no cold season to bring relief after the sweltering summer. But many Englishmen have lived there happily for long periods. Some, however, have allowed the atmosphere of the little town, wedged on a narrow strip of shore, between towering stark cliffs and the sea, to affect their mentality with a form of claustrophobia. There have been tragedies in Muscat, and some people believe that the British Agency is haunted. At Sollum, on the Western Desert of Egypt, during the 1914 war, men were affected in the same way, by being cooped up on a narrow strip of sand, between the sea and the escarpment, though the cliffs behind Sollum were lower, and less forbidding than the mountains which shut in Muscat.

One of the people who is very often mentioned by Loch in his diary, is the young Greek interpreter who accompanied him on his first visit to Muscat. His name was Adey, but Loch often refers to him as 'the little Greek'. Adey was the son of a man of means, the Sharaff (money-changer or banker), of the British Embassy at Constantinople. He and his brother were sent by their father to Europe to complete their education: Adey went to London and his brother to Paris. Adey had social ambitions, and in London he somehow managed to get an entrée into 'the First Society', where he described himself as 'The Prince of the Lebanon'. To support his pretensions, he took to appearing at parties in Oriental dress, and finally he appeared with a green turban on his head, indicating that he was a Haji, who had performed the Pilgrimage to Mecca – he was, in fact, a Christian. It was at this stage in his career that Loch first met him, at a party in Harley Street, and he recognised him again, when he came across him in Bombay in 1818.

Adey's pretence that he was a prince was shattered by meeting, at a party in London, the Turkish Ambassador who lodged a formal complaint with the Foreign Office about the young man who was masquerading as 'The Prince of the Lebanon' – the Lebanon, at this time, being a province of Turkey. Adey was sent for by the Foreign Minister and, after an interview with him, he left England hurriedly and joined his brother in Paris. He stayed there for some time, until he had spent all his money, and he then returned to Constantinople hoping to be received as a prodigal son. But owing to his debts, and the bad habits which he had acquired in London and Paris, 'added to all the predisposed vicious inclinations of the Greek', as Loch says, he had become a notorious character, and his father cast him off.

From Constantinople, Adey made his way by land to India, and eventually arrived at Calcutta where his plausibility gained him many friends, who persuaded the Government to employ him to buy horses for the army in Persia and Arabia. He set off in a ship from Calcutta for the Persian Gulf but, shortly before she sailed, the ship caught fire and was totally destroyed, but Adey survived. Returning to Calcutta, he described his hardships and losses with such feeling that a public subscription was raised for him. With a considerable sum of money in his pocket, he set off again for the Gulf, and was successful in buying a number of horses, which he brought to Bombay.

In Bombay, he produced his horses for inspection by Colonel Baker who was in charge of the remount depot for horses, which were bought for the Presidency cavalry. The Colonel found among them some remarkably fine animals, one of which he admired exceedingly. 'The Little Greek, with all the address of which he was master, begged the Colonel to confer a favour on him by accepting the horse as a gift, knowing quite well that the blunt, honest Colonel would spurn the idea of accepting a present.'

Baker then invited Adey to look over his own stud and to give an opinion of his horses. While displaying one of his finest animals he said to the Greek: 'Mr. Adey, you requested *me* to accept one of *your* horses, so it is only courtesy for me to offer you this one.' To the blunt Colonel's astonishment and dismay, Adey, instead of politely refusing the gift, replied in his broken English: 'Sare, I will show you how different is the politeness of our country to that of yours. *We* always *accept* presents offered by great men, such as Your Excellency. We would consider it an insult, in our low condition, to refuse such.' So Adey got away with the horse.

It was shortly after this incident that Loch arrived in Bombay on his way to the Gulf. Adey at once came on board to renew the acquaintance which he had made with Loch in London, and begged for a passage to Bushire. Loch, thinking that Adey's knowledge of Arabic would be useful, told him that, if he could arrange for a passage with any of his officers, he could join the ship. The midshipmen agreed to his messing with them. Officers were apparently allowed to take passengers in their quarters, if they had the permission of the Captain, for on this trip there were several passengers on board the *Eden*.

During the voyage, Adey showed himself to be both a braggart and a coward. When pirate ships were sighted, he stamped up and down the deck, rubbing his hands, and asking what chances there were of overtaking them and going into action. But when the *Eden* drew near to the pirates, 'the poor little devil would come to me with his hands on his stomach, telling me that he had such "a big pain" that he would be obliged by my directing my servant to give him one small drop of brandy, for he was very bad'. The brandy made him a man again, and he would stay on deck, swaggering around, but when the guns opened, he dashed down the hatchway into the steerage, where he remained 'as if

VII. Rafaa Fort

VIII. H.M.S. *Liverpool*
(*From a contemporary painting*)

IX. A boom under construction

with a fit of ague, until he was routed out by some of the mischievous youngsters'. When two prizes were taken and the pirates on board them could not be found, he volunteered his services, and buckled himself on to one of the ship's cutlasses then, with a pistol in each hand, he went on board the pirate boat, which Old Moffath had already taken possession of.

Adey left the ship at Bushire. He and a Jewish family who had also been passengers in the *Eden* stayed in the same caravansarai. Business took the Jew to Basra and he asked Adey to look after his goods during his absence. One night there were suddenly cries of 'Murder! Thieves! Ruin!' from Adey's room. There was a scene like one from *Gil Blas*. People rushed from their rooms, half asleep, with lights in their hands. Others peered from half-open doors, holding lights above them, to see what was happening outside, and some plunged about, half-naked, among the bales and merchandise in the courtyard.

Adey was discovered, apparently in a state of misery, declaring that his room had been broken into by robbers who had opened some of the chests belonging to his dear friend, the Jewish merchant, and had stolen many of the contents. He described minutely many of the goods which he said had been stolen, and the question was how was he able to describe in detail the contents of the chests which had not been opened and which he had had no opportunity of seeing? It was revealed that a few days before the 'theft', Adey had obtained a number of keys from the owner of the caravansarai, on the excuse that he had lost his own. It was quite obvious who was the thief. The affair was dealt with by the Shaikh of Bushire in a summary way, and Adey was very lucky to get off as best he could.

When the *Eden* sailed, Adey was left at Bushire, but some time later, when Loch went to Basra, the first person to greet him was 'the Little Greek', who was again involved in horse dealing. He at once offered to buy a horse for Loch, but Loch did not fall for this.

Towards the end of his time in the Gulf, Loch met Adey again at Cochin on the west coast of India. Adey had somehow obtained the post of superintending the building of some ships for the Bombay Government, and he persuaded Loch to take home with him in the *Eden* a wooden chair which was supposed to have been made from timber which Adey had recovered from the foundations of an old fort built by the Portuguese in 1497. Adey always had his eye on the main chance, and he was sending the chair as a present to Sir Bryan Martin, the Comptroller of the Navy. This was the last time that Loch set eyes on Adey, but he did hear about some of his subsequent exploits.

Adey went again to England and introduced himself to the family of a naval officer, claiming that he and the officer had been very great friends in India. He ingratiated himself into the good graces of the officer's sister, and eventually persuaded her to marry him. She was a widow with a jointure of £400 a year, quite a comfortable income in those days. Adey managed to obtain most of her money before they parted.

The last which Loch heard of the curious history of 'the little Greek' was, when reading an account of the first part of the Burma war. He saw in a newspaper the name of 'the poor infatuated Greek' among the list of men who were liberated from the dungeons of Rangoon. Loch completes his story of Adey with the words: 'where he is now, God knows. If in the land of the living, he is, in all probability, existing on his wits as he has done throughout his life.'

CHAPTER VII

'That execrable sum of all villainies, commonly
called A Slave Trade.'
The Journal – February 12th 1792

THE *Eden* stayed for three days in Muscat. In addition to
the two seamen who died while she was in harbour, a
third man died on the day that she sailed. From Muscat,
Loch crossed the Gulf and spent a week cruising among the
islands off the Persian coast. On the morning of January 10th,
seven large vessels, answering to the description of Joasmi, were
sighted; they were anchored in the narrow passage which formed
a natural harbour protected by shoals and sandbanks, between
Kishm Island, near Bundar Abbas, and the little island of Henjam.
'All sail was made in chase', and although 'the wind was directly
in our teeth', the flood tide was so strong that the *Eden* was able
to enter the passage which was about two miles wide. Having
no charts, Loch went up to the masthead, to survey the course.
He sighted a long sandbank but, before the ship could avoid it,
she had run aground; but she was soon afloat again. A pirate
ship which tried to run past her, received 'a good peppering', and
the *Eden* then moved closer to the six vessels which were hugging
the shore but, owing to shoals, she only reached 'a long gunshot'
from the nearest ship. The *Eden* then opened her starboard guns
on the pirates, doing considerable damage. The tide changed,
forcing her to get underweigh, and run into the middle passage,
where she anchored in deep water in a position where none of the
pirate vessels could gain the open sea without passing her. Here
she remained 'with her sails chew'd up at the masthead, all ready
for a start, with the guns clear, and the people at their quarters'.
The pirate ships had many advantages over British men-of-war.
Their draught was less, so they could cruise in shallow water,
they were equipped with two lines of powerful oars, like Roman
triremes, and their captains were familiar with the tangle of shoals
and sandbanks which made a labyrinth of both shores of the Gulf.

Darkness came suddenly, as it does in the Gulf, but at ten o'clock, the moon rose over the sea, lighting up the pirate vessels which were seen to be getting under weigh. The tide turned, and one of the pirates tried to run out to sea, past the *Eden*, hauling close-in to the shore. The *Eden* opened fire on her, and she received a shot 'which entered between wind and water, passing from stern to stern'. After midnight, the disabled ship ran ashore on the sandy beach. Another ship, a batil, attempted the same manoeuvre, she had already been damaged by the *Eden's* guns, and this, combined with the strong wind and heavy swell put her out of action; she, too, ended up on the beach. At daybreak, Loch sent a party ashore to set fire to the two pirate vessels. When the men returned, they brought with them three prisoners, two men and a boy, and they reported that 'the beach was strewn with dead'.

On the 11th, the *Eden* was again underweigh and ran into the harbour where the rest of the pirate squadron had been left. Two batils were 'working windward out of the western passage'. The wind had fallen, but they were using their 'long sweeps', rowing close to the shore, and being towed, to help their progress, by gangs of men from the crews, who moved along the beach ahead of the ships, pulling them with long ropes. They were carrying with them the survivors from the ships which had been destroyed. The *Eden* was unable to get within range of the pirates and, by the evening, they were out of sight. A third pirate ship was seen stranded on the shore, and Moffath, with two boats, was sent to destroy her; the boats returned loaded with rice, taken from the hold of the ship. Loch learned that the intention of the pirates had been to set up an 'establishment' at Bassidu on the western point of Kishm Island, opposite Ras al Khaima, which would have given them the control of both sides of the straits at the entrance to the Gulf.

The last scrap with the pirate squadron, or what remained of it, was on the 14th, when early in the morning a pirate vessel was sighted in the open sea. The *Eden* gave chase; the pirate ship, when attempting to tack, almost filled with water, but the crew 'by extraordinary exertions, skill and knowledge of the vessel' succeeded in baling her out and, the wind shifting northward, put her before the wind. 'The powerful sail, which had almost caused the destruction of the vessel, was now the means of carrying her in its arms.' Then the wind suddenly fell, and the ship was able to escape from the *Eden* by using her oars in the calm which ensued.

One of the three prisoners who were brought from the shore had poisoned himself and died soon after coming on board: Loch says 'his corpse turned a pale, livid green'. The other man, too, tried to kill himself, and was found half suffocated, having stuffed a quantity of tow down his throat, which much amused the boatswain's mate 'who rolled out "damn my eyes! Here's a bloody fellow who's been caulking up his throat with oakum"'. The oakum was removed, and the attempted suicide soon recovered. The third person, a boy, had been wounded by gunshot, his wounds were dressed, and by the time the *Eden* reached Ras al Khaima, he was well enough to go ashore. Besides the old man and the boy, there were two other pirate lads in the *Eden* who had been captured in a previous engagement; being young, they were not sent to Bombay as prisoners. Loch says that 'from their treatment by the seamen, they had become almost part of ourselves'.

Loch decided to drop the old man and the three boys at Ras al Khaima. His object in doing this was to let the pirates know about the success of the British ships in other parts of the Gulf. He told the prisoners, before putting them ashore, to inform their Chief that 'if any persons in his power were inhumanely butchered, or any further barbarities were practised against British subjects, then the fate of the Joasmi prisoners who had been sent to Bombay would depend on its Government'. Though Loch knew that he had no grounds for threatening retaliation against the prisoners, he thought that his warning might have a salutary effect. He evidently believed that his words had been effective, for he says that 'afterwards I had the inexpressible delight of knowing that, in consequence of the mode I took of landing these people, and the information transmitted through them, not one subject of the British, either English or Indian, suffered death from the Joasmi in cold blood'. It is more likely that the Joasmi would have been afraid of reprisals from the British ships in the Gulf, than of threats against their prisoners in Bombay.

The *Eden* crossed the Gulf again to Ras al Khaima, where the three lads and the old man were put ashore in a boat which had been taken from the pirates at Kishm. The two boys, who had spent several weeks in the *Eden*, were loath to leave the ship. 'They showed real good feeling and heart at leaving us.' They were probably sorry to return to the life of a junior pirate. When they left, they were given presents by Loch, and a letter was written in Arabic, by 'the old Jew', who was a passenger in the *Eden* from Bombay to Bushire, stating that the things which they had been given were their own property.

After spending some days beating along the Arab and Persian coasts, the *Eden* arrived at Bushire on January 23rd. There she found a convoy of ships at anchor, waiting to proceed to Muscat, where preparations were being made for the expedition against the Pirate Coast. For the next few weeks, the crew were employed in caulking and painting the ship and in repairing and refitting the rigging. The next place which Loch visited was Bahrain.

It was two years since the British had first made contact with the Shaikhs of Bahrain. In 1816, Bruce visited the islands, where he had a friendly reception, and obtained the agreement of the Shaikhs to a 'Treaty of Friendship', but as he had no authority from his Government to make such a treaty, it never came into force. Bruce might have learned a lesson from this, but that he did not do so was shown by the second unauthorised treaty which he made with the Persian Governor of the Province of Fars, at Shiraz in 1822, which led to his downfall. In this so-called treaty, which referred to various matters concerning the Persian Gulf, he described Bahrain 'which has always been subordinate to the Province of Fars', a statement which was completely untrue. The unauthorised treaty was immediately repudiated by the British Government, and Bruce was removed from his post for having attempted to carry out negotiations with Persia without the sanction of his Government. To this day, the 'Treaty of Shiraz' is one of the main arguments which is put forward by the Persian Government to support her claim to the ownership of Bahrain. Bruce was an officer of the East India Company's Marine. According to Loch, who got to know him very well, he was originally sent by the Bombay Government to the Gulf to investigate the possibility of developing some ancient copper and sulphur mines on the Persian Coast a few miles from Cape Kenn. In 1808, he was dealing with commercial matters at Bushire and, by the time that Loch knew him, he was Resident.

He was a keen, energetic man, for whom Loch developed a great liking.

Bahrain at this time was ruled by two brothers, Shaikh Abdulla and Shaikh Sulman, who had absolute control of the country. They were the sons of Shaikh Ahmed bin Khalifah, known to posterity as 'The Conqueror', who, in 1783, led his tribe from Zabara on the Qatar coast against Bahrain, expelled the Persian garrison, and made himself master of the islands. After the conquest of Bahrain, the tribe, which was previously known as the 'Utub', took the patronymic of 'Khalifah'. The system of dual control was frequently adopted by the Khalifah in later years, and at times it worked successfully. Loch refers to Shaikh Sulman, who lived in the fortress town of Rafaa in the centre of the main island, as 'the Shaikh of Bahrain', and to his brother, Shaikh Abdulla, who lived in the fort of Abu Maher in Muharraq, as 'the Shaikh of Arad', which is the old name of Muharraq.

The Bahrain Arabs were not themselves engaged in piracy, but Joasmi ships frequented their harbours, and much of the pirates' loot and not a few slaves found their way to the Bahrain bazaars. After taking Bahrain from the Persians, the Khalifah Shaikhs found themselves in a dangerous position. They expected the Persians to make an attempt to retake the islands but, though there were frequent rumours of Persian preparations, no attack on Bahrain was made. Both the Sultan of Muscat and the Wahabi Chief had invaded Bahrain, and for some years, the Wahabis had exercised control over the islands though the people had never accepted the Wahabi religion. Both these powerful chiefs desired to possess Bahrain. The Khalifah were also faced with the lifelong enmity of the Pirate Chief, Rahmah bin Jabr, Shaikh of the Jalahamah tribe, who awaited an opportunity to destroy them, and spent much of his time inciting the other Gulf rulers to attack Bahrain. Their one means of salvation was to play off their enemies one against the other, and this the Khalifah Shaikhs succeeded in doing with great skill. The early history of the Khalifah in Bahrain is confusing, for every few years they changed their relations with the other Gulf rulers; at one time, they would combine with the Wahabis against the Muscatis, another time the Muscatis would be supporting them against the Wahabis, but by such means they managed to maintain their independence and their grip over Bahrain. Owing to their precarious position, surrounded on all sides by enemies, and not very strong themselves, they were disposed to be friendly with the English if they could obtain from them some support and protection.

Bahrain is a group of islands about half way down the Persian Gulf, some twenty miles from the coast of Arabia. The capital, Manama, is on the northern point of the largest island, separated from Muharraq Island, on which the second largest town is situated by a sea channel 1½ miles wide. The two towns face each other across the water like Dover and Calais.

In 1819 Muharraq was the seat of government, and Manama was the commercial centre. Both towns were surrounded by walls, the remains of which could be found, with some difficulty, forty years ago, though the towns had long since extended beyond the walls. The Shaikhs and the leading merchants had their houses in Muharraq, which was slightly higher than Manama and considered to be more healthy. They occupied large, low stone houses, usually painted white, built around one or more courtyards. Coral stone, quarried from the sea shore, was used for building. The houses of merchants and Shaikhs had roof terraces, arched verandahs, latticed windows, and handsome doorways, decorated with elaborate plaster work. At one time, only the Shaikhs were allowed to build more than one storey in Muharraq, for 'the aristocratic class of the Khalifah', as Palgrave called them, objected to being overlooked by their neighbours. The question of overlooking is still a cause of trouble in Bahrain, and is the subject of many cases in court, though the Khalifah have relinquished their monopoly of building tall houses.

The poorer people lived in barastis, palm branch huts; many of the wealthier families had barastis on the sea shore, outside the towns, which they occupied during the hot months of the year. The Bahrainis were sea-faring people, most of them were engaged in the pearl industry, and much of their food came from the sea, which provided quantities of fine fish of many different kinds. There was hardly a man in the place who did not depend in some way on the sea for his livelihood. In this respect, Bahrain was scarcely changed from the beginning of the 19th century, until oil was found in 1932. Above most of the barastis where the seamen and fishermen lived, there was a pole with a bunch of rags tied to it, which indicated the direction of the wind: today, instead of rags, home-made models of aeroplanes are often used as weathercocks.

Muharraq was defended by a fort on a headland jutting into the sea, which became an island at high tide; in later years it was used as a quarantine station. In deep water, near the fort, was one of the freshwater submarine springs, described by so many travellers in Bahrain. Men dived down to the source and filled leather waterskins with fresh water, holding them tightly closed as they rose through the sea to the surface. This spring, under the sea, provided the main supply of drinking water for Muharraq and for ships in the harbour. Some years ago, the Government tried to control some of the submarine springs, to bring fresh water to the surface in pipes, but this proved impossible, and quantities of fresh water still flows to waste in the sea. Another large fort stood on the shore a mile or two north of the town, which was built by the Muscatis in 1799, when they had a garrison in Muharraq for a few months.

Manama, from the sea, was less showy than Muharraq. The town was on flat ground, a few feet above sea level, consisting mostly of barastis, those along the dirty, muddy beach screening the buildings behind them. At the western end of the town, on the shore, was a group of large fortified buildings occupied by the Amir of Manama. About a mile inland, stood a solid square fort, with towers at each corner, which is now the police head-quarters. In most of the Gulf towns, the main fortress stood a little way back from the town. Along the coast towards the west, gardens and date groves extended down to the sea shore.

The Manama bazaar was the usual labyrinth of narrow lanes, roofed with matting, containing little shops, some built of stone, others of barasti type. The coffee shops and caravansarais were in a square in the centre of the bazaar. But in spite of its rather dingy appearance, Manama had a quiet and peaceful air, and was filled with a gaily dressed, cosmopolitan crowd of Arabs from all parts of the Gulf, as well as Persians, Hindus, and a few Jews from Baghdad.

Some time during January or February, a report had reached Bruce, the Resident in Bushire, that: 'a European Lady and her niece, with her attendants, had been captured and taken to Bahrain, and were there publicly exposed for sale as slaves.' The name of the Lady and of the ship from which she was taken by pirates are not mentioned in Loch's diary – perhaps such details as these were not known to the authorities. Loch was extremely distressed at hearing this news, as he says: 'I cannot describe the feelings I laboured under from the moment I received the intelligence from Bruce of the unfortunate females having fallen into the hands of those merciless savages. I pictured to myself the unfortunate wife of one of the officers of the army in Cutch to be the person, knowing that several of the vessels which had on board the baggage and wives had fallen into their hands previous to me meeting with the first pirates.' It was decided that the European Lady and her niece should be rescued from Bahrain. By chance, there were several ships at Bushire, forming 'a very respectable force'. They consisted of H.M.S. *Conway* and three Company's cruisers, the *Benares*, *Mercury* and *Antelope*. On February 8th, Loch in command of the squadron, sailed from Bushire bound for Bahrain. The squadron met with dirty weather after leaving Bushire, and it was not until the evening of the 11th that the *Eden* reached the outer anchorage of Bahrain, after groping her way through the shoals and coral banks which protect the sea approaches to the islands.

At daylight on the morning after their arrival, Loch sent Moffath and the interpreter ashore in the gig, to explain why the squadron had come to Bahrain, and to ask that someone in authority should come on board to discuss the matter. Soon after Moffath's return, Shaikh Abdulla arrived in his dhow from Muharraq, leaning against the hard stuffed cushions on the carpet-strewn deck in the bows of his boat. Loch received him on board and told him that 'he had received intelligence which he could not doubt', about the European Lady and her niece, and their attendants, having been exposed for sale in the slave market. He gave the Shaikh eight hours in which to produce the ladies, failing which 'unless a satisfactory excuse was produced for not doing so' he threatened to destroy all the ships in the harbour. The Shaikh vehemently protested that there were no Europeans in Bahrain, and swore that he knew nothing about any European Ladies and their nieces. He said that he would go back and 'institute an enquiry', and if any Europeans were found, they would be sent on board immediately – in any case, he would return within the given time. Loch then ordered the *Antelope* to anchor at the south end of the harbour, off Muharraq, to prevent any vessels from escaping.

While Loch was waiting impatiently for the return of Shaikh Abdulla, the Banian (Hindu trader), who had supplied Bruce with the information about the European Lady came on board. He was probably a forbear of some of the Indian merchants who are now in Bahrain for one or two of the firms have been established there for over a century and a half. In later years, the Indian merchants played an important part in the commerce of Bahrain; besides dealing with imports from India, they traded extensively in pearls and, for many years, in the time of Shaikh Isa bin Ali, the great-grandfather of the present Shaikh, the customs were farmed out to a Hindu merchant. During the last war, the Indian merchants did valuable service to the country by importing essential foodstuffs which were rationed, and sold at controlled prices, though they could have made fortunes by importing the goods to other states in the Gulf where there were no controls.

Loch immediately questioned the Banian about the where-abouts of the European Lady, and he received a most surprising reply. 'To my utter surprise and astonishment, as well as joy, the Banian flatly contradicted the statement which he had forwarded to Bruce of there having been a European Lady brought there at all. He stated that he himself had been mistaken, but that several women had been there for some days exposed for sale. On the appearance of the squadron, they had been hastily embarked and returned again to Ras al Khaima. However, he added that there were yet in the harbour several pirate vessels.' When Shaikh Abdulla returned, he confirmed what the Banian had said, and told Loch that the women in question were 'native Indians', and had been taken away by the pirates when the British ships were sighted.

Loch then gave orders for a landing party to deal with the pirate boats, and he told the Banian that he must go with the sailors to identify the pirate vessels, 'that there might be no mistake in the destruction or capture of other property'. Banians are not conspicuous for their bravery, but in this case it was hardly surprising that the Banian 'pointedly refused to do this, stating that it would be his utter ruin, and perhaps the means hereafter of his being put to death'. Loch accepted the Banian's excuse which was a very valid one, and having failed with him, he tried the Shaikh. Shaikh Abdulla was not asked to accompany the landing party, but he was asked to supply some of his retainers to accompany the sailors and show them which were the boats of the Joasmi. He, too, made 'considerable demur', but Loch indicated that unless he agreed to provide the men, he would be detained on board the ship, 'night drawing on, he at last gave his consent'. In view of subsequent events, to which Loch does not allude in his diary, it is interesting to hear from Loch himself what measures he took to ensure that the ships against which he despatched a landing party were, in fact, pirate ships. Knowing that the Banian was unreliable, having completely changed his story about the European Lady, Loch might have suspected that his report about there being Joasmi ships in the harbour was open to doubt.

Boats from the squadron assembled alongside the *Eden* under the command of Lieutenant Daniel, one of Loch's officers, accompanied by Moffath, some officers from the other ships, all the available midshipmen, and a few of the Shaikh's retainers who had been reluctantly provided by Shaikh Abdulla. It was night before the preparations were completed, and darkness added to the difficulty of attacking unknown ships in a crowded unfamiliar harbour. At midnight Loch, on the deck of the *Eden*, heard 'considerable firing of musketry and guns in the harbour'. This continued for some time. An hour later, he saw a signal rocket, fired from one of the boats. This was the signal which had been arranged to let him know when the landing party had gained possession of the pirate vessels. Loch had passed a very anxious hour or two, as he says: 'none but those who are placed in a similar position to the one in which I now was could have the slightest notion of the anxiety, hope and ultimate supreme joy, when the most welcome signal was made.'

The boats returned. Only one of the sailors had been wounded but the pirates had suffered considerable casualties, though many of them had jumped into the sea and swam ashore. The pirate vessels were driven on to the beach by a strong north wind which had come up in the night. One of them was a baggala, the largest type of sailing vessel in the Gulf, carrying a crew of 150 men. 'She was considerably lower forward than aft, having a high poop' which was formed into a sort of castle, defended by the chiefs and principals on board. This class of vessel is from two to five hundred tons burden.'

'The other vessel was a batil, having a crew of 70 to 100 men, and some 60 to 70 tons burden: she was a beautifully built vessel, and sailed remarkably fast. The baggala has an enormous mast, as large as a small frigate, stepped one third from the stern, raking forward, with a mizzen mast abaft. On the main mast is hoisted a prodigious sail, the yard of which is equal in size to a 36-gun frigate. The sail of the batil is larger in proportion, having but one mast stepped one third forward. I had models of these vessels made, when I was in Bushire, and presented them to the Museum of the College of Edinburgh.'

The batil and the baggala were too badly damaged to be taken in tow, so Loch decided to give them to the Bahrain Shaikhs, in return for their – unwilling – co-operation. Before Loch left, Shaikh Abdulla agreed that, in future, he would never allow any British subjects, either Europeans or Indians, to be brought to Bahrain for sale as slaves, at the same time, he once again assured Loch that no Europeans had ever been offered for sale in Bahrain. Loch then asked the Shaikh if he would agree to be a mediator between the British and the Joasmi, to arrange for an exchange of prisoners. The prisoners who were held at Ras al Khaima were to be exchanged for pirates who had been sent for confinement in Bombay. In this matter, too, the Shaikh acceded to Loch's request. Subsequently, an exchange was arranged, and some Indian women, wives of Indian soldiers, were exchanged for some of the pirates. After completing his business with the Shaikh, Loch returned to Bushire.

But this was not the last of the affair of the European Lady and her niece. On arrival in Bushire, Loch's friend Bruce again insisted that, in spite of what the Shaikh and the Banian had said 'there was yet a report of the women being concealed in Bahrain', so 'to set the matter at rest' (although it is difficult to understand how the subsequent action was calculated to do so), a number of trading vessels from Bahrain, which happened to be in Bushire harbour on their legitimate business, were taken possession of by the British. Their captains were taken on board the *Benares*, who proceeded with the Company's cruiser *Vestal* to Bahrain where the captains were displayed as proof that their ships were in the possession of the British. At the same time, Bruce wrote a letter to the Shaikhs, saying that if the European Lady and her niece, and their attendants, were not handed over at once, he would hold the Bahrain trading vessels until he received orders from Bombay.

Once more the Shaikhs denied, indignantly, that there were any European women in Bahrain, and the Banian repeated his assurances that there never had been any European women held there, and he told Bruce that what he said in the beginning was all a mistake. The Shaikh, in his letter to Bruce, complained bitterly about the loss of his trade by the detention of his ships and pointed out that Bruce's action was causing his people to lose a far greater sum of money than the price of any women, even a European Lady and her niece, who might be sold as slaves in Bahrain where, in fact, no women were being held or sold. Bruce appears to have been satisfied with this reply, or perhaps he gave up the whole affair as a bad business. The Bahrain captains were put back in their ships and allowed to leave for home. One of the ships, however, stayed behind.

The Captain of this ship lodged a complaint with Loch that while his ship was held by the Navy, the Marines from H.M.S. *Conway* had stolen from it a valuable bag of pearls. Loch and the Captain of the *Conway* held an enquiry, but were unable to satisfy themselves that there was any truth in the charge, so Loch asked Bruce to deal with the matter. Bruce, on his part, 'passed the baby' to Shaikh Abdul Rasool, the Shaikh of Bushire. The Shaikh sent for the Captain, and asked him a few questions: 'which he prevaricated; his heels were then placed in the bastinado where, after a few strokes, the bundle of pearls was produced from the man's breast. Thus the fellow received his bastinadoes, paid the Shaikh a sum for not receiving more punishment, and a remuneration to those who had inflicted the punishment, and paid all the expenses of the investigation.' Loch's comment on the affair was 'They can run up an account for justice in that country as in others, aye, and squeeze it out of them too'.

As Loch says: 'what was the object of the Banian? I never succeeded in discovering whether it was some mercantile object, or otherwise.' When one reads the story today, there seems to be strong reason for supposing that the whole affair of the European Lady and her niece was a concoction of the Banian, but what could have been his purpose in stirring up such a mare's nest is hard to fathom. But this was not the only matter about which he lied. He told Loch that there were ships of the Joasmi pirates in Bahrain harbour. The ships which Loch's landing party captured, with loss of life, belonged to the Beni Yas tribe, who were not engaged in piracy, and the Bombay Government eventually had to pay compensation for their destruction.

CHAPTER VIII

'So I embarked on a ship, and it descended to the
city of Basra, and we traversed the sea for many
days and nights. We passed by island after
island, and from sea to sea, and from land to
land.'

First Voyage of Sinbad the Sailor, E. W. Lane's translation

AFTER his visits to Bahrain, Loch returned to Bushire
where he stayed in the Residency with Bruce. When he
landed on the pier, the first person he met was 'a good-
looking, well-made man in Persian dress, who accosted me in
such good English, mixed with all the nautical idioms, interlarded
with slang and oaths, which made me doubt at first that he was
not an Englishman'. Loch soon discovered that he was a Persian
who went by the name of 'Rogue Ali', about whom he had
heard from Dent, one of the *Eden's* officers, who had been in
Bushire before. 'Rogue Ali' was interpreter, durbash and general
purveyor to the Residency, and had acquired the nickname because there was another Ali employed by the Resident, who had
been given the name of 'Honest Ali'. 'Rogue Ali' was a well
known character, and is mentioned by other people besides Loch.

From Loch's description, the Bushire Residency, where he
stayed so often during his two and a half years in the Gulf, was
built on the lines of many of the Company's factories in India.
It resembled the buildings of that period which were painted by
the Daniells, uncle and nephew, who, in the first decade of the
19th century, published a set of pictures with the title: 'Views of
Hindostan.'

The Residency was an oblong building about 200 to 300 yards
in length, outside the south-eastern corner of the town walls and
close to the sea shore. Passing through a gate 'under a porch
rather like a portcullis', a zigzag passage led into a 'neat courtyard'. The zigzag passage at the entrance was a feature of all
buildings which might have to be defended, for a straight passage
into a courtyard would be less tenable in case of an attack.

Around the courtyard were kitchens, stores and offices, and on one side, a large, high dining-room with a wide verandah in front of it. On the upper floor, were rooms to accommodate men in the service of the Company, who were at Bushire on duty or furlough; one of these rooms was allocated to Loch. Along another side of the courtyard was a screen of pierced, Persian plaster work, decorated with arabesque designs, which to Loch looked Chinese. This very fine plaster work was once a feature of Arab houses in Bahrain, but it is now regarded as old-fashioned, and has been replaced by uninteresting styles of Western decoration. Behind the plaster-work screen stood a row of enormous water jars made of blue and green earthenware 'such as Ali Baba's may be supposed to have been'. A passage gave access to an inner courtyard, 'in which there were Mrs. Bruce's private apartments, which were hardly ever seen except by intimate friends'. It seems that Mrs. Bruce led a somewhat sequestered life for, although Loch spent much time with Bruce, he only mentions Mrs. Bruce two or three times, without saying anything about her.

The Bushire Residency, which was in the town, was established in 1763, when the East India Company obtained from the Persian ruler, Karim Khan, a firman granting the Company certain exclusive trading rights in Persia. Apart from being closed for a short time on two occasions, it occupied the same site until the middle of the 19th century, when a Captain Felix Jones, of the Indian Marines, after whom a cable ship was named in the present century, obtained from the Persian Government a piece of land on the coast, about seven miles from Bushire, as a summer camp. Gradually permanent buildings were put up on this site, which was called Sabzabad, and eventually, it became the Residency.

Sabzabad, although in many ways an inconvenient and unsuitable building, having been constantly altered and added to by many Residents, without a water supply, and distant from the town of Bushire, was retained until 1946. The Residency was then moved to Bahrain, and the Sabzabad building was handed over to the Persian Government for use as a sanitorium, but whether it was ever used as such, history does not relate. The British naval base which was at one time at Basidu, on Kishm Island, had been transferred to Bahrain in 1935.

The next place which the *Eden* visited was Basra. It was governed by a Turkish Mutasellim who was responsible to the

Pasha of Baghdad, who in turn was responsible to the Ottoman Sultan in Constantinople. The Company's representative, Mr. Colquhoun, who had been there for eight years, had become ill, and Bruce's assistant, Mr. Taylor, had been sent to Basra to relieve him. Bruce thought it desirable to be present at Taylor's installation, and wished a British man-of-war to be at Basra on this occasion. At nine in the morning of February 28th, Bruce came on board the *Eden*, under a salute of 11 guns, with him were his wife, Mrs. Taylor and her sister. The *Conway*, commanded by Captain Barnard, was left at anchor at Bushire.

The voyage to Basra was long and tedious. On March 2nd, the *Eden* ran aground off the 'almost imperceptible island of Corgo', near Karak Island 'but she was afloat again almost as soon as the sails were thrown back'. This was the third time that the ship had been aground since she came to the Gulf, 'owing to the uselessness of the charts'. At Karak, the *Eden* took on a pilot to navigate the river. Loch mentions the white, limey clay near the shore at Karak, which the inhabitants used as soap; at one time this clay was sold in the Bahrain bazaar as shampoo for the hair.

The *Eden* followed the course which Nearchus, the Admiral of Alexander the Great, took in the year 325 B.C., which is described by Arrian. Many pages of Loch's diary are taken up with his efforts to identify the places mentioned in the journal of Nearchus with the places in the Gulf, which he saw and visited, but since his day this question has been discussed and written about by more authoritative writers. Progress up the Persian coast was slow, and it was necessary to keep the lead constantly going. On the 3rd, the snow-covered Bakhtiari mountains were sighted some sixty miles inland, to the northeast. When passing the mouth of the 'Granis or Rohilla' river, Loch mentions 'an English gentleman' who, some years before, suggested a scheme of making a canal to join the Rohilla and the Tab, and to connect the Rohilla with the Bay of Bushire. In return, he asked for the canal transit dues to be paid to him for a specified time. According to Loch, the Persian Government was interested in the scheme, but no agreement was made.

The *Eden* ran aground in the mud shoals again before reaching the river. A kedge anchor was dropped by the ship's boat some distance ahead, and by winding the hawser to which the anchor rope was attached, the ship was pulled off the mud-bank, but the

anchor was lost.   On the 5th, the *Eden* arrived near the mouth
of the Shatt al Arab, two boats were sent out and anchored on
each side of the deep water channel, like buoys; the ship then got
under weigh and crossed the bar with a good wind and a favourable tide.   There was still no sight of land on either side, and it
was not until she had sailed for some distance that the pilot pointed
out to Loch something black, apparently floating on the surface
in the distance, which at nearer view turned out to be a mass of
reeds, growing in places as high as twelve feet.   The ship then
entered the part of the river where both banks were visible, and
Loch could see the walled villages surrounded by date groves and
plots of cultivation.

At one spot, there was a dangerous whirlpool where the river
and the sea met.   'The ship had all sail set, running through the
water at the rate of five or six miles an hour, hustled along at
almost equal velocity by the flood tide, when, all of a sudden, she
was twisted round, in spite of the helm, and would have been
driven on shore, had not the anchor been instantly let go.'   Several times the *Eden* had to send her boats ahead to take soundings,
and to station themselves on each side of the channel before she
could move on.   As they sailed up the river, Loch saw a pack of
jackals chasing some animal, and a large lioness 'going at a round
trot, and, as a dog does at fault, putting her nose to the ground
every now and then.'   The lioness was not more that 200 yards
from the deck, but by the time a musket was produced and loaded,
she was out of sight.   Nearer Basra, where a long narrow island
divides the river, the passage was so narrow that a ship lying at
anchor could not swing without touching one of the banks.

The *Eden* reached Basra at midnight on March 7th, and anchored
off the main wharf; there was 'a beautiful bright moon' which
shed its light on the houses of the city, the gardens and the date
palms.   Early next morning, Loch learned from Taylor who had
been ashore, of the death of Her Majesty Queen Charlotte, which
had taken place on November 7th 1818.   The colours were struck
at half mast, and a salute of 30 one-minute guns was fired.   Later
in the morning, Bruce and Taylor, with their wives and families
disembarked into a boat, known locally as a 'snake', under a
salute of 11 guns.   Loch accompanied them to the British Residency which was in the centre of Basra on the main canal, and
there he stayed during the ship's visit.

Basra, during the early days of the 19th century, was a straggling, dilapidated city, containing not more than 100,000 inhabitants, of whom about half were Arabs, the remainder being Persians, Turks, Armenians, Indians and Jews. There were very few Europeans living in the town, except occasionally one or two of the Carmelite fathers who had a church and a hospital. The town was built along the banks of the Tigris, and on the creeks and canals which were fed from the river. It was surrounded by high walls, with towers at intervals, all in a poor state of repair, yet strong enough to be a defence against the attack of ill-armed Arab tribes. Only a quarter of the area enclosed by the walls was occupied by buildings. Gardens, full of vegetables, brilliant green lucerne, fruit trees and date groves filled the remaining space.

The houses were made with mud bricks, dried in the sun, with roofs carried on the trunks of date palms, which do not lend themselves to this purpose, but neither stone nor timber for building was obtainable in the neighbourhood of Basra. Buckingham, who spent over three months in Basra in 1816, describes the houses as 'badly constructed, mostly deficient in what are held by the occupiers to be conveniences of comforts'. The climate, he says, was 'for half the year intolerable', and the town was 'defiled by filth enough to engender by itself the most pestilential diseases, inhabited by an ignorant, wretched and ugly race of people'. Yet, in spite of the unsalubrious conditions, he surprisingly adds: 'it is usual for invalids to come from India to Basoora for the restoration of their health, and if the seasons are properly chosen, there are few constitutions which would not benefit from the change.' He mentions 'the bracing winter climate, fine fruits, a variety of vegetables and a constant supply of the choicest game'. There has always been very good shooting near Basra, and in 1803, when Samuel Manesty was the British Resident, his shooting parties were famous even in England.

When Loch visited it, Basra was a place of importance to the British, being their principal trading station in the Gulf though, at various times, it had held second place to Bushire. It was the land terminus of 'the Direct Route' between Europe and India. Since the beginning of the 19th century, many travellers went by land from Aleppo, and from other Levant ports, either via Baghdad or direct to Basra, whence the Company's cruisers sailed every month to Bombay, carrying passengers and despatches to India. The desert crossing took between two and three weeks, Europeans travelled with Arab caravans, riding on horses, camels or mules. 'The Direct Route' was much quicker than the long sea journey round the Cape.

A British factory was first established in Basra in 1640. Over the years it occupied various sites in the town, but the factory (or Residency, as it came to be called), where Loch stayed, was chiefly constructed by Manesty, the former Resident. It was a large, imposing, fortified building, made of kiln-baked bricks, on the south bank of the central creek, within easy reach of the Customs House and the Turkish Governor's 'Palace' – buildings which Buckingham describes as 'of the meanest kind, and in the worst state of repair.' In front of the high Moorish walls of the palace, was the battery from which salutes were fired. Moored off the building was the Turkish fleet; (three most extraordinary looking half ketch, half Zubeck rigged vessels), which were incapable of putting out to sea although, in the past, the Turkish fleet of some twenty well-armed vessels was strong enough to command most of the Persian Gulf.

The Residency consisted of two large courtyards surrounded by buildings, with a gateway on the land side manned by sepoy guards. A noticeable feature was the immense stables. Arab horses were the principal export from Basra. Every year, some 1,500 horses were shipped to India, to provide mounts for the troops. The average price of a horse bought in Basra to be shipped to Bombay was 300 rupees: shipping, feeding and landing charges amounted to 400 rupees, and the horse would be sold for about 800 rupees. The best horses were sent to Bengal, and these cost at least 1,000 rupees in Basra, and the profits were considerably larger. But, as Buckingham says, 'the greatest number of these are sent from here by the British Resident on his account'.

It is surprising that the trade was so extensive, for the export of horses from any part of the Turkish dominions was expressly forbidden by the Porte. The trade flourished in Basra because it brought profits to the merchants, the English, and the Governor who found it worth his while to ignore prohibition. Loch's estimate of the Turkish character was probably a reflection of the opinions of Colquhoun: he says that they were: 'overbearing, morose and cruel, with much cunning, yet with a considerable share of good breeding, with a degree of honour incompatible with the rest of their character, adhering strictly to any engagement which they may have formally entered, far superior on this point than either Persians or Arabs.'

From his quarters in the Residency, Loch had a view of the canal crowded with craft of various types, which, owing to the narrowness of the canal, constantly collided, causing noisy disputes, which reminded him of 'the voluble ribaldry of a seaport in Spain'. There was a ferry opposite the Residency. 'The people were transported in a large circular basket made of wickerwork, covered with skins besmeared with bitumen. The ferryman cautioned the people, as they stepped in, how to do so, lest they might overturn his frail barge, and he forced them to sit down. I have seen twelve to fifteen people sitting with their legs set across, as you see a set of children when playing Hunt the Slipper. When the ferryman pushed his vessel off from the shore it rolled from side to side, and all gave a shriek, as if they were immersed in water. The person who guides the basket now begins to paddle, sitting on the gunwhale or side, then you see the whole twirling round in the most ridiculous manner possible. Thus, by an innumerable number of circuits, they eventually reach the opposite bank.' This type of boat, which is called a 'gufa' in Arabic, can still be seen on the rivers and canals in Iraq.

Loch describes the people of Basra as 'a motley crew, some having gaudy dresses, others having merely a shirt of what was once white cloth, or nothing but a cloth round the waist'. They wore a variety of clothes, which in some cases denoted their nationality or religion. Merchants, especially in the cold weather, were handsomely dressed in rich Indian stuffs, with Kashmir shawls, the Persians favouring dark greens and yellows, and the Arabs wearing white or light brown. The Turks, according to Loch, 'delight in very gaudy colours and richness of dress, having quantities of gold and silver lace on their jackets and waistcoats. They are also fond of fine caparisons for their horses.' The desert Arabs and those from the Gulf, wore the same dress as they do today; Jews wore dark clothes, and the Indians wore a mixture of Persian and Arab dress.

On the day after Loch's arrival, he was awakened, 'by a loud, discordant sound of "hic, hac, hic, hac" ', which became so irksome as hardly to be bearable. This was the voice of a begging derwish, who was stationed at the Residency gate. 'He began at daylight, continuing to call out at the full extent of his well-trained voice, only ceasing, to beg alms of some passer-by. He was young, handsome, dressed in a white turban and a loose white garment, bound round the waist with a shawl. Because he was a pilgrim on his way to Mecca, nobody could touch him, or order him to go.' Loch tells the story of a similar nuisance at Bushire, when a derwish established himself at the gate of the Residency. Eventually, Rich who was at Bushire at the time, 'feigned to be a maniac, and so frightened the poor wretch, that he got up and started off at full speed, and was never seen again'.

Loch does not say much about Colquhoun, who was being relieved by Captain Taylor. Colquhoun was an army surgeon, and had previously acted in that capacity during the time of the late Resident, Mr. Manesty, who was an official of the East India Company. When Manesty left, Colquhoun became 'Resident in Charge', but, as Buckingham remarks: 'Colquhoun continued to draw the emoluments of surgeon as well as Resident.' As his principal duty was to look after the health of the Resident, it appears that he got paid for looking after his own health!

The British Resident in Basra kept great state, with sepoy guards provided by the Marine Battalion in Bombay; besides these, he had a large staff of Turkish Chaoushes and servants. The cost of maintaining his establishment was about £5,000 a year, which was then a large sum. The influence of the Resident was considerable, owing to the extensive trade with the British, the frequent presence of British men-of-war at Basra, and the fact that there was another senior British representative at the court of the Pasha in Baghdad. Buckingham describes Colquhoun as having 'sufficient urbanity to extend his protection to both Jews and Christians, without fear or favour, and yet sufficient firmness to resist all encroachments on his privileges'.

The words spoken by King William IV in February 1835, at a private audience which he gave to Colonel Chesney, who was leading an expedition to survey the rivers Tigris and Euphrates, typify the British attitude in those days. 'Remember, Sir,' said the King, 'that the success of England mainly depends upon commerce, and that yours is a peaceable undertaking, provided with the means of opening trade. I do not desire war, but if you should be molested, due support shall not be wanting.'

Colquhoun was a sick man, he suffered from 'the most excruciating headaches'. What troubled him most, preventing him from sleeping, was the catawauling of 'myriads of cats that infest the place'. To prevent being disturbed at night, he ordered his sepoy guard to drive away the cats which assembled below his room. This they did by letting off one of their muskets – although one would suppose that the sound of shots at night would be even more distasteful to an invalid than the noise of courting cats. When the musket was not in use it was put back in the arms rack in the guard room.

'A poor Turkish Idiot' was in the habit of coming to the Residency, where he was given food by the guards. Sometimes, if he did not think that he had been given enough, he became abusive. When this happened, the sentry used to 'swap a musket at him' to drive him away. One morning The Idiot appeared, as usual, and became very aggressive. A sepoy pulled out a musket from the rack, not knowing that it had been loaded for shooting cats in the night. 'He levelled it against the unfortunate wretch, and pulled the trigger.' The Idiot fell dead at his feet.

There was an uproar in the town, and the Residency was surrounded by an angry mob. The Turkish Governor was away in Baghdad, and his young son was acting for him in Basra. The situation was dangerous, and it seemed likely that the populace would attack the Residency. 'It now became necessary for some decided steps to be taken. Mr. Colquhoun assembled his Turkish guards, mounted his horse, and rode boldly through the mob to the Palace.' He informed the young man that he had no intention of handing over the sepoy, but he promised to send a full statement of the circumstances through Baghdad to Constantinople. He also warned the acting Governor that if the Residency was attacked, he would defend it to the last, and would not be answerable for 'any act of desperation committed by his sepoys. This determined and bold conduct of Mr. Colquhoun, brought the young man to his senses, he begged that the whole matter might be considered a mere riot of the rabble, which should immediately be put down. All was now glossed over, and the arrival of the *Eden* opposite the town, assisted in sealing the quiet.'

The Governor returned to Basra before the *Eden* sailed, and Loch with some of his officers watched the Governor's procession passing the street behind the Residency. They were on the roof, having been warned by Colquhoun not to show themselves, for 'there was a great probability of our being shot at, and if so, there was little chance of detecting the culprit, which would make the likelihood of our being fired at more certain'. Loch and his officers, two of the midshipmen and 'old Moffath', were not impressed by the procession which Loch describes as follows:

'The Motsaleum (Governor) proceeded with his guards and regular troops immediately in his rear.' The Governor's bodyguard were in uniform, they wore red jackets, seamed with black cord, full blue Turkish trousers, and white turbans, and carried English muskets and black ammunition boxes and belts. These were followed by a rabble of irregular Arab troops, behind them came the populace. 'There was a constant firing of musketry, beating of tom-toms, yelling, whooping, and a sort of song of the country, similar to that of the jugglers once in England, and a sort of dance, finished by a loud yell, often extremely indecent.' The trouble over the affair of 'The Turkish Idiot' seems to have ended with the return of the Governor, who probably arranged for compensation to be paid to the unfortunate man's relatives.

During his visit, Colquhoun told Loch the story of a man from Kuwait who had asked for protection in the Residency, from fear of being seized owing to his being able to turn base metal into gold. Colquhoun who, according to Loch, was something of a chemist, decided to test the alchemist. The man was given a piece of lead, which he placed with certain ingredients in a crucible over a fire. After the lead was melted, it was allowed to harden again, and when removed, it appeared to be a piece of gold. Colquhoun sent it down to the bazaar, where it was tested, and found to be gold: he had watched the process with the greatest care, but was unable to detect the trick. Although he was sceptical about the alchemist, Colquhoun allowed him to take refuge in the Residency, but when the man went back to the bazaar to collect his belongings, he disappeared. He was seized by some men who had come to Basra from Kuwait, with the express purpose of kidnapping 'the Golden Goose', and he was carried off in a boat, never to be heard of again.

There seemed to be prevalence of amateur alchemists in Basra, for a few days before Loch sailed, another so-called alchemist came to call on Colquhoun, who received him with Loch, Bruce and Taylor. 'After sitting for awhile in the most awkward manner on a chair, not knowing what to do with his legs, finding that there was not room to sit with his legs crossed, he at last squatted on the floor. After some time, he gave Mr. Colquhoun a significant look, which Colquhoun understood, and assured him that he was among friends. The Alchemist stated that he had received a small package of the Salt of Gold, and in a short time he was to be initiated into the method of procuring gold from it. He at last pulled from his bosom, with the utmost caution, a small parcel of paper. On opening it, he told us, in a low voice, that he had received it from a friend, and for a sum of money was to gain the secret.

'But the poor man was disappointed and chagrined in observing us laughing, on his showing us the contents of the paper, and on being informed that it contained nothing more than common, shining talc, ground into powder. I shall not easily forget the poor man's misery, as he swung his body backwards and forwards in agitation. At last, placing his right thumb to his teeth, he gave a shrill whistle, exclaiming "I am taken in! They have nearly ruined my fortune already, and they wish to complete the wreck. Thank God my eyes have been opened." Neither Turks nor Persians ever whistle, unless it is in derision or anger, and then only with a single long one. The man left the Residency at once, apparently more displeased at having been shown up as an easily-imposed-on person, than gratified at having been saved from ruin.'

Having remained as long as was thought necessary, the *Eden* set sail for Bushire on the evening of March 16th, carrying Captain Bruce and his family, and Mr. Colquhoun.

CHAPTER IX

'They rise, they fall,
Now skim in circling rings, then stretch away
With all their force, till at one fatal stroke
The vig'rous hawk, exerting every nerve,
Trussed in mid air bears down her captive prey.'
Field Sports: William Somerville – 1735

THE return from Basra was accomplished more easily than the outward voyage, and on March 21st, the *Eden* was at Bushire, where she stayed until May 2nd. On March 28th, a Bombay merchant vessel arrived from Muscat, which, Loch says, was 'an extraordinary circumstance' for she was the first merchant ship to cross the Gulf alone, without escort. For a long time, no merchant ships had ventured in Gulf waters except in convoy, owing to the danger from pirates.

A few days later, the Company's cruisers *Mercury* and *Vestal* arrived from Ras al Khaima, carrying fifteen Indian women, widows of sepoys who had been taken by pirates and murdered. They had been on board the same ship as Mrs. Taylor, the wife of Bruce's assistant at Bushire, who had been held for some time as a prisoner of the Joasmi at Ras al Khaima, but was later released on payment of a large ransom. The release of the Hindu women in exchange for pirate prisoners at Bombay, was arranged through the Shaikhs of Bahrain, at the request of Loch when he had recently been in Bahrain.

At the same time, Loch received a letter from Hassan bin Rahmah, Shaikh of the Joasmi at Ras al Khaima; it was written in Indian ink, on sea-green paper. In his recent letter, the Shaikh protested against Bruce's behaviour during a recent visit. He complained that Bruce had made 'certain demands for which he had no grounds, and thus broke the treaty and commenced hostilities'. The Shaikh declared that he had not molested any British ships (which was quite untrue). He was apparently referring to an agreement which was made between the British and his predecessor in 1806, but the conditions of this agreement had never been carried out by the Joasmi. Captain Conyers who commanded the *Mercury* and brought the Shaikh's letter to Loch, was considered somewhat to have exceeded his instructions in the negotiations about the arrangements for the exchange of prisoners. The time for lenity was past at last, after years of indecision, which had cost the lives of many seamen in the Gulf, the Bombay Government was taking a strong line and showing a determination to put an end to piracy. The flimsy, impudent excuses of the Joasmi Shaikh were ignored.

It was during this visit that Loch met a young Frenchman who, under the name of Abdul Rahman, arrived at Bushire from Basra in a European ship. He was only fourteen years old, when a ship in which he was travelling from Mauritius to Basra was captured by pirates. All those on board, except this boy and another lad, were brutally massacred. The two French boys were spared on condition that they became Moslems and joined the Wahabi sect. This they did, and for some years, they lived with the pirates at Ras al Khaima, where Abdul Rahman married two wives and produced a family. 'Yet he could not brook the degradation of living with these people, and made his escape', travelling up the coast, sometimes on foot, and sometimes getting a lift in small coasting craft.

For some time, he worked as interpreter for the Navy at Muscat and, after the capture of Ras al Khaima, was made 'Beach Sarong', being responsible for dealing with complaints from boat owners, embarkation, and the landing of supplies. Loch says: 'it is strange that, in spite of the feelings of disgust which he had for the pirates, which were so strong as to make him desert not only them, but his wives and children, yet, after mixing again with Europeans, he found his ideas and manners so changed that he could not be persuaded to return to his home.' He was nineteen years old when Loch met him, 'a remarkably fine athlete, six feet tall, and in Arab clothes he appeared a giant. He had a constant smile on his countenance, and retained all the vivacity of his countrymen, yet his gestures were modulated into those of an Arab.' His face and hands were white, but he stained his hands with henna, and darkened his eyebrows and eyelashes with antimony.

In the beginning of April, Loch went on an expedition inland with Bruce and Major Littlefield; the latter was staying at the Residency inspecting the horses which had been bought for the army in India.   They took the road from Bushire in the direction of Shiraz, stopping at some of the villages which were under the control of the Shaikh of Bushire, whose authority was very extensive.   The weather had become hot, so they usually rode at night, staying during the day at a village.   Much of the country through which they passed was very different to the harsh, barren shores of the Gulf.   The air at night was scented by many flowering shrubs; there was a continuous concert from the bulbuls, Persian nightingales, and fireflies sparkled among the vegetation.   Their pleasant rides through the country were only disturbed when they came near villages and were surrounded by packs of half-wild dogs.

The first village at which they stayed is called by Loch 'Ali-shangu'; it consisted of 'a few miserable huts, and some thatched hovels enclosed in a palm branch fence', which was a caravansarai which the travellers to and from Bushire regarded as 'an absolute luxury'.   Loch was impressed by the industry and skill of the Persian peasants 'who, contrary to the Arabs, are fond of cultivation', although plundered and oppressed by the landlords.   The dislike of the coast Arabs for any form of agricultural employment is still one of their characteristics.   In Bahrain, the cultivators are the aboriginal Shia Arabs, it is almost unheard of for a Sunni Arab to work in a garden or a date grove.   In the villages which they passed, Loch found that it was the custom of the landlord to take one-third of all the produce as rent, but in addition to this, he extracted large gifts in kind, and sent much of his stock – horses, sheep and cattle – to be kept and fed by the tenants, without any payment.   The tyranny and robbery by the landlords, had brought the country to 'a miserable state of almost utter ruin'.

On the second day, they stayed at a house belonging to Bruce near the village of Borazjan.   It was a fertile neighbourhood with gardens and orchards irrigated by an underground water channel, which brought sweet water from some springs in the distant hills. These underground channels, qanats, which were described by Strabo eighteen centuries ago, are much used in Persia, and were at one time, the chief water supply for many of the gardens in Bahrain.   But in Bahrain, most of them have been allowed to fall into disuse, and gardens are now irrigated from artesian wells, which are allowed to flow continuously, with the result that the water table all over the islands is falling rapidly.

The local Shaikh and his retinue came to visit Bruce. The three Englishmen sat on the verandah and the Shaikh and his party sat on the ground in a semi-circle facing them, entertained by a well-known itinerant singer. At one moment, he kept everyone in roars of laughter at his unseemly songs and jokes, the Persians, unlike the Turks and the Arabs, do not mind laughing loudly – the next instant, he would draw tears from his audience, singing of the past glories of Persia, and the deaths of ancient heroes. Loch had no opinion of Oriental music, which he mentions with distaste more than once in his diary. Of this singer he says: 'but if they were pleased with their music, God pity their ears!' To him, it seemed that the singer's main object was 'to see how long and how hard he could remain on one note, at the same time having a constant quaver in his voice'. Bruce told Loch a story about Sir John Malcolm's visit to Bushire a few years previously. There was a band on board the ship in which Malcolm travelled, so 'to please the natives' when they arrived at Bushire, the band was sent ashore to give a public performance at which the audience of Bushiris 'with one accord exclaimed "How hideous, how horrible!"'

The unfortunate singer who performed for Loch and Bruce was blind. During one of the revolutions in Persia, his eyes had been put out. He was at one time a wealthy and important man but, since he was blinded, he made his living as an itinerant singer, dependent on the charity of his fellow-countrymen. Persians used frequently to blind their political enemies. There is a story of a European woman who, when visiting the ladies in one of the Persian royal households, saw a little boy walking about with his eyes blindfolded. She asked him what was the matter with his eyes. He told her he was learning to walk about without seeing because, when he grew up, he would probably have his eyes put out. This habit was not unknown in the Gulf. About thirty years ago, two or three Arabs came to Bahrain from one of the Trucial Shaikhdoms for medical treatment by the American Mission doctor. He could do nothing for them, for each of them had had his eyes burned out with a hot iron.

From Borazjan the party went on to Dalaki, another village which belonged to the Shaikh of Bushire. The inhabitants had revolted against the Shaikh, owing to his oppressive measures, and extreme severity, but on the day of Loch's arrival, the Shaikh's troops had regained control of the village, and were in occupation of the fort. The place seemed silent and deserted, for all the villagers had fled; when they reached the fort, they had to beat on the door for some time before it was opened. They were let in by the Shaikh's troops, and spent the night there.

Loch and his companions slept on the roof of the tower. In the evening, they were amused by watching one of the guards on a roof below them. First, he carefully collected a quantity of straw which he put in a heap, he then stripped off his clothes, and put a light to the straw, next he picked up each garment, and held it in the smoke, so that it billowed out, and the many thousand inhabitants of his clothes fell crackling into the flames! Having thus de-loused his clothes, he put them on again 'thus he supposed himself to have clean linen for at least another month, and he appeared to be most comfortable after the cleaning, at which there was no great wonder'. However, he seems to have left out his body and his head!

The next stop was Rohilla, near the river of that name, which was about fifty yards wide, but so impregnated with sulphur, 'mixed with black naphtha' that the water could neither be used for drinking or for cultivation. This place was not a very great distance from the area where a century later oil was discovered, and the 'sulphurous streams' to which Loch refers, may have come from oil seepages. Sir John Malcolm's falconer met the party at Rohilla, where he had prepared for them a most comfortable hut under some trees, which they occupied for three days, when they spent their time hunting and hawking. Loch found hawking 'the most interesting of all the sports I have ever witnessed'. It seems to have been his first experience of falconry, though it was still popular in Scotland and in parts of England. As recently as thirty years ago, the Malcolms of Poltalloch in Argyllshire, kept hawks, and hunted with them. Loch describes their first morning's sport.

Soon after daylight, the party went off on horseback across the plains where gazelle were likely to be found. There was little cover, only small stunted shrubs, tufts of stiff grass which was used by the Persians for making fine mats, liquorice plants, and an occasional tamarisk tree. The falconer and his son carried hawks on their wrists, hooded and fastened to the rider's gauntlet by a jess, a short leather throng around the bird's legs, which could easily be slipped off. On reaching a likely place, one of the birds was unhooded; it sat on the rider's wrist, moving its head round looking for game. After riding some time, a gazelle sprang up ahead, and was seen racing away. The hawk's jess was slipped, and it launched into the air, moving with great speed, and no apparent effort. At the same time, a brace of silukis, Arab greyhounds, were released, but they had no chance of overtaking the gazelle, though they rapidly outran the horsemen who were going at full gallop in pursuit. The hawk skimmed along, flying a few feet above the ground, rose higher in the air when it was on a line with its quarry, and then dropped down on to the head of the gazelle, which tripped and fell. In an instant, the hounds reached it, followed by the falconer's son. He immediately cut the gazelle's neck, and gave the hawk a piece of the bleeding flesh, and while it was engaged in eating the meat, he popped the hood over its head. A second gazelle, which was put up, provided a longer run. Again the hawk and the two greyhounds took part in the chase, but it was some time before the gazelle was brought down. The hawk dropped on its prey, but the gazelle continued to run, and was only defeated when the hounds caught up with it.

In Bahrain, where falconry has long been the favourite sport of the Shaikhs, hawks and greyhounds are never used together. The quarry is usually a bustard, and the season for hawking is when the migrating bustards come to the islands. Silukis hounds are used for coursing hares which are still fairly plentiful in Bahrain. On the main island, there are a few gazelle and, on one of the smaller islands, there are both gazelle and black buck; the latter were imported from India many years ago. But the Shaikh does not allow any of these antelopes to be shot or hunted, unlike the situation in Qatar or Saudi Arabia, where gazelle are run down by Arabs in cars, and slaughtered with machine guns. On the Western Desert of Egypt, as in Persia, silukis and hawks used to be employed together for hunting hares or foxes.

On April 11th, Loch was back at Bushire, where he remained for three weeks. The Shaikh of Bushire had recently bought a ship of between five and six hundred tons, and as the *Eden* was about the same tonnage, he wished to see her, though the construction of a man-of-war was very different from that of a merchant ship. The Shaikh's ship was the first that Persia could boast of, except for a man-of-war built by order of Nadir Shah

XI. A Trucial Coast Arab

X. Pearl diver

from wood imported from Mazanderan 'which was afterwards wrecked at the head of the bay of Bushire, where her bones were to be seen at the period I am writing'. Persia had a long seaboard in the Gulf, but she has never had a navy of any importance though, in the first half of the 18th century, the Persian Ruler, Nadir Shah, attempted to create one.

The Shaikh came on board the *Eden* with a salute of guns, and after going round the ship, Loch entertained him in his cabin: he was given fruit and coffee, and the Shaikh complimented Loch on the excellency of the coffee, made by 'Honest Ali' who had been borrowed for the occasion to help Loch with his guests. Shaikhs, when they visit British men-of-war today, are always given coffee, invariably they politely praise it though, as it is usually made in the English way, they find it almost undrinkable. 'The Shaikh was apparently much gratified with the reception which he met with', so Loch hoped that the visit 'might have a good effect in preventing impediments being thrown in the way of our merchant vessels in discharging and embarking their cargo'.

On May 2nd, the *Eden* left Bushire for Bombay. A few days later, four 'country vessels' were sighted, which may have been pirates; the *Eden* attempted to catch up with them, but at nightfall they escaped. Next day, 'two strange sail' were seen; the *Eden* overtook them, and found that they were two of the Sultan's frigates returning from a cruise down the south coast of Arabia. One of Loch's difficulties was the recognition of ships from a distance, for there were no means of identifying trading vessels, ships of the Sultan's fleet, or pirates, who frequently used captured vessels.

On the same day, in the afternoon, six large sailing dhows were seen near the Quorns, at the entrance to the Gulf. 'The wind was light and baffling, and inclined to calm now and then, and the ship was unmanageable.' Next day, the weather was the same, but 'oppressively hot'. Neither the *Eden* nor the six vessels 'could have steerage way. The dhows lowered their enormous sails, hoping that, as the hulls were not seen from the deck, we would not observe them at all.' Then the breeze came up, and when the dhows saw the *Eden* coming towards them, with all sails set, they made sail, keeping close together, showing no signs of haste. 'As we closed on them, they drew nearer to each other, I now observed their determination to attack and board us, three on either side. It was, of course, my object to avoid this, owing to the disparity in numbers, they having on board their four vessels no less than 800 men, the *Eden* having 118 at this period.' It appears that two of the dhows were captured vessels, being towed by the others. 'The advantage in gun was greatly in our favour, we having 36 of large calibre, they having 14 of smaller calibre, and ill served; besides which, we had the advantage in point of manoeuvre.'

It was a beautiful, clear, moonlit night, and the breeze which had come up was favourable to the *Eden*. At 11.30 p.m. the *Eden* was within pistol shot of the pirates. The helm was put to port, and the three pirate ships on the larboard bow were given the larboard broadside of round and grape shot. At the same time, as the ship swung round, the marines on the gangway poured their muskets into the pirate vessels. This forced the pirates to sheer off, some of them in a crippled condition, with their sails flapping round the masts, and the ships almost unmanageable.

The *Eden's* helm was now put hard a'starboard, and her guns were brought to bear on the other three pirates, forcing them to stretch every stick of canvas, hauling in for the shore. The first ship reached Ras al Khaima with great difficulty. All sail was made again in chase of the other pirates; they were three large baggalas. One of the dhows in tow was picked up by the *Eden's* boats, the chase then continued. The pirates, in their hurry to escape, ran their vessels on to a coral shoal close to the shore, and the sharp, jagged teeth of the coral rocks tore through their bottoms. But they were near enough to the shore for the men to escape, flinging themselves into the water, and swimming ashore. The *Eden* hauled out into deeper water, to avoid the same fate as the pirate dhows, once again discharging her starboard broadside at them. Those of the crews of the pirate ships who were able to do so, eventually made their way to Ras al Khaima. The pirate ships which had been taken, were afterwards repaired by men of the Sultan's frigates, and were taken to Muscat. Not a man from the *Eden* was touched, although there were many shot marks on her hull and sails.

The dhow which had been cut adrift and picked up by the *Eden* contained two people from Muscat, a gun laskar who had been taken prisoner, and a pirate who had slipped into the boat when the fighting started, hoping to make his escape. The Indian laskar had been captured some time ago, and was probably kept alive to help with the guns. The prisoners reported that there had been heavy casualties among the pirates. After this successful engagement, the *Eden* sailed for Muscat, which she reached on May 15th.

In Muscat, Loch met Captain G. Forster Sadlier, of H.M.'s 47th Regiment, who had been sent by Lord Hastings, the Governor-General of India, on a mission to the Sultan of Muscat, and to Ibrahaim Pasha, who commanded the Egyptian forces in Arabia. The object of the mission was to persuade the Sultan and the Pasha to co-operate together with the English against the Joasmi pirates and the Wahabis. On his way to Muscat, Sadlier went on board the *Conway*, in which Colquhoun was travelling to Bombay, and was told that, for some months, there had been no 'depredations by the pirates', and communications between Basra and Katif were now open.

When Sadlier's ship anchored in Muscat harbour on May 17th, the concussion from the saluting guns caused his thermometer to fall and smash – perhaps a bad omen! Sadlier had several interviews with the Sultan; he met the Sultan's brother, Salim, who had lately returned from Persia, where he had been seeking help against the Joasmi, and the Sultan's Minister, whom he described as drowsy and lethargic. But he failed completely to persuade the Sultan to agree to co-operate with the Pasha. Whenever the Pasha's name was mentioned, the Sultan 'expressed himself with much vehemence', reviling the Pasha for his acts of cruelty against the Arabs. He told Sadlier that 'to allow his troops to associate on shore in concert with the Turkish army' might be fatal to him. Said Ruete, in his biography of Said bin Sultan, says that 'the Sultan had nothing in common with the Egyptians, but everything to fear at their hands'. He absolutely refused to allow his troops to take part with the Egyptians in any operations. Sadlier pointed out to the Sultan the advantages to Muscat and other States in the Gulf, which would result from a combined effort by the British, the Sultan and the Egyptians against the pirates and the Wahabis, but the Sultan remained adamant. He told Sadlier, as a further argument against combining with the Egyptians, that some of the pirate chiefs were already making overtures to him, and were prepared to submit to him. He considered that his forces, and those of the British, were fully capable of dealing with the pirates, and he offered ships, men and all possible help to the British, such as allowing them to use some of the islands which he controlled. Although the Sultan disagreed with the point of view which Sadlier had put to him, his reception of Sadlier was most friendly, and he insisted on calling on him in the 'sooty and tottering apartment' where Sadlier lodged in the bazaar. Loch, in his dairy, gives in full a copy of the despatch which Sadlier sent by his hand to Sir Evan Napean, the President and Governor in Council in Bombay. In this despatch, he mentions that one of the reasons why the Sultan was so opposed to the idea of cooperating with the Pasha was because it was generally known that the Turks had pretensions to Bahrain, which the Sultan himself hoped one day to recover.

From Muscat, Sadlier went to Bushire, and there he heard that the Pasha was going on the Pilgrimage, and then returning to Egypt. He crossed the Gulf, meaning to land at Katif, but his ship ran aground off the coast some twelve miles from Katif. He was rescued by pilots, who were sent to his aid by Rahmah bin Jabr, the pirate chief, who occupied a fortress on the coast. The Turkish Governor of Katif refused to see him, but demanded the services of a doctor. The ship's doctor went ashore, but as no horse was provided to take him to the town twelve miles distant, he returned to the ship. The Governor was only suffering from what Sadlier calls: 'an endacious appetite!'

The Governor was in a state of great agitation because he had received orders to hand over control to the Shaikh of the Beni Khalid tribe, who had been appointed as Turkish representative in Hasa. He did all that he could to oppose his successor, refusing to allow the Shaikh to enter the town with more than two attendants. The Shaikh, very wisely, stayed outside. Meanwhile, Sadlier says: 'the Turk armed himself in his chamber, which resounded with his vociferations, and applied himself to "regulating" his accounts, being an adept at converting tens into hundreds and vice versa!'

On June 28th, Sadlier left Katif on the first lap of his journey across Arabia. The journey was dangerous, the Egyptians were withdrawing and the Bedouin were becoming aggressive. The Arabs who accompanied Sadlier were thoroughly unsatisfactory; he calls them 'hordes of robbers' who never ceased trying to extort more money from him. He mentions one surprising fact, that his party was followed over the desert by Bedouin girls, 'thus forsaking a life of innocence for the most horrid state to which human nature could be debased, that of a common prostitute!' He ascribes their lack of morals to the Turks. The country had been devastated, towns and villages were left in ruins, and all that could be taken had been carried away. There were hardly any horses left, but when Sadlier reached the Hejaz, he found that the Pasha had acquired a stable of 300 of the finest horses in Arabia. As Sadlier struggled on, he began to realise that his mission was unlikely to be successful, the Egyptians were concentrating on the Hejaz, and he realised that it was improbable that the Pasha would 'enter into projects for the acquisition of territories which he could not possibly retain'.

On August 26th, Sadlier reached Rus, to find that the Pasha had left for Medina on the previous day. On September 6th, he reached Bir Ali, where the Pasha's harem and family were encamped. He was given a meal by the Italian doctor. His horse having fallen dead, after a thirty hours ride, he had to continue his journey on a camel. Finally, he caught up and had a meeting with Ibrahaim Pasha, who received him with civility, and apologised for the 'inconvenient' march which he had undertaken. 'Inconvenient' was a mild word to describe Sadlier's experiences! Sadlier presented the Pasha with a sword, a gift from the Governor-General, and delivered the despatches which he had brought from India. But Ibrahaim Pasha would give no reply to the propositions contained in the letters, saying that such matters would have to be referred to his father, Mohammed Ali, the Viceroy of Egypt. Evidently it was too late to interest him in the British suggestion that he should support the English and the Sultan in their expedition against the Joasmi pirates. He did, however, tell Sadlier that he had written twice to the Sultan 'but as no measures had been adopted for furthering plans' he had abandoned the intention.

Sadlier waited for many weeks for replies to the despatches, which he had brought from India. Meanwhile, he reported back in a letter to the Government in India that 'the object of the mission relative to a joint co-operation against Ras al Khaima (the pirate capital) has proved impracticable from circumstances which could not have been foreseen'.

Towards the end of his time in the Hejaz, Sadlier was involved in a quarrel with the Pasha. Before Sadlier left, he was told that he was to be given a horse and a mare to take as gifts to the Governor-General. He was not allowed to see them. The Pasha's servants brought for him to see the 'horse furniture' which was in a 'tattered condition of ragged appearance'. Sadlier had been asked to give an opinion about the gifts, and he said what he thought of them. The Pasha was very annoyed that Sadlier considered them unsuitable, and he cancelled the gift of the horses, and threatened to return the sword. It was soon after this that Sadlier finally left by sea, for he had been unable to obtain an escort to return with him across the desert to Basra, which he had planned to do.

Very little credit has ever been given to Sadlier for the journey which he made, under excessively difficult conditions. He was the first Englishman to cross Arabia from east to west, and he did so at a time when a journey by a European traveller was fraught with danger. For his feat, he received no recognition, though later travellers, who did the same journey with far better equipment, gained much praise and publicity.

CHAPTER X

'Notwithstanding the meanness of Bushire as a
town, it is the best, excepting Bussorah only,
that now exists in the whole of the Persian Gulf.
It possesses considerable importance as the only
port of such an extensive empire as Persia.'
Travels in Assyria, Media and Persia:
J. S. Buckingham – 1829

THE *Eden* sailed from Muscat on the evening of May 16th,
'to the inexpressible joy of all on board, for the weather
had been more oppressively sultry than can be conceived,
never at the coolest time of the day, under 96° in the shade'. In
Muscat, unlike the other Gulf ports, there is no real cool season.
In Bahrain and Kuwait, during two or three months in the winter,
Europeans have fires in their houses and wear thick clothes. The
climate of Muscat, combined with the mental depression caused
by the huge, forbidding black mountains which encircle the town
and harbour, has taken toll of many British lives. When the first
Political Agents were posted to Muscat, not long after Loch was
there, it is recorded that three of them died within the space of a
few months.

When the *Eden* sailed, she had a prisoner on board; he was one
of the pirates who had been captured in the last engagement.
While in port, he was in charge of a sentry, but when the ship
was well away from Muscat, he was allowed to move about
without a guard. On the morning after they sailed, it was reported to Loch that the prisoner was not to be found, and it was
assumed that he had jumped overboard, and had perished in
the sea.

It was not until Loch's next visit to Ras al Khaima that he heard
what had happened to his prisoner. The sea was warm and, as
he says, 'as smooth as glass'. The pirate had managed to swim
ashore, and then, hiding during the day among the rocks, feeding
on shell fish and walking down the coast at night, he had finally
made his way back to Ras al Khaima. His adventures were

known there, and he boasted to the people of the town about his escape from the British ship. 'When the place was invested, he used all his exertions to foil us in its capture', fearing that he would fare ill at the hands of the *Eden's* crew, if he was captured again.

Loch says that the sentry had the man in his charge until they were seventeen miles from Muscat – not necessarily seventeen miles off the coast. The incident is not as remarkable as it would seem, for many of the Gulf Arabs are almost as at home in the sea, as they are on dry land, being accustomed to spend many hours in the water when diving for pearls. There are sharks in the Gulf, but they rarely attack human beings: stinging rays, saw fish and poisonous jelly fish (which are seasonal), are a greater danger to human beings than sharks. Loch describes the sea snakes which he saw after leaving Muscat 'which appear, when swimming in the water, to be from 12 to 16 feet long'. These snakes, in the upper part of the Gulf, are never more than four or five feet long, though their appearance in the water is deceptive. He speaks of them as 'venomous as to cause death to fowls, which were presented to their bite', the crew evidently tried some experiments with sea snakes. They are dangerous looking creatures, of a greenish yellow colour, with black stripes, but the Arab divers have no fear of them, they catch them in their hands, and swing them about, when they meet them in the sea.

On May 24th, the *Eden* put in to Bombay where, four days later, the China fleet arrived. This was a great occasion, and men came from distant stations to get their letters from home, and to view the numbers of eligible young ladies, 'wives to be', as Loch calls them who had come to India to find husbands, preferably wealthy nabobs. 'Generally speaking, in India, officers make the best husbands, for they are frequently young and uninjured by the climate', says the author of *The Good Old Days of the Honble John Company*. But for the *Eden* it was an unhappy visit, cholera was raging in Bombay, and six seamen died while she was in port, and a seventh man died as she sailed out of the harbour, when he had only been ill for two hours. 'The disease had attacked so many, that the main deck was lined with hammocks of the invalids, besides numbers lying on deck, in a dreadful state of agony from the spasms which they suffered.' Considering the cramped conditions, and the inadequate medical arrangements, it is surprising that not more than seven men died.

Between Bombay and Ceylon, the *Eden* met the full force of the Southwest Monsoon, and was driven off her course, but on June 11th, the wind shifted and the weather became fine. The crew were able to dry their clothes and bedding, for a week the ship's company 'had hardly a dry stick on them, owing to torrents of rain and the waves breaking over the ship'. Next day, the *Eden* anchored off Trincomalee, 'where there is, every evening, while the land breeze lasts, a delicious odour of aromatic shrubs, reaching a distance of many miles'. The ship stayed for a few days at Trincomalee, which Loch says was 'a neat, well-built, small town'; after which, Loch got orders from Admiral Sir Richard King to proceed to Madras.

Landing at Madras was no easy matter in those days, owing to the heavy surf. Locally built flat-bottomed boats, made of planks bound with fibre ropes, were used: they reminded Loch of 'great oval washing tubs'. The crew, a dozen or more men, propelled them with bamboo poles with flat pieces of wood at the ends, the steersman using a similar oar. As the boat approached the breakers 'the crew shouted a wild, uncouth song'. At the edge of the breakers they held the boat by backwatering, then, after a heavy sea had broken, they drove it through the surf, shouting together, 'Ya Allah, Ya Allah!' The men employed on the masoolas, as they were called, were evidently Moslems. After crossing several waves of breakers, the boat was thrown high and dry on the beach.

Loch's friend, Colonel Mansel, who travelled out from England with him, was waiting on the shore to meet him, so Loch hurried to get out of the boat. At once he was surrounded by 'a crowd of wretches, all most officious to be of service'. He heard Mansel shout: 'your cloak, your cloak!', and looking round he saw his cloak in the hands of an Indian, who made off into the crowd: he never saw his cloak again.

The view of Madras from the Roads was very impressive. The churches and fine houses, faced with a type of plaster which gave the appearance of marble, were surrounded by luxuriant gardens producing 'a most agreeable effect'. The principal building was the fort of St. George, which contained the large barracks, public offices, the Treasury and the houses of many of the officers and officials.

'In Madras, no-one moves out in the heat of the day who can remain within doors, but at sundown, there is to be seen on the

Mount Road, the most perfect crowd of horsemen and carriages of all descriptions, both open and closed. There are chariots, gigs, and curricles, bandys and bullock-carts.' The costumes of the people were as varied as the vehicles. The European ladies wore handsome fashionable dresses, officers rode by in 'gaudy uniforms', and there were civilians in short white jackets and white trousers. The rich Indian merchants were attired in beautiful, gorgeously coloured robes with embroidered turbans and shawls. Hindus were 'lightly covered with white muslin, the black skin of their bosoms being exposed to view, without covering on their legs'. Everybody seemed to be driving as fast as possible, as if they were trying to win a race.

On July 2nd, Loch was back at Trincomalee, refitting and taking stores on board, the ship was leaking so badly that she had to be recaulked. Here, two of the officers died. One of them was a young Lieutenant called Rushworth, a popular and promising young man. He and some of his friends were hunting jackals; thinking that he had fatally injured one, he dismounted from his horse to put it out of its misery. He put his foot on the animal's head, whereupon it seized him by the heel, lacerating the tendon. 'He complained slightly', and was taken on board the ship. 'Within a few hours, lockjaw ensued, and he shortly breathed his last.' Loch describes the funeral, which was attended by many naval and military officers.

After spending a week doing survey work, Loch returned to Trincomalee, and relates an incident which occurred during his absence. There was in Trincomalee, an English woman called Mrs. Brinkman, the widow of a Dutchman. She was the hostess of 'the Inn of Trincomalee: the very picture of a Hostess, being short, fat, good-looking, and having the appearance of not at all disliking the contents of her own cellar and larder'.

Mrs. Brinkman had to go to Colombo on business: as usual, she travelled in a palanquin, carried by porters, though 'her weight must have been no joke for the poor coolies'. On her way back, she met a herd of elephants, which was not an uncommon occurrence on that road, but one of the elephants was attracted by Mrs. Brinkman's palanquin, and approached it. Seeing this, the porter dropped the palanquin and fled.

The stout Mrs. Brinkman managed to extricate herself from the palanquin. She then rolled for some distance, got up, and waddled as fast as her fat figure would admit, to the security of a big tree, behind which she hid. From there, she watched the elephant demolishing her palanquin. Eventually, Mrs. Brinkman had to trudge on her poor feet all the way back to Trincomalee. Loch describes the affair, as 'a most ludicrous accident, which nearly proved fatal'.

On August 20th, the *Eden* sailed for Muscat. Owing to the monsoon, Loch was compelled to make the southern route, running south across the Line to meet the south-east Trade Wind, crossing and recrossing the Line to fall in with the Southwest Monsoon. At times, on this voyage, the ship covered 190 miles in twenty-four hours. On September 30th, after a voyage of 4,190 miles, the *Eden* reached Muscat. Their stay in Muscat was short, the crew of the *Eden* must have been glad of this, for September in the Gulf is the worst month of the year. Loch heard that the pirate fleet had captured some trading vessels down the coast, so two days later, the *Eden* was again under weigh in pursuit of the pirates. Off Barka, a town on the Oman coast, 'the man at the chains had but time to sing out "shoal water, Sir"', when bump! she was on a coral reef'. However, after some time the ship was extricated from the shoal, and anchored off the town. During the night there was a total eclipse of the moon.

Next morning, pirate vessels were sighted standing out from Barka, towing a prize along the coast. The *Eden* gave chase, but the wind was 'light and baffling, and the *Eden's* sailing having a good deal fallen off, in consequence of our having struck so often on the ground, we could do no more than give the vessels a good fright, and force them to destroy their prize, after the *Eden's* guns had been opened on the sternmost'.

The next port of call was Kishm island, a dependency of Muscat. The Shaikh, who was given a salute of three guns, came on board with presents of goats, vegetables and fruit, including pomegranates the size of large oranges, of the finest flavour and texture that Loch had ever eaten. At Kishm the ship took on water, which was of good quality, sweeter than the water which they obtained elsewhere in the Gulf.

Back in Bushire, the news was that the pirates, under a truce, had sent a 'wakil' (representative) to discuss with Bruce certain proposals to be put before the Bombay Government. But on his way from Ras al Khaima to Bushire, the pirate wakil, disregarding all ideas of truce, had indulged in a little piracy, attacking and capturing several vessels which he sent back to Ras al Khaima. For this reason, he and his ship were detained at Bushire by the British, until instructions arrived from Bombay.

The lot of representatives sent by the pirates to negotiate with the British was not always enviable. A wakil who was sent a few months previously, returned home, having agreed with the British to what he thought were favourable terms. The pirates thought otherwise. The wakil's beard was plucked out, he was mounted on a donkey, facing its tail, and driven round the town, followed by a mob of men and boys, pelting him with filth.

The wakil whom Loch met at Bushire was an old man. He and his followers were not in custody, but were allowed in the bazaar under surveillance, in spite of which they had already made one unsuccessful attempt to escape. When he stayed with the Bruces at the Residency, it was Loch's habit to take a walk on the flat roof of the building every morning at dawn. Several times he saw the old wakil steal down to the beach – anyone who has lived in an Oriental seaside town would guess his purpose – but in this case he used to take out a little telescope and sweep the horizon. Loch told Bruce what he had seen, and a stricter watch was kept on him. One morning Loch saw the wakil on the shore as usual, so he stayed awhile watching him. As it grew lighter, three pirate ships became visible on the horizon: Loch signalled to the *Eden*, which lay at anchor off the town, and in no time, the ship's boats were lowered, and started in pursuit of the pirates; but when they saw that they were being followed, the pirate vessels changed course, and were soon out of sight.

A few days later, Loch discovered that a vessel from Dubai, whose people were in league with the pirates, had slipped through one of the passages among the sandbanks and entered the inner harbour. Dubai is a town on the Arab coast, now the capital of one of the Trucial Shaikhdoms, which, owing to its position on the banks of a twisting inlet, is often euphemistically described as the 'Venice of the Gulf'.

The Dubai ship was hurriedly unloading her cargo, and Loch had discovered – though he does not tell us by what means – that Shaikh Abdul Rasool, the Shaikh of Bushire, had been bribed to facilitate the escape of the pirates on board the ship. Loch signalled to the *Eden* ordering the pinnace, manned and armed, under

Moffath's command, to proceed to the inner anchorage where he would meet them. He hurried to the harbour, alone, and gave orders to Moffath to board the Dubai vessel and take possession of it. Immediately he was surrounded by an angry crowd of men, among them was Shaikh Abdul Rasool, who threatened him with violence unless he countermanded his orders. By this time, Adey the interpreter had joined him. 'Of course, the only answer which I could give was that I was doing my duty, and I refused to comply with their demands.' By now the sailors had taken possession of the ship. Loch told the Shaikh that 'if he permitted the slightest insult, far less any injury to be offered, most severe retaliation and vengeance would ensue'. He threatened to complain to the Government of Persia as well as to the Bombay Government, and should it be thought that he had acted wrongly, he would take the blame.

The Shaikh seems to have realised that he would get into trouble if he obstructed Loch, so he invited him into the caravansarai which was on the shore of the harbour. They were followed by a mob, but the Shaikh ordered the big doors to be closed. He and Loch had a long conversation; Shaikh Abdul Rasool said that it was not Loch's seizure of the vessel that angered him, but the fact that Loch had ordered its capture in his harbour, in sight of all his people. Loch then accused him of trying to help the pirates to escape, pointing out that to do so was against his own interests, as the pirates preyed on the trading vessels of Bushire, and were as much the Shaikh's enemies as the enemies of the British. Finally, Loch walked out of the caravansarai back to the Residency, as if nothing had happened, 'receiving neither molestation or insult'. The matter was reported to Bombay, but it was never again referred to by the Shaikh. After this affair, Loch and Shaikh Abdul Rasool became on good terms. Shortly afterwards, during one of the Moslem festivals, Shaikh Abdul Rasool gave a dinner party for Loch, Bruce, and the ship's officers, to demonstrate that all was now peace and happiness.

The dinner was in the Shaikh's 'palace' in a long narrow room, running the whole length of the building. Rooms were narrow because roofs were carried on palm trunks, which were not strong enough to bear any great span. It is only during the last forty years that timber beams, and latterly, steel beams have been used in the construction of Arab houses in the Gulf. The meal was served in European style, at a table provided with plates, knives and forks, the guests sat on chairs. Shaikh Abdul Rasool must have been very advanced, and familiar with Western ways, for only thirty years ago, a meal served in European style would have been most unusual in an Arab or Persian house in the Gulf. The Shaikh sat on a chair at the side of the room, joining in the conversation, and giving orders to the servants, but not partaking of the meal. Some old-fashioned Arabs still keep to this custom, but today an Arab host usually sits and eats with his guests.

The menu included kabobs, stewed meats, chickens with rich fruit sauce, and a roast kid stuffed with peaches, nuts and rice. For dessert, there were figs, green almonds, and many kinds of preserved fruits. The beverages consisted of different kinds of sherbets, one was made from the seed of a species of willow, 'which gave it a most delicious flavour', and red and white Shiraz wine. Sir Robert Ker Foster, who travelled in Persia at this time, says that the wine was manufactured in secret by Armenians, and that 'when good it should be a little sweet, with the flavour of dry Madeira'. Loch says that the red Shiraz wine was from the same vineyards which supplied the vines which were imported to Constantia, at the Cape of Good Hope, which produce the finest South African wine.

The Shaikh sat smoking and talking during the meal, but every now and then he left the room, 'for the purpose of taking some deep draughts of his favourite Shirazi, which was evident on his return, for his intoxication was apparent'. Musicians played and sang during dinner, one of their drums was 'not unlike, in size and shape, the fig drum of Smyrna', others were made from coconut shells covered in parchment. Loch had no appreciation of 'the uncouth sounds' of Oriental music. The party ended with fireworks, 'which were but a poor display', although the Bushiris thought them 'exceedingly grand. . . . We returned in the evening to the Residency, very much pleased with our entertainment, the Shaikh appearing no less so.'

One of the principal exports from Bushire was horses: they were raised on the plains of Kazaroon, and were a cross-breed of Arab and Turkoman stock. Many of the more wealthy Persians in the neighbourhood of Bushire were engaged in breeding and trading in horses. Loch often watched them being shipped from Bushire, and he noticed the cruel manner in which they were loaded into boats from the end of the stone jetty, which caused frequent casualties. There was a fine crane at the pierhead, which had not been erected, and one day, Loch asked Shaikh Abdul Rasool why he did not use it. The Shaikh said that it would cost a great deal to put it into working order, and to keep it running, without any financial return. Loch's interest in it was mainly on account of the horses, so he offered to send his ship's carpenter and a party of men on shore to put it together. The Shaikh was profuse in his thanks, but again he complained about the cost of running the crane, so Loch suggested that he should make a small charge for its use.

Loch little knew that what he suggested to the Shaikh was the very thing that the merchants of Bushire wished to avoid. They knew their Shaikh only too well. Immediately he instituted a system of charges, ostensibly for the use of the crane; but in fact, he imposed a new tax on everything which was shipped from the pier, irrespective of whether the crane was used or not. In this way, he developed another method of squeezing the merchants for money, with the apparent support of the British.

The Shaikh had, perhaps, some excuse for extracting as much as he could from his people, for he himself was constantly under pressure from his overlord, the Prince of Shiraz, to pay more tribute. Though the Shaikhs of Bushire were virtually independent they were nominally subject to the Prince of Shiraz, and through him, to the Shah of Persia. The people of Bushire, which had a population of about 5,000, were not Hawala Arabs, as were most of the inhabitants of the Persian coast towns. The Bushiris were of mixed Persian and Arab stock, many of them came originally from Oman and intermarried with Persians. At one time, three families controlled Bushire: two of them were long established, and the third family came later from the Arab coast, and gained an ascendency over the others. From this family which belonged to the Abu Meheeri tribe, came two Shaikhs, both called Nasr, predecessors of Shaikh Abdul Rasool. One of them led an expedition against the Khalifah at Zabara in 1780, three years before the Khalifah took Bahrain and transferred what had been a Persian dependency into an Arab principality. Nasr was heavily defeated by the Khalifah at Zabara, his sword was taken and is still a family heirloom, and he became known in Arab history by the derogatory name of 'Nasur', the diminutive of Nasr. One

Shaikh Nasr, in about 1765, became a Shia, and married a Persian lady, 'in hopes of being appointed Admiral of the Persian fleet' – according to Niebuhr. But the marriage did him no good, for he became 'odious to his subjects and to his neighbours, and his children are no longer counted among the Arabian nobility'.

The Bushiri Shaikhs had accumulated much wealth, for the port which they controlled was the only one of importance on the Persian coast though, as Buckingham said, 'as a seaport, Bushire had no one good quality to recommend it'. In Loch's time, it was a busy place, visited every year by about twenty merchant ships from Bengal and Bombay, and by trading vessels from Basra and the Gulf ports. But trade was crippled by overwhelming pressure and exactions. The merchandise, when landed, was carried by mule caravans over the mountains to the interior of Persia. All along the route, those who were in a position to oppress the people beneath them, took their toll. The Shaikh, to satisfy the rapacity of the Prince, and to fill his own treasury, fleeced both the merchants and the minor Shaikhs to whom he farmed out towns and villages. The lesser Shaikhs in their turn, extorted as much as they could from the impoverished peasants. From the 'vacillating and tottering Persian Government' at the top, down to the village headman, there was corruption, persecution and oppression. Whenever the demands of the Prince became too outrageous, Shaikh Abdul Rasool threatened to remove himself and all his followers, and the people of Bushire, to the island of Kharak, leaving Bushire desolate. This was a very real threat, and it deterred the Prince from taking extreme measures against the Shaikh.

For some time, the Prince of Shiraz had coveted Bushire, he planned to oust the Shaikh and to put in his place one of his own sons. While Loch was in Bushire, news reached the Shaikh that the Prince was about to embark troops at Bundar Rig, 120 miles north of Bushire, with the object of occupying the island of Kharak, where the Shaikh had a fortress in which he kept his treasure. But the plan was not carried out, probably because, as usual, the Persian authorities were unable to obtain ships.

It was some time after Loch left, that Shaikh Abdul Rasool's reign came to an end. After managing for many years to circumvent the wiles of the Prince, he allowed himself to be persuaded to visit Shiraz; perhaps he wanted to see his son, who was

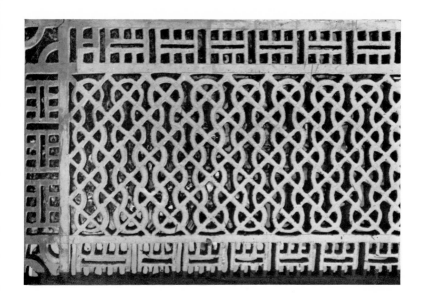

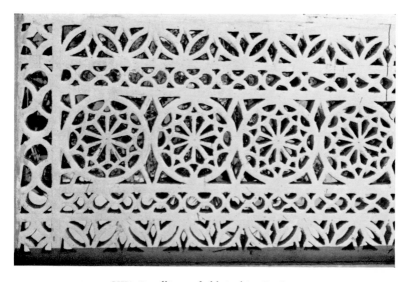

XIII. Panellings of old Arabian Design

XIV. Arab with falcon

XV. Selukis

there, ostensibly for his education, but in fact as a hostage for his father's good behaviour. He was given solemn assurances of safety, and is said to have been attracted by the offer of the hand in marriage of the Prince's daughter. Another reason for his visit was in order to discuss with the Prince plans for retaking Bahrain.

As soon as he entered the city walls, he was seized and imprisoned. It was proposed that he should be put to death, but if this were done, probably much of his treasure in Bushire and Kharak would be seized by other people, so an enormous ransom was demanded from him. It was collected, and paid, and the unfortunate Shaikh was allowed to return to Bushire, shorn of much of his wealth. On his way home, quite close to Bushire, he was attacked by a band of brigands, led by a man who had a grudge against him. After a desperate fight, he was killed and hacked to pieces. Although he had been notorious for his severity and for the exactions which he had levied on merchants, Wellsted describes him as 'not ill fitted for the people over whom he rules', and when he died 'the better class of people' in Bushire, 'bitterly regret his loss'.

One morning, Loch was in the courtyard of the Residency when an Arab horse from Nejd was brought in to be shown to Bruce. Suddenly, there was a buzz of chatter among the servants and hangers-on in the courtyard. A remarkably handsome old man, tall, well dressed, with a stately demeanour, and a long white beard, made his appearance. He was led into the courtyard by his son, a good-looking young man, and was greeted with 'a low obeisance' by all the Persians who were present. The old man was blind.

The horse was led up to him. He caressed it, feeling the texture of its skin and measuring every part of its body and legs with his hands. He then gave his opinion on the merits of the animal, pointing out its proportions, and drawing attention to certain defects which had not been noticed by those who judged the horse by the eye instead of by the more correct rule of measurement.

There is some doubt about the identity of this old man, who, according to Loch, was called Abdul Futtah, though from his history, which Loch describes, he was probably Ali Khan, who was famous as the finest judge of horses in Persia. In 1788, he had shown a disposition to aspire to the throne, opposing the then ruler, Agha Mohammed Khan. Ali Khan and his followers met Agha Mohammed Khan on the battlefield, but before the fighting started, Agha Mohammed sent his brother alone, to propose a parley. Ali Khan agreed to this with some reluctance, and went with a few of his men to the enemy camp. He was lulled with wine, and then seized, and his eyes were put out 'in the most cruel and painful manner by hot irons'. For a long time he was kept in prison, then, during the anarchy which followed the murder of Agha Mohammed, he was liberated, and when Loch met him, he was receiving a small pension from the East India Company.

Loch always enjoyed his visits to Bushire, where the climate was better than elsewhere in the Gulf. Even in the summer, he remarked on the delightful coolness of the early mornings, besides, it was possible to ride inland towards the range of mountains which made a background to Bushire. Often he accompanied Bruce on visits to the mountain villages.

Loch used to be awakened in the quiet of the early morning by 'the fine sonorous voices' of the muezzins calling the faithful to prayer from the minarets of the seven mosques, three of the mosques belonged to the Sunni sect, and four to the Shia sect. Though Loch admired the sound of the muezzins' voices, the Bushiris were notorious for their harsh, ugly accents, and their corrupt pronunciation of Persian. Buckingham's opinion of the Bushiris was 'a disagreeable mixture of the Arab and the Persian, in which whatever is amiable in either character is totally rejected, and whatever is vicious in both, is retained'. Today, in some of the Gulf towns, the call to prayer is relayed on loud speakers, which saves the muezzin the trouble of having to ascend the minaret, but defects in the machines are apt to produce strange gurgling sounds which spoil the effect of the chanting.

After the call to prayer, the flat roofs of the houses, where people slept in the summer time, were all a-bustle. Hawkers appeared in the narrow streets and lanes, crying their wares, selling cakes, made of honey and almonds, fresh milk, prawns, sweetmeats, and dried locusts. From every courtyard sounded the clang of pestles and mortars beaten in time to the song of the women who were pounding the coffee beans for the day. Soon strings of laden mules and camels started off through the town gates, on their long journey through the mountain passes to Shiraz and beyond, followed by the blue-clad women water-carriers, with their goat skins on their shoulders. They brought fresh water from springs in the date gardens, some miles away, which they sold in the town. The well water in Bushire was brackish, though Loch says 'strange to say, after becoming accustomed to it, the water appears sweet to the palate'.

The people of Bushire, among whom were many Armenians, and a few Jews, were mainly occupied in trade. 'The greater part became merchants in some way or other ... all look on their superiors with awe, but when it is in their power, they oppress those under them.' They were fond of good living, and they smoked and drank coffee from morning till night: they drank wine, too, but not in public. Of the coastal Persians, Loch says: 'an Englishman may land in any part of the coast of Persia, and will be assisted from place to place, certain of experiencing good, and even kind treatment everywhere – otherwise it will be his own fault.' Another characteristic which he mentions more than once was the Arab's 'great hatred of labour. Seldom does he cultivate more ground than is absolutely necessary for himself. A man is rich indeed if he possesses some horses, goats and one or two camels.'

Loch was in Bushire during the festivities at the end of the month of Ramadhan, when the town took on the atmosphere of a fair. Walking through the bazaar, he came upon a group of people watching a strolling player, a little hunchback. Laid on a carpet before him, were a number of different dresses, which he put on and off with great rapidity, 'at the same time, altering his appearance, so that you would not swear that it was the same man'. The audience were delighted with his performance, and he kept them in roars of laughter, but in the middle of the most amusing part, he stopped, rolled up his carpet, and moved some distance away. The crowd followed him. He then went among them, begging, and only continued his act when he thought he had received a suitable reward for his performance.

In another place, there were tumblers and mountebanks, and a 'Pahlawan' (a champion athlete). These men used to travel from village to village, challenging the local strong men to feats of strength. They still ply their trade and sometimes visit the Arab towns in the Gulf, but now-a-days, they are more likely to be seen pitting their strength against a motorcar, in gear, with the engine running, or lying on the ground supporting a board, over which a car is driven, than performing the old-fashioned weight-lifting tricks.

The next thing which Loch came across was an unmistakable 'take-off' of himself and Shaikh Abdul Rasool. The man who played the part of Loch had somehow got hold of a naval cocked hat, which he wore perched on the top of his turban, and a straight uniform sword, which was slung at his side. He imitated Loch paying a visit on the Shaikh, strutting about and grimacing and bowing, going through all the gestures which an Englishman is supposed to make. He mimicked the awkward manner of a European who finds that he has to sit on the floor, first looking for a chair, then subsiding on the floor, drawing his legs underneath him with his hands, with great apparent difficulty and exertion. 'Then followed a most ridiculous mock interview between the Shaikh and myself, which, I have no doubt, was remarkably well imitated, for it caused bursts of applause, particularly owing to my being there, enjoying it as much as they did.' Even today, nothing delights an Arab audience more than watching the repercussions of a European, who is being cleverly and intelligently mimicked, in some sort of theatrical performance.

CHAPTER XI

'A pirate is the enemy of the human race.'
                                        Coke.

LOCH made a long stay in Bushire, waiting for the expedition to arrive from Bombay. In the meantime, there were political developments on the Pirate Coast. Sultan bin Seggar, the Shaikh of Sharja, and Rashid bin Hameed, the Shaikh of Dubai, who, in the past, had been allies of the Joasmi, were alarmed at the prospect of the combined campaign by Britain and Muscat against the pirates, in which they might well be involved. They decided to shake off their allegiance to Hassan bin Rahmah, Shaikh of the Joasmi, and to make peace, if they could, with the Sultan of Muscat. But the Sultan was now in a very strong position, and showed no inclination to treat with them, besides, he had been advised by Sadlier, the envoy from the Bombay Government, not to believe their protestations of friendship.

Shaikh Hassan now found himself deserted by his friends. The Wahabis, who had been his strongest allies, had been crushed by Ibrahaim Pasha, and were in no position to help him; his neighbours in Dubai and Sharja no longer regarded him as the strong man of the Gulf, and wanted to break away from him, and his representative, 'the old Wakil', whom he had sent to Bushire to discuss terms between the Joasmi and the Bombay Government, had achieved nothing. The 'Old Wakil' in fact was being held by the British, owing to his piratical escapades on his way to Bushire.

The Shaikh decided to look elsewhere for support. At this time, the Shaikhs on the Persian coast, such as the Shaikh of Bushire, were more or less independent, and made alliances with the rulers in the Gulf without reference to the Central Government, which, as long as the Shaikhs paid tribute, left them to themselves. Shaikh Hassan decided to seek help from Linga, one of the larger ports on the Persian coast, which possessed a number of vessels. Even in recent times, Linga used to send a considerable number of large dhows to the pearling banks. The Shaikh of Linga agreed that his fleet would bring supplies of dates from Basra to Ras al Khaima, to provide for the defenders who expected to be besieged there. He also agreed that some of the pirate ships should join the Linga fleet in order to carry out piracy at the top of the Gulf, under the protection of the Linga ships, which were unlikely to be interfered with by the British. The Shaikh knew how difficult it was for the British to identify pirate ships when they were not actually engaged in piracy. 'So under this deception', as Loch puts it, the Joasmi would continue their piratical activities. Much of this information was given to Bruce by Rahmah bin Jabr, the famous (or infamous) pirate chief of the Jalahamah tribe, whom Loch met in Bushire for the first time. Rahmah bin Jabr is mentioned several times on different occasions in Loch's diary, but to obtain a more composite picture of him, all that is known of him has been put together.

In the markets and coffee shops of the coastal towns of the Gulf, old men still tell stories of the life and death of Rahmah bin Jabr of the Jalahamah tribe, who was for half a century the implacable enemy of the Khalifah Shaikhs of Bahrain. He was one of the most vivid characters that the Gulf has produced, a daring freebooter, without fear or mercy. The only other men about whom one hears the same stories constantly told by the Arabs, both of very recent times, are the late King Abdul Aziz Al Saud and Sir Percy Cox, who served in the Gulf in the first decade of this century.

Today, young Arabs regard the stories about Rahmah as 'old wives' tales, but the men of the Khalifah family and of the Jalahamah tribe, who now live peacefully together in Bahrain, still think of him as an historical figure. He is one of the few Gulf Arabs of the early 19th century, who was described by more than one contemporary eye witness, both Buckingham and Loch met him frequently, he features prominently in Nabhani's history of Bahrain, and is mentioned by several Arab and European writers.

His career started many years before Loch came to the Gulf, and it ended, dramatically, some years after Loch had left. He is said to have begun his life as a horse-coper, with the money which he made, he bought a boat, and with twelve companions, he started his career as a pirate. His next venture was a 300-ton vessel, manned by 350 men. His story is the epitome of a tribal feud, typical of those feuds which used to disturb the peace of the Gulf. There are still frequent quarrels among the Shaikhs, and the tribes, but they are now more likely to be caused by boundary disputes over oil bearing seas or lands, than by the clash of personalities.

Early in the 18th century, the Utubi tribe, progenitors of the Khalifah, and the Subah, ancestors of the ruling house of Kuwait, emerged from the Arabian desert, and settled at Grane, which was on the Arab coast at the top of the Gulf. Both tribes trace their descent from the famous Aneza tribe, and so claim kinship with the Saud family of Arabia. They built a fort at Grane, which became known as Kuwait, Kut being the Arabic word for a fort.

In about 1766, the Khalifah, which was the name by which they were later known, accompanied by the Jalahamah, a sub-tribe of the Utubi, moved down the coast to Zabara on the Qatar peninsula opposite Bahrain. Bahrain was, at this time, held by a Persian garrison. Since the Portuguese occupation of Bahrain, which lasted for about a century until 1622, the islands had been constantly over-run by different Arab tribes. In 1718, Bahrain was held by the Omanis, but by 1783, it was a dependency of Persia.

The Khalifah came to Zabara to be nearer to the pearl banks, for since settling in Kuwait they had become a sea-faring people, engaged in pearl diving and trading at sea. Zabara had little to commend it as a settlement, it is an arid, salty stretch of coast, with a few wells containing brackish water. The Khalifah built a town defended by a strong fort, whose ruins and those of a large mosque, can still be seen. They became prosperous, and were joined by other Arabs, many of them coming from Basra after the city was taken from the Turks by the Persians in 1776.

The presence of a flourishing Arab settlement on the Qatar coast, only thirty miles across the sea, was a threat to the Persians in Bahrain. The Khalifah began to make forays into Bahrain, and the Persians retaliated in 1782 by sending a fleet and a military force, commanded by the Shaikh of Bushire, to reduce Zabara. The Khalifah refused to surrender when called upon by the Persians to do so, and in the battle among the white sand dunes on the coast, the Persians were ignominiously defeated, and they retired to their ships. The Khalifah Shaikh, Khalifah bin Mohammed, described as 'artful and politic', is said by an Arab historian to have 'poured rains on the people from the clouds of his bounty'. But it seems that he missed out Rahmah and the Jalahamah tribe, who already had a dispute with the Khalifah about pearling rights. Rahmah and his people returned disgruntled to Kuwait. Finding, however, that the Subah tribe did not welcome them with open arms, they again shook off the dust of Kuwait from their feet, and came back to the Qatar coast, settling first at Ruwais, and later at Khor Hassan, where they engaged in indiscriminate piracy.

In August 1783 the Khalifah, supported by the Subah of Kuwait, made an attack on Bahrain, and drove out the Persians, who never again occupied the islands. Rahmah, perhaps attracted by the prospect of loot, abandoned his quarrel with the Khalifah, and brought his pirates to assist them in the conquest of Bahrain. After establishing themselves in Bahrain, the Khalifah Shaikh, Ahmed, known as 'the Conqueror', divided up the rich date gardens among those who had fought for him, keeping the best for himself and his family. Once again, Rahmah considered that he and his tribe were ill-requited. They finally broke with the Khalifah, and became for two generations their most bitter enemies. From his lair in an inlet on the Qatar coast, Rahmah's strong fleet, manned by bloodthirsty pirates, preyed on the shipping of Persia, Bahrain and Kuwait. He avoided conflict with the Wahabis, whose sect he had joined, and carefully abstained from any aggression against ships sailing under the British flag, claiming that the British were his friends. Whenever Bahrain was attacked, he joined her enemies, and he spent much of his time visiting the various rulers of the Gulf, trying to persuade them to attack Bahrain.

The Khalifah now ruled in Bahrain and Zabara, and controlled most of Qatar, Bahrain became the centre of the pearl trade, and her merchants in their big sailing boats, traded extensively with India, paying for the goods which they bought, with the money which they got from selling pearls. Shaikh Ahmed died in 1795, and was succeeded by his son Sulman, who reigned for over twenty stormy years. In the early part of his reign, his brother, Abdulla, shared with him the responsibility of government. But Bahrain did not remain for long at peace. In 1799, the Sultan of Muscat, Sultan bin Ahmed, seized some Bahrain ships in Muscat harbour on the pretext that they had not paid dues to him, then, with some encouragement from Persia, he declared war on Bahrain. The Khalifah, deciding that discretion was the better part of valour, knowing that they would receive no support from the aboriginal inhabitants of Bahrain, who were unlikely to help their latest conquerors to repel yet another wave of conquerors, retired to Zabara, their refuge in times of trouble.

The Sultan occupied Bahrain without opposition. He built a fort at Arad, on Muharraq island, and left there his young son Salim, with a small garrison. Soon afterwards, the Sultan was killed in an engagement with pirates, on his way back to Muscat from Basra. The Muscat occupation only lasted for a few months. The Khalifah sought help from the Wahabis, and the Wahabi Amir, welcoming the chance to get a foothold in Bahrain, sent a force under Ibrahaim Faisan to Zabara, which supported the Khalifah when they landed in Bahrain, and without much difficulty, expelled the small Muscat garrison. But the Wahabi chief, who had come ostensibly to help the Khalifah, remained in Bahrain as their master. They found it almost impossible to dislodge their powerful ally, so once again, they returned to Zabara, leaving the unfortunate people of Bahrain to be savagely persecuted by the Wahabis, who regarded the Shias as worse than infidels.

By 1810, the power of the Wahabis was on the decline; owing to the need to defend their country against the Egyptians, who were advancing from the west, they reduced the garrison in Bahrain. Again, the political pattern of the Gulf changed. The Khalifah secretly sent an envoy to the Sultan of Muscat, asking him to help them to dislodge the Wahabis. The Sultan was engaged in hostilities with the Wahabis, and was unable to provide any men or ships, but he gave the Khalifah money, and presented the Shaikh with a sword, whose name is 'Salmuni'. Among the Arabs, swords of historical interest are given names, and are regarded as heirlooms. Finally, the Khalifah were able to expel the Wahabis, and Faisan and his men joined Rahmah on the Qatar coast, and became his partner in piracy, seizing many Bahrain ships, and putting the crews to death. About this time, the Khalifah, seeking new allies, appealed without success to the British for support in maintaining their rule in Bahrain.

Finally, the Khalifah took the offensive against Ramah. One

dark night, they brought their fleet close to the pirates' anchorage. Rahmah, seeing some lights at sea, told his friend, Faisan, that it must be the Khalifah fleet. Faisan regarded this as impossible, believing that the Khalifah Shaikhs were still captives in the Wahabi capital, where some of them had been held as hostages. At daylight, the Bahrain fleet was seen off the coast. Owing to the superior strength of the enemy, Rahmah thought it prudent to avoid an engagement, knowing that the Khalifah were unlikely to make a landing. Faisan jeered at Rahmah, calling him a coward, which was a trait of which Rahmah could never be accused. Against his better judgement, Rahmah decided to fight. Led by Rahmah in his big ship *Al Manowar* (a name evidently acquired from the English), the pirate fleet sailed out of the harbour, and soon the ships of the two fleets were joined in battle. The ship commanded by the son of the Shaikh of Bahrain was alongside *Al Manowar*, and in the hand to hand fighting the young Shaikh was killed, then both ships caught fire and sank. Rahmah, whose arm had been badly burned, found himself in the sea, and he and Faisan clung to a floating spar, until they were rescued. It is said that while they were hanging on the wreckage, Rahmah reminded Faisan that he had recommended avoiding battle with the Khalifah. The pirates suffered a defeat, and shortly afterwards, Rahmah left Qatar and settled in the island fort of Dammam on the coast of what is now Saudi Arabia. He soon recovered from his setback, and in 1816, hearing that the Sultan was again preparing an expedition against Bahrain, he hurried to Muscat and offered his services against his enemies, the Khalifah. The Wahabis were on bad terms with the Sultan, and Rahmah's sudden change of loyalty angered them. They turned his followers out of the fort at Dammam and, for some years, Rahmah had no fixed base. When not at sea, he and his pirates spent their time between Muscat and Bushire.

When Buckingham was at Bushire in 1816, Rahmah arrived with a fleet of nine ships, and about 2,000 men, most of them being negro slaves over whom he had absolute authority, 'he is some-times as prodigal of their lives, in a fit of anger, as he is of those of his enemies who he is not content to slay in battle, but basely murders in cold blood after they have submitted'. Buckingham tells how, when some of Rahmah's men used mutinous expres-sions, he put them into the big wooden water tank in his ship, fastened it down, and left the men in it till they suffocated, and then threw their bodies into the sea.

Of his appearance, Buckingham says: 'his figure presented a meagre trunk, with four lank members, all of them cut and hacked and pierced with wounds of sabres, spears and bullets, to the number of perhaps more than 20 wounds. He had a face naturally ferocious, and ugly, now rendered still more so by several scars and the loss of an eye. This Butcher Chief affects great simplicity in dress, manners and living. He carries simplicity to a degree of filthiness which is disgusting. His usual dress is a shirt which is never taken off from the time it is first put on, till it is worn out, no drawers, or covering for the legs, a large black goat's skin cloak wrapped over all, and a dirty handkerchief thrown loosely over his head.

'He was not only cherished and courted by the people of Bushire', though this did not prevent him from seizing their ships, or from blockading Bushire on several occasions, 'but he was courteously received and respectfully entertained when he visited the British Factory'. One day, Rahmah arrived at the Residency at breakfast time, and was invited to drink tea. 'Some of his followers took chairs around him, they were as disgustingly filthy as could be imagined, and did not scruple to hunt for vermin in their skins, of which there was abundance, and throw them beside them on the floor.' The idea of a ferocious pirate drinking tea, at breakfast, is somewhat out of keeping, but being a Moslem and a Wahabi, he would not have touched liquor.

Another time, Rahmah came to the Residency to show his wounded arm to 'some medical gentlemen from the Company's cruisers'. The wound was made by grape shot and splinters, the arm was one mass of blood for several days. He gradually recovered, however, without surgical aid, the bone of his arm between the shoulder and the elbow being completely shivered to pieces. The fragments progressively worked out, and the singular appearance was left of the forearm and elbow connected to the shoulder by flesh skin and tendons, without the least vestige of bone. Some years later, he acquired a silver tube, which was fixed round his arm so that it was 'capable of exertion'.

Buckingham was disgusted at the way Rahmah was treated by the British officers. One of the Englishmen asked him 'with a tone of encouragement and familiarity' whether he could still kill an enemy with his boneless arm. He drew his dagger, and supporting the elbow of his damaged left arm with his right hand, he grasped the dagger in the clenched fist of his left arm, and drew it backwards and forwards, saying that 'he would like to have the cutting of as many throats as he could effectively open with this left hand'. His words were greeted with applause. It is not perhaps surprising that Rahmah claimed to be the friend of the British.

In June 1816, the Sultan of Muscat, Said bin Sultan, made another attempt to subjugate Bahrain. He had with him, Rahmah and his pirate fleet, and three ships from Bushire, provided by the Prince of Shiraz, carrying Persian mercenaries from the coast. It was a strong force, but not an auspicious expedition. Bruce, the Resident, had recently been in Bahrain, where he found the Khalifah well prepared to resist invasion, and he had tried, unsuccessfully, to dissuade the Sultan from attacking the islands. Rahmah and his pirates were not easy people to handle, and the Persians, who themselves had aspirations to the ownership of Bahrain, were unlikely to view with pleasure the prospect of Bahrain becoming a dependency of Muscat.

The Sultan's army landed on one of the islands, according to the local history it was Sitra, but some writers suggest that it was Arad. For two days, there was no sign of opposition, and the Sultan said to Rahmah, 'your Utubi seem to be dead'. Rahmah, himself from the Utubi tribe, replied: 'if their flags are not seen tomorrow morning, then you may believe that they are dead'. At daybreak next morning, the flags of the Khalifah appeared among the date trees. 'See', said Rahmah, 'there are my Utubi, now put your trust in God!' There was a short fierce battle, in which the Muscat forces were badly beaten, and driven back to their boats, leaving many casualties on the field, including the Sultan's younger brother, Hamed. The defeat of the Sultan was partly due to the treachery of the Persian troops, who went over to the enemy during the engagement. The Persians urged the Sultan to come to Bushire after his defeat at Bahrain, promising to supply him with reinforcements to make another attack, but he discovered that there was a plot to seize him in Bushire, so he returned to Muscat. Again, Rahmah urged him to make another effort to take Bahrain, but the Sultan refused at that time to do so.

The political scene changed again. The Persians adopted a

friendly attitude towards the Khalifah, sending an envoy, Sekunder Khan, to Bahrain, bearing presents and robes of honour for the Shaikhs. He offered them terms if they would declare their allegiance to Persia, but they declined to lose their independence. It was now the turn of the Khalifah to become friendly with the Wahabis and the Joasmi pirates of the coast, thus producing another change in the situation. The Joasmi had, for some time, frequented Bahrain harbours, selling much of their booty in the bazaars. These constant changes in loyalties, if they can be so described, are difficult to follow, but there was one person who held steadfastly to the same policy, that was Rahmah, whose *idée fixé* was to destroy the Khalifah.

When Loch met Rahmah in November 1819, the old pirate was trying to persuade the Persians in Bushire to join him in an attack on Bahrain. Loch says of him: 'he was as great a pirate as those of the Joasmi tribe with this exception, he protected British trade, and was at peace with Basra and Bushire, but at war with every other part of the Gulf. This man was the terror of the Gulf, not being very scrupulous as to whom he attacked, neither giving or expecting quarter . . . he exercised his crimes under the cloak of religion . . . his avarice was equal to his cruelty and brutality.'

Loch describes Rahmah as being 'about five foot seven, nearly sixty years of age, stooping considerably, with a quick waddling gait at this season of the year, wearing a large, black goat's hair cloak, the hood similar to that of the Capuchins, drawn close round his head. Thus his small, but sharp-featured face peered from under the bonnet-shaped hood, giving him the appearance of some hellish old sorceress, rather than the man whose name was enough to create alarm wherever he carried his feuds.'

'In going through the streets, he was gazed at by all, and followed by a crowd of children. Above his cloak, he had slung over the left shoulder, hanging on the right side, a huge sabre and in his girdle a pair of pistols. His address was abrupt, and extremely forbidding, his voice sharp, and loud, speaking as rapidly as he could pronounce the words. When seated, he had a trick of placing his sword under one leg and over the other, drawing it half from its scabbard, and forcing it back with a loud snap. Again, drawing first one pistol from his girdle, then the other, examining the priming, as if to be certain all was fit for service, then cocking them, and half-cocking them, making it not comfortable to be near him, lest the trigger should slip from his fingers, and the pistol go off.'

It was apparently well known in Bushire that part of Rahmah's fleet was waiting to attack the convoy of ships from Linga on the Persian coast, which was bringing the year's supply of dates to Bahrain. The Persians of Linga had lately become friendly with the Shaikhs of Bahrain, and this aroused Rahmah's anger.

Loch's second meeting with Ramah was in 1820, shortly after the Treaty of Peace had been signed by the Shaikhs of the Pirate Coast and by the Bahrain Shaikhs. Loch was at Bushire, when Rahmah came there to be informed about the decisions which had been made in the treaty in which he himself had taken no part. When he arrived, he had with him two or three attendants, among whom was his eldest son, 'a lad of about twenty years of age, of middling stature, rather good looking and most contrary to his father, of a wild manner and countenance'. This was Bishr, who, after his father's death, continued the feud against the Khalifah until he himself was killed fighting.

Rahmah was told by Bruce that, in future, he would not be allowed to act in a piratical manner, and should make up his mind to retire to his fortress at Katif, which at this date was his headquarters, and live there quietly, 'or he must expect to receive such chastisement as the Pirates of Ras al Khaima had done'. It was explained to him that there was now hardly a ship in the Gulf which did not carry some property of British, or British Indian subjects, who would suffer if he captured them. It was not surprising that during this conversation, when he was told that he should live a quiet, peaceful life in the seaside town of Katif, 'he showed most restless, ungovernable and irritable temper'. However, he did eventually agree to retire to Katif, on the understanding that 'neither he, his Tribe or vessels should receive insult or molestation, and should trade on the same footing as others, but should he be attacked by any other tribes, of course he was absolved from remaining quiescent'. The last condition was probably proposed by him. One can well imagine that it passed through his mind that, if he attacked a ship, it would be very difficult afterwards to determine whether his or the other ship was the aggressor!

Loch did not meet Rahmah again, but not long after this interview, he became embroiled in a quarrel with one of his neigh-bours. He ordered his youngest son to take command of his fleet, and to attack a very much stronger force. The boy was defeated, and returned a fugitive to his father in Katif. 'The old iron-hearted Pirate could not brook the thought that his son should outlive a defeat and retire in the face of the enemy, even if the odds were heavily against him.' Calling him a 'dastard son of a dog' for daring to come back and report a failure, he had the boy bound and thrown into the sea to drown, as a warning to his followers. Somehow the boy loosened himself, and he was picked up by a boat several miles astern. For many months, Rahmah did not know that his son had survived, and when he did hear, he never uttered his son's name again. The son was killed some years later, during the storming of a fort.

It was too much to expect a man of Rahmah's character and reputation to adopt a peaceful way of life, and give up piracy and fighting. It seems that he did desist from indiscriminate piracy, but he continued to harrass the vessels of his enemies in Bahrain. Twice the Bahrain Shaikhs tried to come to terms with him, the second time in 1823, they agreed to a pact of friendship, but it only lasted for two years, then hostilities were resumed. The veteran pirate, scarred with wounds of a hundred fights, now quite blind, was still a power in the Gulf. He commanded a formidable fleet, manned by ruthless Arab pirates and his negro slaves, lately he had enlisted a number of Baluchis to serve under him, who were well known in the Gulf as first class fighting men.

In 1826, Shaikh Abdulla bin Ahmed was cruising with part of the Bahrain fleet, near the coast of Arabia, when he learned that Rahmah was on board his ship *Ghatrusha* in the Bay of Katif, where many of his followers were living. He himself had settled again at Dammam. Rahmah could have returned to Dammam by land, but he decided to do battle with the Khalifah. Believing himself still invincible, the old man 'took the garments off the forearm of endeavour' as the Arab history has it. He prepared for action, and his great ship moved slowly away from the walls of Katif, propelled by the oars of the negro slaves, watched by the townspeople from the shore. The ship passed through the bay to the open sea, where the Bahrain fleet was assembled. The enemy waited for him until he reached the deep water, then all together, with sails set and long lines of oars breaking the water, they bore down on him.

As the enemy ships closed in, Rahmah stood on the high poop of his ship with his eight-year-old son at his side, and his favourite slave, Tarrar, behind him, who told his master that the commander of the nearest boat was Shaikh Ahmed, son of Shaikh Sulman. Shrill above the din of battle, the sound of cannon and musket shots, the drums and war songs, and the creaking of oars, Rahmah's voice screamed insults at the son of his enemy.

The two great sailing dhows crashed together, with a screech of rending sails and sharp reports of snapping wood. The men of Bahrain, led by Shaikh Ahmed, armed with a sword and a little round shield, slowly fought their way over the sides, and on to the deck of *Ghatrusha*, hacking a passage through the pirates who were defending the ship, using swords and spears and daggers. Many men perished, and the blood ran down the decks and stained the sea around the two ships.

Fighting desperately, the pirates were slowly forced back, foot by foot, towards their blind leader who was on the poop above the powder magazine. As the fight raged, Rahmah heard the tale of it, shouted to him by the slave, Tarrar, how one by one the pirates fell before the swords of the boarders. The fighting swayed to and fro, but always the pirates lost ground. The enemy reached the foremast. They were among Rahmah's bodyguard, closing in on him. He, Rahmah, the Jalahamah, the scourge of the Gulf, was about to become the captive of the Khalifah.

Crying out the words of Queen Zabba, 'with my own hand, not by the hand of Amr', Rahmah snatched a firebrand, and plunged it deep into the powder magazine below him.

There was a vivid flash of fire, a roar as of thunder as the two ships burst apart. When the pall of smoke lifted, nothing remained but smoking wreckage. Rahmah, his young son, his companions, and many of the enemy including Shaikh Ahmed of Bahrain, were dead. So passed Rahmah bin Jabr al Jalahamah 'the personification of an Arab sea robber'.

CHAPTER XII

'How yet resolves the Governor of the town?
This the latest parle we will admit:
Therefore to our best mercy give yourselves
Or, like to men proud of destruction,
Defy us to our worst.'
Henry the Fifth – Shakespeare

BRUCE had been told by Rahmah the Pirate that the Shaikh of Linga was in league with the Joasmi and the Linga fleet was to meet some of the pirate ships up the coast above Bushire. For this reason, when three large ships arrived from Linga, Bruce and Loch decided to seize them, and to confiscate their weapons, although they were ostensibly on a peaceful trading trip. The crews were disarmed, the captains were taken on board the *Eden*, and the vessels were anchored alongside her. Loch admits that 'the seizure of the vessels may appear strange, they belonging to a country with which we were at peace'. If by 'country', he meant Persia, his action was of small consequence for the Shaikh of Linga acted independently of the Persian Government, which would probably have approved of action aimed at destroying the power of the pirates. The Persian Government had, in fact, offered to co-operate with the British against the Joasmi but their object was probably to get possession of Bahrain and their offer came to nothing. Among the arms which Loch took from the Linga seamen were swords with the name 'Andrea Ferrara' engraved upon them.

On October 19th, Loch received information that 'the long looked for expedition had at last left Bombay, and were soon expected to arrive in the Gulph'. Next day he weighed anchor 'with a nice little breeze from the north-west', and made sail out of Bushire harbour. He had with him, a cumbersome convoy, three Linga ships, a pirate vessel which had been taken by the *Mercury* at the top of the Gulf, and the batil in which 'the old wakil' had come to Bushire, the old man himself was in the *Eden*. Accompanying the *Eden* were the Company's cruisers *Mercury* and *Nautilus*. The crews of the pirate ships remained in their vessels in order to manage them.

On the 22nd, three strange dhows were sighted, and the *Eden* made all sail in chase, but during this operation, one of the prizes in tow sprang a leak, the men on board were taken off, and she was scuttled. Meanwhile the ships got away. Two days later, the *Eden* met the Company's cruiser *Tornati* on her way to Bushire. She had been sent to fetch Bruce to Ras al Khaima, and to inform Loch that H.M.S. *Liverpool*, a 50-gun man-of-war, which carried the Commander-in-Chief of the expedition, was on her way to Ras al Khaima which she would probably reach before the *Eden* arrived.

Nothing daunted, Loch decided to press on, 'getting rid of all encumbrances'. He transferred the Linga captains back to the *Nautilus*, and ordered her commander to take them and their ships back to the Persian coast, and let them go, as it was now too late for them to give any help to the pirates. He kept the pirates' envoy in the *Eden*, then 'with most tantalising light winds', he sailed for Ras al Khaima, arriving there on November 30th, dropping anchor close to the *Liverpool*, which lay off the town. But as the *Eden* approached Ras al Khaima the Wakil's ship managed to slip away, and the crew tried to push her into the harbour. She was intercepted by some of the boats from the *Liverpool* and destroyed on the beach. The slippery old Wakil must have watched the failure of his men to save the ship with regret.

As soon as he had anchored, Loch sent the Wakil ashore in a boat, landing him some distance from the town whence he trudged into Ras al Khaima. He was soon back again. He came out in a boat to the *Eden* with last minute proposals from the Joasmi Shaikh for a peaceful settlement, 'that might avert future blood-shed'. But his proposals were unacceptable, and he was sent on shore again and informed that 'he need not return with any further propositions, for nothing less than the total destruction of the pirate vessels and all that constituted their present strength would satisfy'. At the same time, Loch handed over to him the weapons which had been taken from his followers, presumably because he had come in the capacity of an envoy – although he had not behaved like one.

Ras al Khaima was the most strongly fortified town on the

Pirate Coast. It stood on a narrow isthmus running northeast, some three or four miles in length and less than a mile wide, with the open sea on one side and on the other side, a creek which provided safe anchorage for dhows. On the sea side, it was protected by a long sand bank like a breakwater enclosing a strip of deep water, where light dhows could anchor close below the town walls. At the mouth of the creek there was a bar only passable at high tide; the tide rose and fell about six feet. Large ships, such as the *Liverpool*, had to lie in the open roadstead, where they were exposed to the full force of the northeast wind, which blows fiercely in the winter and causes heavy seas.

The town had a sea frontage of about half a mile, and a depth of a quarter of a mile. The walls, which had been rebuilt since the 1809 expedition, had crenellated towers at intervals, on which cannon, taken from captured ships, were mounted. The towers were connected with the walls by parapets, giving access to all parts of the battlements. The walls were made of coral stone and mud, and were as much as fifteen feet wide at the base, narrowing towards the top. On the land side, the walls extended to the edge of the creek, with strong towers at each corner. In the centre of this wall was the town gate, defended by two square towers. The citadel, a high, massive building made of stone, faced the gate. In the centre of the town, there was another large, round tower surrounded by a high wall which enclosed an open square. The principal houses were of stone, but there were many barastis as well.

The vicinity of the town was flat and sandy, with date groves towards the east. The coastal plain extended inland for some miles, to a range of limestone mountains, rising to a height of several thousand feet, with sharp, jagged summits. As Loch says, 'to say the least of it, Ras al Khaima was no mean or insignificant work of defence'. It was a very tough proposition for a landing party.

The expedition was the most powerful force that had ever appeared in the Gulf, larger and more effective than the expedition sent against the pirates in 1809. The troops consisted of about 3,000 fighting men, of whom 1,600 were Europeans, from the 47th and 65th Regiments, with a company of artillery. There were three British naval ships, H.M.S. *Liverpool*, H.M.S. *Curlew*, and the *Eden*, nine cruisers of the British East India Company, and a number of transports. In addition to these, were the Sultan's fleet, and his land forces. Sir William Grant Kier, a distinguished soldier who had seen much service in Europe and India, was in command of the expedition. He was a humane man, and his moderation when he finally concluded a treaty with the pirate chiefs of the coast, was considered too lenient by some of the authorities of the East India Company in Bombay. There is a suggestion, in the book on General Perronet Thompson, by G. Johnson, that the naval and military commanders did not see eye to eye at the time when the treaty was made, which is not an unusual situation on occasions such as this.

On November 28th and 29th, preparations were made for the landing, and officers from the *Liverpool* reconnoitred the coast, looking for a suitable place on which to disembark the troops. The other ships had gone to Kishm to take on stores of wood and water, for the wells in the neighbourhood of Ras al Khaima were brackish. Shortly after midnight on November 30th, a man in the look-out in one of the ships which were anchored some distance from the town, sighted several vessels belonging to, or in league with, the pirates, stealing along the coast in an attempt to enter the harbour. It was a fine clear night, and the moon was shining brightly. The *Liverpool* was of too heavy draught to come closer in, but within half an hour, the *Eden* was under way and near enough to the enemy to open fire, having previously hoisted her boats out. One of the largest vessels, a baggalow, was driven close to the shore, and the *Eden* anchored as near to her as she could, in only a little more water than she drew.

The boats, carrying every available officer and man, pulled towards the pirate ship. As they got near, the sailors gave three cheers, preparatory to boarding her. They were close to the ship, in a minute they would be on her deck. Suddenly, there was a tremendous explosion which echoed in the mountains, followed by a long, hollow sound, which was carried over the still water, and the vessel burst into flames.

The pirates had laid a train to the powder magazine, calculating that, when the ship blew up, the sailors would be on board. It was well timed, but the sailors' lives were saved by what seemed to be an Act of Providence. As the boats went into action, there had been an unexpected delay. The tampion of one of the guns became jammed, and the advance of the boats was held up for a few minutes until this was rectified. If this had not happened, a hundred men would have lost their lives. Boats from the *Liverpool* now joined those of the *Eden*, and gave chase to the pirates whose ships were driven ashore under the town walls, but the men on board them were able to escape and join the defenders. When the boats returned, the *Eden* ran out into deep water, and anchored near the *Liverpool* leaving the pirate vessel burning on the beach, its flames lighting up the walls of the town from which the disappointed defenders looked down.

The Sultan arrived on December 1st with his squadron of three large ships, and the troops which he had arranged to provide when he discussed the plans of the campaign with Sadlier. Several thousand of his Arab troops were to operate from the land, marching up through the mountains from Muscat, but they took longer to arrive than had been expected, and it was not until after the town had fallen that they made their appearance. Loch was much impressed by the seamanship of the officers of the Sultan's navy.

'It was natural to suppose that, in a nation so rude and so little accustomed to manage ships of any sort, to say nothing of ships of war, that there would be great irregularity, and much noise on board them. Indeed, the general supposition among us was that they would hardly have been able to manage them at all. But judge of our astonishment, when the ship, on board which the Imam was, ranged close under the stern of the *Liverpool*, saluting her with fifteen guns, with as great precision of time between each gun fired as was possible. Every stitch of sail was then shortened at once, and in an incredibly short time, they were furled, and the anchor let go, all without hearing a word except the orders which were given, and as well done, as many of our crack ships of war.'

Next day, the *Curlew* and the other ships of the expedition arrived, and Loch was given detailed orders about the landing of the troops. He was in command of the landing operations, which began before dawn on December 3rd, in fine, cold weather. The boats, loaded with troops, moved in a long line towards the beach, with gunboats, under the command of Captain Walpole, on the flanks. As they drew near the shore, at dawn, guns from the ships opened fire on the town, distracting the attention of the enemy who probably expected the landing to be made nearer to the town. There was no opposition, 'in a crack, all were landed

137

on the beach, with two six-pound pieces'. The troops formed up, and advanced rapidly to some higher ground about 100 yards ahead. 'The people of the town were taken unawares, and did not conceive that so many troops could be put ashore in so short a time.' By the evening all the stores, tents and equipment had been landed, except the heavy ordnance which was to be brought on shore later.

That night, an advance party pushed forward and took up a position within range of the enemy's front line defences, where they set up the light guns; it was intended that the heavy guns should be placed here when they were landed. On the morning of December 3rd, the General and his staff visited the battery and outposts. They were seen from the enemy lines, 'which roused a peppering of musketry from the defenders, as well as from their ill-served guns. It was with great difficulty that the General could be persuaded to retire.' The earthworks were extended, and sites for the heavy guns were prepared.

The guns had been brought in boats to the beach where the troops had made their first landing. It was difficult to man-handle them on the isthmus, so the boats were ordered to move along the coast to a point as near as possible to the forward post, escorted by gunboats. When they arrived, 'the people' began to unload them. While the drag ropes were being put round them ' "rousing them" up, according to the phrase', Loch and Walpole 'took a turn towards the tower on the beach at the end of the wall, when off went one of the enemy guns'.

'I perceived the shot coming directly towards us. It struck the ground about twenty yards in front, made a rebound, and I had but time to give my friend Walpole a shove, and to bob my own head, when it passed between us. It made another recouche, and passed over the heads of about 200 seamen, without injuring a single man.' The mortars were landed and dragged under cover, before the enemy fired another round. This incident reminded Loch of the siege of Gibraltar, when two boys were placed in every battery to call out a warning when they saw shots or shells emerging from the enemy cannon. Cannon balls of the type which were used by the pirates, can still be found in many places in the Gulf. They are round stones about eight inches in diameter; in Bahrain they are sometimes used as garden ornaments.

On the morning of the 3rd, there was much activity around the town. A body of men made their appearance in the distance, coming from inland, but seeing the troops, they changed their direction, and approached the town by way of the creek, which they crossed, rushing towards the gates. From the town, pirates poured out, waving swords and spears and firing guns. The shots and the excitement led the British to suppose that the Sultan's troops had arrived before they were expected, and were now making an assault on the town. But the newcomers turned out to be Arab reinforcements from other towns on the Pirate Coast, who were being welcomed by the firing of guns by the defenders. This was 'the mode of salutation to the different Arab chiefs who came to the assistance of Ras al Khaima'. Soon after the main body of the reinforcements had entered the town, a solitary man, riding on a camel, bearing a large red flag, made his appearance. He was greeted with shots from the troops who were now within range, but ignoring the bullets he rode at full speed towards the town and reached the gates unhurt. 'This is one of the many instances of the extraordinary personal intrepidity of these people, who are naturally brave and ferocious, and are also enthusiastic in their own religion. But our troops had a yet stronger proof of their personal and collective bravery on the night of the 3rd.'

A British and an Indian regiment were assigned to the two batteries as working parties, to prepare emplacements for the guns, piquets having been thrown forward to protect them. The main body of the two regiments was encamped in the rear, among date groves about half a mile from the town. The heavy guns had been dragged some way from the shore, and were left with the ropes attached to them, under a guard.

A little before midnight, a shot was heard from the batteries, then shooting broke out among the piquets and the main advance guard, which appeared to be retiring. The pirates had made a determined sortie from the town. By creeping on their hands and knees along the beach, they had managed, without being seen, to get behind the batteries where the light guns were sited then, leaping to their feet, they attacked the piquets with no other weapons than their swords and spears, cutting down many of the troops and spearing others. A number of men were killed in this engagement, including the colonel who was in command of the advance party. The troops rallied, and after a charge and some hard fighting, the enemy were driven back, 'with great slaughter, taking care to carry with them the greater part of their dead and wounded, many of whom were females who had joined in the sortie'. The Joasmi women had shown themselves to be as brave and ferocious as their men.

Reinforcements were sent up, and by next day the lost ground had been regained but 'there was hardly a single survivor' from the forward piquets which had been first attacked. It was found that the pirates had dragged the heavy guns some seventy yards forward, close to the town walls, hoping to take them for their own use. According to Loch, the British and Indian troops suffered 'a loss of about 200 in killed and wounded, including several officers, the pirates neither giving nor expecting quarter and, owing to their savage brutality, they received none from our troops'.

During the next two days, while the ships kept up intermittent fire on the town, the troops consolidated their position by digging earthworks across the peninsula, with gun batteries at intervals. The Sultan's troops held a position on some high ground in the rear. One of the difficulties facing the attackers was that the shore batteries alone could not effect a breach in the walls, and it was impossible to bring the ships within easy range of the town. Loch made an attempt to take the *Eden* into the deep water inside the shoal, which extended along the front of the town, but 'as the Devil would have it, she took to the ground on the eastern point where she hung, in spite of all our exertions, till the turn of the tide'. The *Liverpool* and the cruisers, when they opened fire, found that their shots went wide, owing to the distance and the elevation of the guns, although the 24-pounders on the *Liverpool*'s main deck did some execution. The land batteries concentrated on the north-west corner of the main tower, expecting to demolish it without much difficulty, but 'this solid piece of masonry' stood up against the gunfire and there were no signs of a breach.

On the 7th, the General, finding that attempts to shell the tower from the sea were producing little effect, decided to land a number of seamen from each ship to reinforce the land batteries. At dawn on the following day, the batteries started a steady pounding at the target, which was kept up, as far as possible, without a pause. After some time, the tower began to show the effects of this sustained barrage. 'Here and there large masses of masonry peeled off, and rolled to the ground.'

During the previous night, under cover of darkness, the enemy had thrown up trenches and earthworks a short distance in front of the attackers' lines. The weather changed, it became cold and rainy and, on the 8th, torrents of rain descended. The rain did not affect the guns, which were heated by constant firing, but it damped the muskets and small arms of the troops. 'This was the moment when the pirates thought it a favourable opportunity to sally forth in another sortie.' The attack was beaten off, two of the *Liverpool*'s 24-pounder's which had been brought ashore, came into action, with grape shot and canister, and the troops whose muskets were usable opened fire. The pirates retired into the town, again with considerable loss. By the evening, the shore guns had made a breach in the wall.

During the night of the 8th, there were parleys between the General and the agent of Shaikh Hassan bin Rahmah, the Chief of the Joasmi, about the surrender of the town. But it appeared that the object of the pirates was to gain time, and no agreement was reached. Loch suggests that the defenders had already decided to evacuate Ras al Khaima and wanted to prevent any more shelling until the tide was so low that they could leave the town by crossing the creek, and so gain access to the mainland. The shelling of the town was continued with renewed vigour.

The end of the operations came suddenly, and was a complete anti-climax. At dawn on the 9th, 'a number of black specks were seen ascending the breach in the citadel'. They were a small party of marines and troops, under Captain Marriat, one of the General's A.D.C.s. They stormed the tower and gained possession of it, and soon the Union Jack was flying on the top of the battlements. The pirates had left the tower when 'the Forlorn Hope', as Loch calls them, made their attack, and only one of the defenders remained. He did some execution by shooting at the troops with his matchlock through the loopholes, until he, too, finally escaped into the town.

As soon as signals were visible, the Company's ship *Aurora*, which was anchored off the eastern point of the town, signalled that the inhabitants of Ras al Khaima were leaving the town from the inland side, crossing the creek which the British did not know was fordable on foot. The crossing of the ford put in Loch's mind the passage of the Red Sea by the Israelites. The fall of the citadel was the signal for a frantic rush by the inhabitants who, according to Loch, numbered some seven or eight thousand men, women and children. Their only object was to get away from the enemy, whom they believed to be as savage and merciless as themselves. Old men, women and children went first, crowding into the water, pushing and fighting to escape, the weaker fugitives falling into the deep holes, and pulling down those who tried to save them. Behind this helpless rabble came the fighting men, 'these murderous wretches now reduced to so many miserable creatures contending with the sea'. They struggled to get across before the turn of the tide, which would sweep them off their feet, expecting any moment to be attacked by the ships' boats. From the town rose a great column of smoke and flames for, before they left, the pirates had set fire to the barastis, whose matting and palm branches burned fiercely. During this 'heartrending scene' the troops stood quietly watching, and not a shot was fired, owing to the orders which had been given by the General. 'Thus did they proceed to the opposite shore, the aged and infirm supported by their relations, and the children clinging to their mothers.' From the shore, they struggled on towards the mountains, where they knew that they would be safe from attack. The scene which Loch witnessed was the finale of Ras al Khaima as the centre of the pirates of the Gulf.

For some time the troops could not enter the town, owing to the danger that their ammunition might be ignited by the burning barastis. When finally they got inside they found that two-thirds of the buildings had been destroyed, and only a few of the large stone houses were untouched. By ten o'clock on the 9th, all was quiet, and the fires had burnt themselves out. Loch took a walk round the town. All that was to be seen of the defenders were a few bodies among the smouldering ruins, of people who had either been shot or were unable to escape. The only live creatures were one old woman and three cats.

On the 10th, Major Colebrook and Major Stenhouse were sent by the General to parley with the pirates. They went, alone and unarmed, to the gardens and the foothills where the people from the town had retreated, explaining to them the reasons for the destruction of Ras al Khaima, and telling them that the British wished to discuss what was to be done in the future. Loch says that this had 'a remarkable effect'. Meanwhile the engineers prepared to demolish the citadel, and some of the other fortified buildings which were too far from the shore to be used by the garrison, which was to be left at Ras al Khaima. The Shaikh's house and the adjoining buildings were to be prepared for occupation by the troops. The fort, which had been mined, was demolished on the 13th, and on the same day, the *Eden* sailed for Kishm to replenish her supply of water. Some days previously, when she had attempted to get close to the shore, she had discarded almost all her water, to lighten the ship.

During Loch's absence, the *Liverpool* and two cruisers carried out an attack on Zaya; later they destroyed a number of pirate vessels and some of the fortifications in other smaller Pirate Coast towns, including Umm al Qaiwain, Ajman, Sharja and Dubai. Zaya was a pirate town about twelve miles north-east of Ras al Khaima, where the Shaikh, Hassan bin Ali, was holding out with a considerable force. The town was on a creek, surrounded by date groves, and defended by a fortress on the top of a high precipitous cliff which was thought by the Arabs to be impregnable. Owing to the height of the fortress from the ground, the attackers had some difficulty in getting the guns trained on to it. After a stout defence, the fort surrendered on December 22nd; an Indian boy, who had escaped from the pirates, had reported that the defenders would have surrendered before, but the Shaikh kept on fighting and was finally reduced to firing the guns himself. The *Eden* arrived at Zaya on Christmas Eve, having returned from Kishm, and two days later she sailed for Ras al Khaima in company with the *Liverpool*.

Back in Ras al Khaima, Loch found that, as a result of negotiations with various pirate chiefs, and owing to the fall of Zaya, their last real stronghold, the pirate Shaikhs had offered to 'abstain from all further hostilities, and to give up their former life of piracy', on condition that their lives, and their people's lives should be spared. As their vessels, strongholds and supplies were now in the hands of the British, this demand was acceded to. Hassan bin Rahmah, Shaikh of the Joasmi, then came to the General to discuss terms; Loch was present at the meeting.

'Hassan bin Rahmah, whose very name a few months previously instilled terror in the minds of those throughout the Gulph, now came to the General, suing for peace and mercy, and a sad sight it was to see this haughty, bold chief, obliged to make his obeisance, broken and defeated. This person's appearance was much what you would expect of such a character. He was of middling size, his features marked, strong and prominent, with a full, brilliant hazel eye, constantly on the enquiry of what was passing in the minds of those present.'

'A circumstance took place at this interview which gratified and pleased me in no small degree, though I must say that it gave me a very different feeling when I saw the object of it. Captain Bruce, Dr. Dukes and Captain Thompson were each well versed in the language, and were present as interpreters. On the mention of my name, Hassan bin Rahmah enquired which I was. On my being pointed out, he rose, came forward, and seized me by the hand, as if he had found a friend among those who surrounded him. The many communications which had taken place between us, was the cause of his conduct. I could not help feeling the abject state that this poor man was now plunged into.'

'There was now a long argument about the exact meaning of the word "Amaum", which was used in the General's proclamation to the chiefs before they came to pay their respects and (if I may call it) homage. They claimed the meaning of the word to be perfect forgiveness of all that was past, and freedom to act in future as they thought proper. The schism between the Interpreters ran so high as nearly to create as much bad blood between the different parties as betwixt Gulliver's Big and Little Endien.'

The other interpretation of this word which, in fact, means 'protection', was that it implied that the lives of the Arabs should be spared, but all other conditions should be left in the hands of the General. The General seems to have taken a middle course, for he allowed Hassan bin Rahmah to go 'with perfect freedom, and to do, act, or go where he pleased, under the pledge of discontinuing his former course of life. To ensure his so acting, Ras al Khaima was to be razed to the ground, with the exception of the Shaikh's house, and the different stone buildings surrounding it', which were retained as barracks for the garrison.

The truce between the British and the pirate chiefs was the origin of the term 'Trucial Shaikhdoms', which became the designation of the territories of the pirate tribes of the Oman coast. Preliminary agreements were made with each individual Shaikh, and on January 8th 1820, a 'General Treaty of Peace' was signed, which included the Shaikhs of Bahrain, whose representative came to Ras al Khaima to sign the treaty on their behalf.

The inclusion of the clause about slavery was mainly due to Captain Perronet Thompson, aged thirty-eight, the General's interpreter, who drafted the treaty. He was a Methodist from Yorkshire, whose Swiss ancestors came from Château d'Oex. His parents, strong abolitionists, were friends of Wilberforce. Thompson, who was first in the Navy and then in the Army, was not the usual type of military officer; he had very definite political views and, when in charge at Ras al Khaima, seems to have tried to instil the local bazaar with his ideas of economics. In 1803, he was a midshipman, later he was commissioned to the 95th Regiment, and served in Sierra Leone, where he became Governor. In 1812, he was back in the Army; he was promoted to Captain in the 50th Foot, and after service in Spain, he was transferred to the 17th Light Dragoons, who were in India, because he wanted to learn Arabic. When he sailed for the Persian Gulf as General Keir's interpreter; he brought with him, in one of the cruisers, his wife and four-year-old son. After the fighting, they lived in a tent on the shore, and Mrs. Thompson wrote the copies of the treaties. Even from his very sympathetic biography, it is clear that Thompson was a difficult man to get on with, unpopular among the East India Company officers, and probably among the naval officers as well. His opinion of the Navy, at the time of the treaty, was that they had 'no ideas of treaties, or of anything less substantial than an oak plank'. This was the man who was left in command of the garrison at Ras al Khaima when the main body of the expedition withdrew in July 1820. Besides commanding the troops. Thompson had been appointed 'Political Agent for all matters connected with the Arabian tribes'.

The garrison which Thompson commanded consisted of about 1,200 British and Indian troops. Most of the officers of the Indian troops belonged to the East India Company and resented being under the command of Thompson, a 'King's officer!' He said of them, in a letter, 'when you give them an order, instead of executing it, they write you a letter to say why they can't!' The officers themselves complained that Thompson was always interfering. It was not a happy situation, made worse by bad living conditions, a very trying climate, lack of fresh water, sickness and disease. In July, owing to the many deaths from illness, Ras al Khaima was evacuated, and the garrison moved to Kishm island which had the reputation of being a healthy place. Thompson himself was ill and was ordered to go to Bombay. He travelled in a ship bound for Muscat, which took seventeen days to arrive but, having got to Muscat, he went back to Kishm.

Inland from the little port of Sur, about 100 miles south of Muscat, there was a Bedouin tribe called the Abu Ali. They were the only Omani tribe to adopt Wahabism, and were, therefore, intensely disliked by the other tribes, and by the Sultan, against whom they had been in rebellion for some years. It was reported to Thompson, and confirmed by the Sultan, that some of the Abu Ali tribe were engaged in piracy. Thompson had orders 'to repel any act initiative of a renewal of piratical outrage', but he had been warned that he was to make quite certain that piracy was being carried out before taking any action and, in any case, to confine his operations to the coast. The Sultan asked Thompson for help in suppressing piracy by the Abu Ali.

Thompson sent a messenger, carrying a letter of remonstrance to the tribe at the place on the coast where piracy was said to have taken place. The messenger had to swim through the surf to reach the shore. History does not relate whether he delivered the letter, but when he prepared to swim back to the boat, he was set upon by two Arabs and some negro slaves and hacked to pieces. Thompson, later, received a message from the Abu Ali, saying that they had no wish to quarrel with the British and would hand over the murderers. The fact that the murderers were with the Abu Ali was regarded as a proof of the tribe's guilt – a fallacious argument. This incident decided Thompson to take action, in concert with the Sultan, against Abu Ali.

A military expedition consisting of about 350 British and Indian troops commanded by Thompson, and about 2,000 Arabs, under the personal command of the Sultan, landed at Sur. After a march of about sixty miles, they arrived within sight of the town of the Abu Ali, which was surrounded by date groves. The troops with the British leading, advanced in open column around a date garden, into which the Arabs had retreated. Suddenly, the whole enemy force rushed out from the garden and made an onslaught on the British. Before any orders could be given, the Arabs were among the British and Indian troops, hewing them down with their long razor sharp swords, which they wielded with two hands, lopping off the limbs of their opponents. There was an appalling slaughter; no quarter was given, the surgeon, who was ill, was dragged from his palanquin and butchered, and within a few minutes, 7 officers and 249 men lay dead or dying on the field.   The remnant of the force fell back with the Sultan's troops to a small fort some distance from the Abu Ali stronghold, where they were able to defend themselves.   Meanwhile, some of the Sultan's Arabs, having no stomach for more fighting, began to desert.   The Sultan had displayed bravery and gallantry throughout, and had been wounded while saving an English soldier; when he found his own people deserting, he called on them, saying; 'let those who are desirous to do so, leave me to my fate'.   His men rallied, and the survivors of the ill-fated expedition started on their march to Muscat, bringing with them a number of wounded. They reached Muscat five days later.

Thompson was left at Kishm for some time, and then, in May 1821, he was taken to Bombay, under arrest, and tried by court martial.   The President of the court was General Lionel Smith who had commanded the expedition against the pirates in 1809. Thompson was charged with rashly undertaking the expedition, contrary to the orders which had been given to him, and 'disgraceful conduct'.   He appears to have tried to put the blame for the disaster on to the conduct of the officers and men under his command.   He was found guilty of undertaking the expedition contrary to orders, and of making untrue statements about the conduct of his officers and men, but he was acquitted on the charge of 'disgraceful conduct'!   He was sentenced to be publicly reprimanded.

The defeat of a British force by Bedouins 'in which British arms sustained a disgrace which they never before experienced in Asia' created a furore both in India and at home.   Most people blamed Thompson for the affair.   Wellsted, who visited the scene of the fighting some years later, found it impossible to believe that the Abu Ali had ever been engaged in piracy, for at that time they had no boats, they were not sea-faring people and lived inland, engaged in agriculture, and in looking after their flocks.   They told Wellsted that they had always wished to be at peace with the English, though not with the Sultan, with whom they were engaged in a religious war.

In January 1821, a large expedition proceeded from Bombay against the Abu Ali; this time there were over 1,200 Europeans, and 1,700 Indian troops, with six guns.   Once again Sir Lionel

Smith appeared on the Persian Gulf scene, this time in command of the retaliatory force, despatched against the Abu Ali. They landed at Sur on January 29th, and encamped there. This expedition, too, narrowly escaped disaster. 'Strange to say', as Wellsted comments, the General and his staff made their camp two or three miles distant from the main body of the army, probably assuming that, being about fifty miles from the Abu Ali town, there was no danger.

In the night, the Bedouin made a surprise attack on the camp, killing one officer and wounding three, killing and wounding about fifty men, cutting the tent ropes and spearing the soldiers as they struggled out of their tents. The General and his staff narrowly escaped annihilation, due it was said to treachery of some of the attackers. The troops formed up, and the Abu Ali retreated.

On March 1st, the troops appeared before the town of the Abu Ali, and were immediately attacked by the Arabs who charged and, in some places, broke through the lines in the face of 'murderous fire of grape and musketry'. The Arabs threw themselves on to the troops, seizing their opponents' weapons with their hands. Though heavily outnumbered, the Arabs fought with savage courage, but were eventually beaten off, leaving many casualties on both sides, and retired to their fort. Their women then came out to drag their dead and wounded off the battlefield.

After some time, two women with a flag of truce appeared from the fort with an offer of surrender. The General insisted that the Abu Ali should hand over all their arms, giving them a time limit in which to do so, but they continued to fight. The artillery then came into action, and made breaches in the walls of the fortress, but still the Arabs did not surrender. Finally, a flag of truce was displayed on the tower, and the carnage ceased. Of the 800 Arabs who had entered the fort, about 500 were slain; the British casualties were about 200.

The fort was demolished, the date gardens were cut down, and water channels were destroyed. Some of this devastation was said to have been carried out by orders of the Sultan, although the Moslem religion forbids the destruction of date trees. The British then marched back to the coast, taking with them about 150 prisoners, including the Shaikh of the tribe and his brother.

The whole of this disastrous affair met with 'the most unquali-

XVI. An Arab dance

XVII. Falcons

XVIII. Old style Arab houses

fied reprobation from the Court of Directors', who censured not only Thompson, but the conduct of the second expedition. They disapproved of the insistence on the surrender of arms, the destruction of water channels and date groves, and the bringing of a large number of prisoners to Bombay. Many of the prisoners died from smallpox and cholera, the remainder were sent back to their home. Wellsted adds a footnote to his description of the event in which he says: 'I learn with pleasure that, notwithstanding the severe strictures of the Court of Directors for his conduct of this expedition, the military career in India of Sir Lionel Smith (a son of the celebrated Charlotte Smith) and that a brilliant one, was marked by repeated acts of benevolence and humanity to the natives, and that he piqued himself, with justice, on those traits.' General Sir Lionel Smith later had a distinguished career in the West Indies. Thompson, too, did not suffer permanently for the part he played in the disastrous Abu Ali affair. He rose to the rank of General; when he retired, he became a 'Radical propagandist', a Benthamite, the editor of the *Westminster Review*, and was Liberal M.P. for Hull. Both Lionel Smith and Thompson in their later years did much towards the abolition of slavery.

At the time of writing, the Abu Ali tribe are still very independent, and continue to be Wahabis. They have a great reputation and are feared by their neighbours. They are on good terms with the Sultan. Once in the past, when the Sultan was having trouble with the people of Muscat, the Abu Ali got into their boats, and came to his aid. On their arrival, the Muscatis immediately submitted to the Sultan.

CHAPTER XIII

'The Khalifah family, if we except certain dis-
sipated habits, accounted for, though hardly
excused, by wealth and power, are a very toler-
able set of men.'
          Central and Eastern Arabia: W. G. Palgrave – 1865

'The moon hath risen clear and calm,
And o'er the Green Sea palely shines,
Revealing Bahrein's groves of palm,
And lighting Kishma's amber vines.'
          Lallah Rookh: George Moore – 1816

LOCH'S next assignment was a mopping-up expedition.
After Ras al Khaima was taken, news was received that some
Joasmi ships had left the Pirate Coast before the arrival of
the British expedition, and were sheltering in Persian ports and at
Bahrain. It was thought that they might form the nucleus of a
new pirate fleet, so Loch was given orders to hunt them out and
destroy them. He left Ras al Khaima on January 3rd 1820, with
Bruce on board, accompanied by the *Curlew* and the *Nautilus*.
The squadron spent two weeks cruising along the Persian coast,
during which time they met the full force of the winter gales.

They passed Kharak Island, whose inhabitants, Loch was told,
'have red hair and fair complexions, a relic of the Danes'. It was
the Dutch who occupied the island for about twelve years in the
middle of the 18th century; if they did leave any descendants, the
intervening two centuries have obliterated all signs of them. They
were driven out of Kharak by Mir Mehenna, a Pirate Chief from
Bundar Rig, whom Niebuhr described in 1774, as 'the most
execrable tyrant who ever existed, distinguished through this
country for his vices and cruelty'. He made his servants murder
his father in his presence, because the old man preferred his other
sons; he killed his mother because she reproached him for his
crimes, and he caused a brother and sixteen relations to be assassin-
ated in order to gain the throne. He had two of his sisters

drowned, because neighbouring shaikhs had asked for them in marriage, which he regarded as an insult.

At Asaloo, Bruce and Loch went ashore, and 'waited on the Shaikh, informing him that we had learnt that several pirate vessels had taken shelter there, which must be given up and destroyed'. As usual, there was difficulty in identifying the pirates, but the Shaikh pointed out one ship which was taken possession of. At Nabend, two more pirate vessels were found to be in hiding. Two of these were taken and burnt, the other two, although chased by the ships' boats, managed to escape. With five pirate dhows to their credit, the squadron crossed the Gulf to Bahrain, arriving on January 21st.

When they approached the islands, Loch dispatched the *Nautilus* ahead, to take up a position at the southern exit of the harbour, which was between the two islands, to prevent any ships escaping. The *Eden* and *Curlew* moved in towards Bahrain; they had no pilots and, in spite of incessant soundings, the *Eden* ran aground but was soon afloat again, 'by throwing all the sails aback'. In present days, even with the help of charts, it is not an uncommon occurrence for ships to run aground when approaching the outer anchorage off Manama which is three miles from the shore. But there is now a new deep water anchorage on the south side of Manama, where six ships can anchor alongside a pier. The *Eden* and *Curlew* moved in to within musket shot of the beach, close to where the Bahrain war vessels lay at anchor.

Two dhows, at anchor in the harbour, were recognised as belonging to the Joasmi, and a party was sent in the ship's boats to take possession of them, which they did without opposition. The dhows were brought alongside the *Eden*. A message was then sent to the Shaikh, 'explaining my orders, and the absolute necessity for destroying all vessels belonging to the pirates, thereby cramping their future power in such a manner as to prevent their holding their heads up'. At the same time, Loch sent a request for horses, so that he and Bruce might ride out to Rafaa, about eleven miles inland, to meet Shaikh Sulman and Shaikh Abdulla.

On his first visit, when he was investigating the case of 'The European Lady and her Niece', Loch saw very little of Bahrain, but this time, he stayed for a week, and went ashore several times. His opinion of Manama was that 'the aspect and situation of the town was far superior to any I had seen in the Persian Gulph, although much of it is formed of date branches, yet with neatness and cleanliness not to be observed elsewhere. The people also appeared to be of a very superior class. Outside the town are fields in the highest state of cultivation, intersected by rows of date trees. Further inland are large date groves, kept in excellent order, but what struck me most forcibly at this season of the year, were the fields, groaning under the most beautiful crops of clover. The cattle were fed on it, which produced most excellent milk and butter, such as we had not tasted since leaving England.'

The date groves of Bahrain, irrigated by innumerable little streams of clear water, flowing from deep pools and springs, and the fields of brilliant green lucerne beneath the trees, which grows all the year round, are still a beautiful and refreshing sight. But many of the date palms are now being cut down, to make way for wide, dual traffic motor roads and, near the towns, whole date groves have been demolished to provide space for Western-style bungalows and houses, which at the present time bring in more money than dates, contrary to the injunctions of Abu Bakr, successor of the Prophet forbidding the destruction of date trees.

When the horses arrived, Loch and Bruce set off for Rafaa, escorted by a son of one of the Shaikhs and his retainers. After riding through several miles of date groves, they emerged into the open country and began to ascend the hill, passing through the vast area covered with ancient burial mounds which, surprisingly, Loch does not mention; perhaps he assumed that they were the natural conformation of the country. In recent years, a Danish archaeological expedition has been digging in Bahrain, and has discovered a city and temples, buried under the sand, dating from 2500 B.C.

Finally the party arrived at the town, which is now known as East Rafaa, so called because another Rafaa, near the Shaikh's country palace, has been built some miles west of the older town. Dryden's translation of Virgil's Aeneid describes such a place:

'High o'er the vale a steepy mountain stands,
Whence the surveying sight the nether ground commands.
The top is level – an offensive seat
Of war; and from the war a safe retreat.'

In 1820, Rafaa was a strongly fortified hill town, with a large population. The main fortress was built by Shaikh Sulman bin

Ahmed who lived in it, on the site of an older building which was once the headquarters of the Hawala Arabs who ruled Bahrain in the 18th century. From the plateau on which the town stands, Loch looked southwards across a bleak expanse of stony desert, broken by rocky outcrops, enclosed by a limestone escarpment, to Jebel Dukhan, the Mountain of Smoke, rising steeply from the plain. Camels grazed off the sparse vegetation among the boulders, the only other living creatures were gazelle, desert hares and iguanas. On the summit of the mountain was a tower, the highest point in Bahrain, of which only the foundations now remain. A watch used to be kept on this tower for the approach of any enemy ships.

To the east, some miles below Rafaa, Loch could see the island of Sitra, heavily wooded with date plams, with fish traps, made of reed fences, sticking out into the sea like arrow heads defending the coast.

When Loch and Bruce arrived on the top of the hill at Rafaa they found the two Shaikhs sitting on a long stone bench built against the wall at the side of the gate of the fortress. Their descendants still sit there in the evenings and discuss the doings of the day, though the younger men in Bahrain now find more entertainment in going to cinemas, watching television, or listening to Western music on their wireless sets. The Shaikhs were attended by about 200 guards, wearing white headcloths and long white robes, tied round the middle with a shawl. Each man carried a sword and a musket, and had a soft leather cartouche full of ammunition. The guards were formed up in two lines on each side of the Shaikhs. As the Englishmen dismounted, Shaikh Sulman came forward to greet them with the usual Arab salutations, and invited them to join the two brothers on the seat. After 'some unmeaning compliments were passed', a hubble-bubble and coffee were called for, 'the latter I partook'.

Shaikh Sulman then rose and asked Loch and Bruce to follow him, giving orders that only his brother, Shaikh Abdulla, should accompany them. 'Off he strutted, leading Bruce and me round one angle of the fortress, then down the north-eastern side of the rising ground until we came to the mouth of a cavern cut from, what appeared to me, to be the solid rock or sandstone. Into this we were conducted. To what this place was to lead, neither Bruce nor I could in any way divine, but we were embarked on

this expedition, and it was our desire and duty to follow it out.'
The passage which they entered almost immediately became too
low for walking upright, but after groping their way for some
distance, they arrived at a spacious room, cut out of the rock. At
first it was difficult to see in the room, for there was no light
except what came in through the passage. Soon, however, their
eyes became accustomed to the partial darkness.

The Shaikhs sat down and invited Bruce and Loch to sit beside
them. For some time, the two Shaikhs carried on a whispered
conversation, leaving their guests sitting silent and wondering.
This is a custom to which Arabs are addicted, and is not considered
bad manners. This whispered conversation was followed by a
long silence. Shaikh Sulman then explained why he had brought
them to this place; it was because he wished to find out the *real*
reason for their visit to Bahrain, for he and his brother could not
believe that they came only to destroy some pirate vessels. The
Shaikhs were most anxious to know whether the expedition was
intended as a threat to Bahrain, which they evidently suspected.
They also thought that the British might be in league with their
enemy Rahmah bin Jabr who boasted that he was on good terms
with the British. Shaikh Sulman explained that, if a conversation
had taken place anywhere else, it would surely be overheard so
they held the discussion in this secret, underground room. The
Shaikhs asked to be informed, candidly, why the ships had come.

'Of course, we could only answer that the cause of our visit was
solely for the destruction of pirate vessels, which he had given
shelter to. To prevent any of his own vessels falling a sacrifice,
either through erroneous information, or through a mistake, he
had better point out those of the pirates.' The Shaikhs were
assured that they need not fear another visit, unless they persisted
in helping the Joasmi and their adherents.

The next point which the Shaikhs took up was the question of
Muscat. They asked whether the British had come to some
arrangement with the Sultan about Bahrain. Loch and Bruce
had no official information on this subject, 'but we assured him
that we knew for a certainty that there was not and, as far as our
information reached, there was no desire or intention of interfering
in any way with them, if they proved by their conduct, a desire
to withdraw entirely from the pirates and would act on peaceable
terms with our vessels and trade. We again enforced on his mind

the necessity of putting an end to the possibilities of the pirates ever becoming an object of terror in the Persian Gulph. It was for this reason that pirate vessels, wherever they had taken shelter, must be destroyed.' The existence of this secret room in which the conversation was held, under the fortress of Rafaa, is unknown to anyone today, the entrance was probably blocked up many years ago and there are now no signs of it on the face of the cliff.

The Bahrain Shaikhs would have had even more cause for suspicion and anxiety had they known what was being discussed in Bombay about the fate of Bahrain. The Sultan of Muscat, who some years before, was regarded as a 'mauvais sujet' by the Bombay Government, because he came to power by the assassination of his relative, was now high in the estimation of the English who appreciated his valuable co-operation, and admired his courageous opposition to the Joasmi pirates. Without the Sultan's help, it would have been very difficult to overcome them. The Sultan was now the most powerful ruler in the Gulf, and it was his ambition to dominate the other Gulf states, but he had failed in his attempts to take Bahrain. There were people in the Bombay Government who advocated sacrificing Bahrain to Muscat. Sir Evan Napean, the Governor of Bombay, favoured the policy of handing Bahrain over to Muscat, with some arrangement by which Muscat would pay for a British garrison to be stationed at Kishm, in order to prevent a recurrence of piracy. Other members of the Council did not approve of this scheme, the principal opposition coming from Francis Warden, the First Secretary. He opposed the betrayal of the Khalifah who had fought so hard to maintain their independence; eventually Napean's plan was abandoned, greatly due to Warden's argument.

The Shaikhs appeared to be satisfied with the explanations which were given to them about the reason for the visit, and perhaps in order that the British ships should not tarry in Bahrain, they consented to send officers to point out the pirate ships in the harbour. The party then returned, through the passage in the rock, and made their way back, up the cliff, to the gate of the fort, where they sat down again on the bench. 'Soon afterwards, a most beautiful horse was driven across in front of where we were sitting, returning again at full speed, it was then caught, mounted, and put through its paces. Of course, it was not possible to avoid expressing my feelings of admiration. The Shaikh then turned to me, saying that the horse was brought out on purpose, to know if I admired it, so that he might have the satisfaction of presenting it to me, in return for the handsome telescope and fowling piece which I had sent him on my first visit.' Senior officers of the Navy are often given horses by friendly Arab Shaikhs, but they usually find that a horse is a difficult gift to deal with. Perhaps it was easier to accommodate a horse on board a sailing ship, than in a modern sloop or cruiser. Gift horses have usually been passed on to someone in Bahrain, which does not offend the donor, as Arabs when they receive presents, frequently give them away at once.

It was late before Bruce and Loch bade farewell to the Shaikhs, and set off 'in great state' on their horses to Manama, accompanied by the Shaikh's son and a mounted escort. Where the palm groves begin, they arrived at what Loch calls 'a canal' which was the stream which passes under the little bridge called 'Radm al Kawari', known to Europeans by the name 'Wiggly Bridge'. There is a ford known as 'Al Muktah' across the water, closer to the sea, where there is a short cut from Manama to Rafaa, this ford is still used by riders on horses and donkeys. It was at this place that they crossed. Bruce, who was leading the cortege, attempted to ride through the water. He reached the middle of the stream, when his horse suddenly lay down in the water, and began to roll, in spite of kicking and beating and abuse from Bruce. 'All state and ceremony were now at an end, and there was a roar of laughter.' The horse was a gray, but when Bruce finally succeeded in making it get up, it looked like a black horse, being covered with mud. Bruce, too, had mud clinging to his clothes. It was late in the evening when the party reached Manama, Bruce in a very bedraggled condition. When they got on board, they found Captain Walpole, of the *Nautilus*, very worried at their non-appearance, having made up his mind that they had been kidnapped by the Shaikhs. He had sent several people on shore to make enquiries, but all he could learn was that Bruce and Loch had 'proceeded on horseback into the interior'. Apparently, they had not told him that they were going to visit the Shaikhs at Rafaa.

Although it was late, and nearly dark when Loch came on board he decided that the pirates must be dealt with at once, otherwise they might escape. Boats from the two ships were prepared to tackle the vessels. They returned during the night, having destroyed two pirate ships, bringing with them three more. 'This was done without molestation, although not without considerable show of resistance which was kept under by the persons sent by Shaikh Abdulla bin Ahmed.' While the boats were away Loch heard that several other pirate dhows were preparing to sail through the southern passage so, as soon as the boats returned, they were sent off again with the same officers and men. They did not return till the following day 'but, unfortunately, unsuccessful'. Loch says that 'all were knocked up with so many hours hard work'.

Next day a boat with a large red flag was seen approaching. It carried a messenger from Rahmah bin Jabr, 'the old Butcher, as he is well named', who was established in the fort of Katif on the mainland, where he lay in wait for Bahrain ships. Rahmah offered to help the British 'with every disposable man, so that he might avenge himself by cutting the throats of all those in power in Bahrain and their adherents, and washing his hands in the blood of his enemies. Bruce and I informed the messenger that the expedition was sent to the Persian Gulph to put an end to all piracy and murderous warfare, which was to the detriment of trade, more particularly that of the English. Whoever committed such acts hereafter would suffer as those at Ras al Khaima had suffered. His proffered assistance was declined with disgust, and he was informed that our feelings were rather to support those in Bahrain against him than him against them.'

On the 24th, Loch and Bruce had midday dinner with Shaikh Abdulla at Muharraq. Loch had made it a condition of their going that the Shaikh should meet them on the shore. 'The reason for so doing was to humble him in the eyes of his own people as a punishment for his duplicity, cunning and prevarication, and for his having thrown every obstacle in our way when I visited the island at the time of the report about the European Lady and her Niece. It was through him too that the Joasmi received shelter in the port which was a market for their plunder.' Since the business of the European Lady, Loch had taken a strong dislike to Shaikh Abdulla, but for the Shaikh to meet the Englishmen on the shore would not have impressed the Arabs as anything unusual.

When the ship's boat arrived near the shore, the Shaikh was

not to be seen so Loch decided to turn back, but just as they moved off a messenger arrived with the news that the Shaikh was on his way, so the boat pulled in again. The Shaikh was seen coming down to the shore with a large crowd of Arabs. He apologised for being late, saying that he was saying his prayers, an excuse which is often heard. The party landed and were led to the place where they were to dine, but at once they were hemmed in by the crowd who came to see 'two such extraordinary looking people'. It became almost impossible to move owing to the press of people until the Shaikh 'made a sign to his men who began to lay about them with date sticks, which they carried for the purpose, and the people in the crowd began to yell, and to run helter skelter'. It reminded Loch of 'what I had often seen in our own country, when a crowd collected round a dancing bear so as to impede his showing off his feats. The Showman, taking his long pole, would sweep it round in a circle breaking the toes of those who did not retreat, but in the case of the Arabs people received blows on all parts of their bodies, to the no small amusement of those who escaped.'

They ate their meal in a large barasti in which the Shaikh held his audiences and administered justice. Two chairs and a table, on which were plates, knives and forks, had been placed at one end of the room for Loch and Bruce; the Shaikh, with some of his favourites, sat on the floor on their right and other guests sat at the lower end of the room. To sit at a table eating a meal, while the host and the other guests sit on the floor is uncomfortable and not conducive to easy conversation. It is pleasanter to join the party on the floor, but perhaps Loch and Bruce would have regarded this as *infra dig*. A couple of chickens on a mound of rice in a pewter dish, were placed on the table with bread and salt and sherbet to drink. Similar large, round dishes were set on the ground down the centre of the room, and the Arabs grouped themselves around them. 'The Shaikh's dish was pilawed fowls and rice mixed with herbs.' This usually consists of chicken, rice, sultanas and almonds. Before eating the Shaikh tucked the long sleeves of his white robe above his elbows. 'He then divided the chicken in the neatest manner, taking hold of the drum sticks of the fowl, and by a sudden twist engaged the two legs, then taking the two pinions he tore off the wings. The rest of the dissection was not so agreeable a sight as with his fingers he tore it to pieces. He then dug his hand into the rice, first placing a piece of fowl on the rice, which he did with a thin piece of un-leavened bread. He then kneaded the piece of fowl with the rice into a ball, as large as the mouth could well contain, which was placed in the two front fingers of the right hand, and by a sudden jerk of the thumb he chucked it into his mouth.'

Loch says that between each mouthful, the Shaikh dipped his fingers in water; if this was the case fashion in table manners must have changed for at Arab meals, it is customary to rinse the hands only before and after the meal. Today, instead of sherbet, which used to be made of pomegranate juice, the guests would be given Pepsi Cola, or some such bottled beverage, the chickens would probably be frozen birds imported from America, and the meal would be completed with Walls' ice cream. It is surprising that, on such an occasion, a sheep, or even a goat, had not been provided for the feast, but perhaps there was a shortage of them at that time.

After dinner Shaikh Abdulla dismissed most of the Arabs from the barasti, and although he had been present at the discussion at Rafaa on the previous day, he once again expressed his doubts about the intentions of the British. He found it difficult to accept the assurances of Loch and Bruce and feared that the British might adopt a policy of supporting the Persians, the Sultan, or even Rahmah bin Jabr, all of whom had pretensions to Bahrain. Again Loch and Bruce reiterated their assurances that the British had no intention of interfering with the independence of Bahrain. To emphasise this Loch told Shaikh Abdulla of the reply which he had given to the messenger from 'that bloodthirsty old Pirate, Rahmah bin Jabr'. Coffee and a hubble-bubble were then handed round and Loch and Bruce, escorted by the Shaikh, walked down to the shore and embarked in their boat.

Shaikh Abdulla bin Ahmed, for whom Loch had such a dis-taste, had a long and turbulent life after Loch left the Gulf. Until 1825, when his brother, Sulman, died, he continued as joint ruler. During these years, the two brothers defended their country against Rahmah bin Jabr who was killed in 1826, and against Rahmah's son, Bishr who carried on the feud against the Khalifah in much the same manner as his father until he too was killed. Shaikh Sulman was succeeded by his son Khalifah who became joint Ruler with his uncle Abdulla, but Khalifah was killed near Katif, fighting against the Wahabis. The Bahrain Shaikhs had at this time established their rule over part of the Arabian mainland as well as over Qatar. Khalifah's son Mohammed aspired to take his father's place as joint ruler and after some time he was awarded a measure of authority by Shaikh Abdulla, which was the signal for an outbreak of family quarrels among the sons, nephews and grandsons of the old Shaikh.

In 1828, the Sultan of Muscat attacked Bahrain in spite of the efforts of the British to dissuade him from doing so. He landed with a large force but preparations had been made for the defence of the islands, such as blocking the entrance of the harbour by sinking numbers of boats filled with rocks. The Sultan was defeated with heavy losses and narrowly escaped being captured, he was saved by his Nubian guards, who carried him, wounded, back to his ship. For many months after this engagement the people of Bahrain used to find the bodies of the Muscatis washed up into their fish traps. Once again, during the fight, some of his Arab troops changed sides, this time it was the Beni Yas tribe who deserted him and joined the Khalifah. In 1829, a peace was made between Bahrain and Muscat.

The combination of Shaikh Abdulla and his great nephew Shaikh Mohammed bin Khalifah was not a happy one. Bahrain became devastated by civil wars, as each Shaikh brought in Arabs from the mainland to support his cause. There was a general exodus of the Shia inhabitants to other places in the Gulf such as Katif and Muscat, to avoid being involved in the quarrels of the Khalifah, owing to this the population was greatly reduced. Shaikh Mohammed was a forcible personality. There are conflicting descriptions of his character. One writer describes him as 'a man who combined in himself the worst qualities of a tyrant, the most unbridled lust, and greed for wealth, an uncontrollable temper, ignorance and impatience against restraint'. Elsewhere it is said of him, 'His good deeds bear testimony of his fine resolve and sound judgement, he was master of great courage and fortitude, and had the merits of shrewdness, majesty, gravity and cheerfulness'. Thirty-five years ago, an old man who, as a youth, had met Shaikh Mohammed when he was living in exile at Mecca, described him to me as 'short and stout, very fond of women, even in his old age, and a great talker'.

During 1837, Shaikh Abdulla had trouble with the Qatar tribes who owed allegiance to the Khalifah. They revolted against his rule, and were joined by three of his own sons. They and the Shaikh of Abu Dhabi, made raids on Bahrain. Shaikh Abdulla was surrounded by rebellious relations, whose conduct frequently involved him in trouble with the British; he was threatened by the Turks, the Persians, the Wahabis, and by the Sultan of Muscat, and his ships were constantly attacked by Bishr, the son of Rahmah the Pirate. In 1841, after ten years of anarchy, Shaikh Mohammed was expelled from Bahrain by his great-uncle, after a battle in which Manama was sacked by the supporters of Shaikh Abdulla, to the detriment of many Indian traders, whose cause was taken up by the British. Shaikh Mohammed soon returned, with a strong force of mainland Arabs, and routed Shaikh Abdulla, who retired to the fort of Dammam on the Arabian littoral. He never again set foot on Bahrain.

Shaikh Abdulla's last years were very like those of his old enemy Rahmah bin Jabr. He had, at one time, a number of vessels and a strong force, and he became a focus for all enemies of Shaikh Mohammed who now ruled the islands. The Shaikh of Kuwait, and other people, tried on many occasions to patch up the quarrel between Shaikh Abdulla and Shaikh Mohammed, but the proud, headstrong old man refused all reasonable offers.

In 1843, Shaikh Abdulla started his long peregrinations around the Gulf, seeking help to recover his lost kingdom. At times he was strong enough to make piratical attacks on Bahrain shipping but, more often, he spent his time visiting the Gulf rulers, trying to obtain their help. From Persia, he got empty promises, the British refused to be drawn into a family quarrel, the Wahabis treated him with scant attention, and the Sultan of Muscat gave him no encouragement. Some of his sons deserted him, and made their peace with Shaikh Mohammed, and gradually his followers left him. For some years, he was almost alone, but he continued to trail round the Gulf, pouring out his grievances to anyone who would listen.

A story is told about him at the Wahabi court, in his old age. He was seated at the lower end of the Amir's audience room, when Bishr bin Rahmah arrived from Bahrain with a message from Shaikh Mohammed, with whom for the moment he was on good terms. He was cordially received, and given a seat above Shaikh Abdulla. But Bishr refused to take a more honourable place than the old Shaikh's, so the Amir invited the two of them to sit one on each side of him.   They left together, Bishr on a fine white mare, the old man riding a mangy camel.   After going some way, the younger man offered Shaikh Abdulla his mount, but the old man rebuffed him, saying that he had only accepted a favour in the audience chamber because the Amir had asked him to do so, and he would never accept anything from one who supported his grand-nephew.

In 1858, he set off on his last journey to Muscat to appeal once more to the Sultan.   He was about eighty years old, ill and disappointed.   He reached Muscat, and died there a few days after his arrival.   His descendants still live in Saudi Arabia, and visit Bahrain every year, to receive an annual subsidy from the Shaikh.

CHAPTER XIV

'The principall and best that are found in all the
Orientall countries and the right Orientall
pearles, are between Ormuz and Bassora, in the
straights, or Sinus Persicus, in places called
Bareyn, Catiffa, Julfar, Cameron and other
places in the said Sinus Persicus, from whence
they are brought into Ormuz. The King of
Portingale hath also his factor in Bareyn, that
stayeth there onlie for the fishing of pearles.
There is a great trafficke used with them, as well
in Ormuz as in Goa.'

Discours of Voyages into ye Easte and West Indies:
J. H. Van Linschoten – 1598

'Do churls
Know the worth of Orient pearls?
Give the gem that dims the moon
To the noblest, or to none.'

Friendship: R. W. Emerson – 1803-1882

BEFORE leaving Bahrain, Loch and Walpole told Bruce
that they would like to see some pearls as they wanted to
buy a few, if the price was reasonable. In the evening an
Arab came on board and enquired for Bruce. 'On his being
ushered into the cabin my inclination was to have him immediately turned out, his appearance being so mean, ragged and filthy.'
But, much to Loch's surprise, when Bruce came in, he welcomed
the Arab warmly, telling Loch that this person, who looked like
a beggar, was one of the richest pearl merchants in Bahrain. 'I
could hardly believe my eyes, "Rich merchant!" I repeated to
myself, looking at the dress and appearance of the man.' Loch's
explanation of the man's appearance was that 'had he been known
to have such riches, or if he had lived in a style which would
suggest that he was better off than his neighbours, the Shaikh
would have found some pretext to have him seized and would
force out of him the greater part of what he possessed'.

Customs die slowly. In quite recent times some of the wealthy old pearl merchants in Bahrain, many of whom were self-made men who started life as divers, affected an appearance of poverty and lived in mean little houses. In their youth they had known that it was unwise to make a display of wealth, which might attract the attention of rapacious overlords and, in their old age, they continued to live as they did when they were younger, although there was no longer any danger of being fleeced. Among the present generation of Arabs, those who have become rich – and sometimes those who wish it to appear that they are prosperous – have no compunction over ostentatious display of wealth. In these days, this takes the form of larger and more expensive cars, air-conditioning units, television sets and radios and, in a smaller way, elaborate cameras which rarely seem to produce worthwhile pictures. Many of these goods are bought on the Hire Purchase system.

Bruce asked the pearl merchant to show his wares, although normally nobody who was thinking of buying pearls would examine them by artificial light. 'He pulled out, from a woman's shaped pocket, which hung from his waist under an upper garment, a dirty coarse bag which he placed on the table.' The bag was probably made of red cotton for pearls were always tied up in bags of this material. 'Opening it, he displayed such a sight of pearls as I had never seen before, more like what is related in *The Arabian Nights*.' The old man poured the pearls into a large dish, which had been placed on the table, and then began to grade them by sifting them through a number of little brass sieves which he had brought with him. In this way, he sorted the pearls into different sizes, the largest being 'about the size of a small horse pea', and the smallest ones being tiny seed pearls, which used to be exported to China for making into medicine. There was another use for seed pearls. Large, fine pearls were kept in small tins, full of seed pearls which, according to the Arabs, are the best material in which fine pearls should be kept. The seed pearls not only preserve the larger ones but, say the Arabs, improve their lustre. Loch and Walpole wanted to buy some of the larger pearls, but the pearl merchant was only prepared to sell the lot, and for this he asked a price which was much more than they were willing to pay.

Loch's diary contains a description of the pearl diving, but he

XIX. A pearling dhow

XX. Gufa boats on the Tigris

XXI. A drum, tumboora and tambourine

XXII. Playing a tumboora

was not in Bahrain during the diving season and he writes from hearsay, so some of his facts are incorrect. He gives the population of Bahrain as 30,000, and the number of dhows in the pearling fleet as 'several hundred'. The present population is 180,000 and thirty years ago, when the industry was flourishing, over 20,000 men in some 500 diving dhows set forth from Bahrain to the pearl banks every year, and produced a catch which was worth about £1,500,000 sterling.

The diving industry and the methods of diving, which have been described by many ancient and modern writers, have changed very little throughout the ages. Some of the dhows belonged to the captains who sailed them, others were owned by merchants on shore. The profit from the sale of each boat's catch was divided in fixed proportions among the captain, the divers and the pullers, the last being the men who pulled up the divers from the sea bed when they came to the surface. In theory the system was a fair one, but many abuses crept into it. The merchants charged exorbitant interest on the money which they put up to finance the dhows and the captains charged heavy interest on the money which they advanced to the divers, who were irresponsible and improvident, and always in debt. Once a diver became indebted to his captain he was virtually a slave and could be handed over to a shopkeeper or to another captain in payment of a debt, being compelled to refund a large proportion of his earnings every season. When he died, or was too old to dive, his sons, if he had any, inherited the debt and had to dive for their father's captain. Tavanier, writing in the 17th century, says 'divers get no advantage from their labours, if they had anything else to employ them, they would quit the trade'. Conditions changed when some thirty-five years ago, the then Shaikh of Bahrain, the grandfather of the present Ruler, introduced far reaching reforms throughout the industry which at the time were strongly opposed, but afterwards appreciated. The Diving Law, which was promulgated by Shaikh Hamed was afterwards adopted by other Gulf Shaikhs. Under the new laws, rates of interest were strictly controlled by the Government, debts could not be inherited and each diver had an account book, checked by Government diving clerks, showing his indebtedness to his captain.

Divers use no mechanical apparatus; they descend into the sea with two ropes, one weighed by a stone, which they release when they reach the bottom. Their nostrils are closed with a clip like a clothes-peg, their fingers and big toes are protected with leather sheaths, and they wear string bags round their necks, in which they put the shells. A man collects six or eight shells at each dive; when he wants to come up, he signals by a jerk of the rope, and his mate on board the dhow hauls him to the surface. Diving is carried out in relays and divers do not stay below for much more than a minute. Loch's statement that divers stay submerged 'for five or six minutes', indicates that he did not himself see diving in progress. The oyster shells are heaped on the deck, and opened next morning before the day's diving begins, so no diver knows whether the pearls which are found were in his catch, or in some other diver's catch. Diving is a tough occupation, but not as unhealthy as many people suppose. Divers expected to make enough in the season, which lasts for four-and-a-half months in the summer, to enable them to live during the rest of the year without working, and there was always the chance of a big catch which would fill their pockets for some years to come. Arabs have an inclination towards gambling, and it is this which attracted them to the diving industry.

One of the unforgettable sights in Bahrain used to be the departure of the pearl fleet from Muharraq. With a favourable wind, the big pearling dhows moved out to sea under their great lateen sails or, on a still day, they were propelled by their enormous oars, each pulled by two men. Today the few pearling dhows which remain, have auxiliary oil engines. In Loch's time, the Shaikh used to provide some of his 'vessels of war', to guard the fleet during the season. For this service, the Shaikh levied a tax which brought him about £10,000 a year, but, as Loch says, 'in addition to this, there were many extortions'. In later years, ships of the British Navy patrolled the neighbourhood of the pearl banks, some of which were forty miles from Bahrain.

There was never a regular pearl market in Bahrain; the merchants did their business in coffee shops, or in their own houses. After changing hands several times most of the pearls were sent to Bombay and, in later days, from Bombay to Europe and America. Now, there are several shops in Bahrain where pearls and necklaces can be bought over the counter as in a jewellers' shop in Europe.

What Tavanier said in the 17th century came to pass in the 20th century for after oil was found in Bahrain, in 1932, there was no shortage of employment, and most of the divers did 'quit their trade'. The same thing happened when oil was found in Kuwait, and in Qatar and in Saudi Arabia. Now the Arabs of the Trucial coast, who used to be employed in diving, are forsaking the sea and working for the oil companies. The pearl industry, upon which most of the Gulf Arabs have depended for their livelihood from time immemorial, is almost a thing of the past, only a few diving dhows go out from Bahrain, which used to be the centre of the industry. Its decline began when Japanese cultivated pearls made their first appearance in the markets of Europe and America. Then came the discovery of oil in Bahrain, and some years later, oil was found elsewhere in the Gulf. The production of oil provided well paid work for large numbers of men, who preferred working in the oil fields to diving in the sea. Today, hardly any Bahrainis are engaged in diving.

The *Eden* left Bahrain on January 27th, carrying 'considerable freights of pearls'. Naval vessels, as well as those of the East India Company, frequently carried freight such as pearls and bullion which was described as 'treasure'. The pearls from Bahrain were destined for Bushire and Bombay. Loch had discovered that the Bahrain merchants were in the habit of under-declaring the value of their pearls in order to pay less freight, so he decided to teach them a lesson. On reaching Bushire he deposited the largest and most valuable consignment of pearls with Bruce, and informed the Bushire merchants that, most unfortunately, their pearls had been 'mislaid'. He assured them, however, that he would, of course, be responsible for the amount on which freight was to be paid if the pearls were not found within a certain time. He then left Bushire for a week or two.

On his return he sent for the Bushire merchant who was to receive the pearls and said that, as they had not been found, would he accept a draft for the amount in the invoice. The Bushiri merchant told Loch that he could not agree to any arrangement without consulting the owner of the pearls, who came from Bahrain, as fast as he could. On arrival, the owner of the pearls admitted to Loch that his consignment was worth more than double the amount shown in the invoice. Bruce was now brought in to explain to the merchants Loch's 'real motive for having detained the pearls, hoping that it would be a lesson in future, for his pearls might have fallen into hands not so likely to deliver them to him or to his consignee'. At the same time, to compensate them for the delay, Loch said that he would make no charge for the freight.

'If the merchant thought my conduct strange before, he now considered that I was quite mad! He had at first conceived that I wished to keep the pearls', in order to pocket the difference between their real value and the invoice price. 'But when he was convinced that he had his parcel in his hands, and that I declined to charge *any* freight, he thought that there was some trick!'

He broke open the sealed bundle of pearls, examined each one, and then re-examined them, and counted carefully the pearls on the strings. Then he sat musing for some time. At last, he exclaimed, 'I cannot understand this'. Once again, Bruce had to explain why Loch had taken this action, which was in order to make him and the other merchants more honest in future. After pondering over this, all the merchant could say was: 'It may be so, but I don't see how that can be accomplished.'

On February 3rd, Loch writes: 'I this day received a letter from a Gentleman attached to the Factory at Bassora informing me that communications between it and Baghdad had been completely cut off in consequence of Arabs having come down the Tigris in such force as to prevent any boat passing up or down, to the great detriment of our trade.' The letter added that Taylor who was Resident at Basra, 'had often stated his desire to have some ships' boats at his disposal for the purpose of opening communications'. Loch, after discussing the matter with Bruce, decided that it was his duty to go to Basra, 'in order to be of service as was in my power'.

River traffic between Basra and Baghdad was often interrupted, usually owing to attacks on the Turks by Bedouin tribes. Sometimes it was due to quarrels among the Turks themselves who engaged in civil wars. On one occasion, owing to disturbed conditions, Taylor withdrew the British Residency from Basra to Mohammerah. Another time Rich, in Baghdad, was besieged in the Residency. In addition to local skirmishes and guerilla warfare there was a state of war between Persia and Turkey.

Two days later the *Eden* left Bushire and after picking up a pilot at Kharak sailed for Basra. She crossed the bar on the 7th, meeting very bad weather at the mouth of the Shatt al Arab, and it was not until the 20th that she anchored in the river some twenty-five miles below Basra. Loch went ahead in his gig to ascertain the position, Taylor, who had not asked for the *Eden*, did not seem over enthusiastic about her arrival. He told Loch that the Turkish Governor, with a large force in sixty boats, had gone up the river to open the way to Baghdad, but since they left no news had been received so he suggested that the *Eden* should remain at anchor, down the river, 'until the fate of the fleet was known'.

Loch returned to his ship next day, and for ten days the *Eden* lay at anchor. Loch was a sociable man, and he cannot have enjoyed kicking his heels for ten days with nothing to do, and nobody to visit, but he made the best of it. Colquhoun, on Loch's previous visit, had given him 'a famous spaniel', and Loch and Moffath took the dog ashore several times when shooting. Taylor had warned them to be careful of the villagers. A few months ago, the officers from one of the Company's ships went shooting, Arabs from a village became 'most officious in beating to find game', which was so successful that all the officers let off their guns. Immediately, the Arabs sprang on them, wrenched the guns from their hands and made off, leaving the officers astounded, and staring at each other. Loch had a double-barrelled gun, Moffath's gun was single barrelled, before starting they agreed that one of them would always keep a barrel loaded. When they landed, five Arabs hurried to help them to find game, urging them to shoot, but owing to Loch's precautions 'they were foiled in their looked-for spoil'. On the 27th Loch received a letter from Admiral Sir Richard King, the Naval Commander-in-Chief, thanking the officers and men of the *Eden* 'for their conduct before Ras al Khaima. The hands were turned up, and the letter was read to them, to their no small gratification.' On the same day Taylor arrived in his snake boat from Basra. He and Loch went to examine the Haffar Cut, a canal through which part of the fleet of Alexander the Great proceeded from Susa to Babylon. All through his diary, Loch shows the greatest interest in the voyages of Alexander, and his Admiral, Nearchus.

While he was with Taylor, they passed a camp of water gipsies.

Loch refers to them as 'Illiots' (a word which I cannot trace). They had come down the Karoon river in a large vessel, and set up a camp on the shore with tents and awnings made of cloth of many colours. They travelled from town to town on the different rivers and canals, making baskets, mats and coarse earthenware and mending kettles, pots and pans. The same gipsies are still to be seen in many parts of the Middle East, as far apart as the Persian Gulf and the middle of the Sudan where they are known for their skill as tinkers. In the 19th century in England, gipsies were often referred to as 'Arabs'.

On March 4th, Loch received orders from Captain Collier to return to Bushire where he arrived six days later to find the *Liverpool* at anchor in the harbour with General Sir Grant Kier and his staff on board. The rest of the expedition had sailed direct to India. After a short stay in Bushire, Loch was ordered to return to Basra as there was still no news about the Turkish Governor's expedition up the river. Once again the *Eden* made her way across the bar, and up the river to Basra, but this time she anchored near the Residency and Loch stayed on shore with Taylor.

One morning, when Loch and Colebrook were taking their usual exercise on the flat roof of the factory, they saw a handsome, well-dressed Turk being carried by a servant into the building. Later they met him, with Taylor, on whom he had come to call, and Loch heard his story.

For some time, he had been paralysed, having lost the power of his legs, and so had to be carried by a servant. He was born in Smyrna, and went to sea as a youth, in course of time he acquired a ship. He traded between the Levant ports and became prosperous: he married, and had a family, and bought property in Smyrna. He then sailed to the Barbary coast where he was equally successful. During the siege of Gibraltar by Spain, which lasted from 1779 till 1783, he heard of 'the miserable state in which Gibraltar was placed, for want of supplies and provisions'. From Algiers, he used his ship with great skill and daring to carry supplies into the harbour of the beleaguered fortress. After the siege, as a reward for his services, the Governor of Gibraltar, General Sir George Elliot, afterwards Lord Heathfield, obtained for him a life pension from the British Government.

He was invited to visit England, 'and enjoyed all the delights which he met there. When the poor old man's conversation brought back the joys which he had experienced during that sojourn, his countenance lit up, and his eyes sparkled with delight as, putting the first three fingers of his right hand to his mouth, blowing a kiss from them, he exclaimed: "dear England, dear England! I am happy for England!"'

Having sold his ship, he went back to Smyrna to settle down with his family but he found that they had all 'fallen victims of the plague'. Owing to his long absence his house and property had been confiscated by the Government, and he was unable to obtain any redress. Since then he spent his time travelling from place to place, living on his pension. He had come to Basra with the fleet of the Governor, who had eventually succeeded in clearing the river passage and driving back the hostile Arabs. The old man stayed to dinner, 'drinking wine, contrary to the Mohammedan rule' which he probably learned to do in 'dear England'. He returned, as he had come, carried on the back of his servant. Loch does not mention his name.

While Loch was at the factory a theft occurred. Some trinkets were taken from somebody staying there by one of the servants. Taylor sent for a 'conjuror' to recover the stolen property. 'All the domestics were assembled round the necromancer, who sat on the ground repeating prayers and verses and making grimaces.' He then produced a piece of spring wire, shaped like a swan's neck, with a little bell loosely attached to the end of it. He fastened the wire on to each of the servants, one by one, so that the bell hung over the person's heart, not touching his body. The more the person's heart beat the more the wire vibrated, causing the bell to tinkle. While he did this, he whispered into the ears of the servants. Each one was then ordered to go outside and collect a handful of dust which he was told to place in a corner of the room. On the completion of this performance, sure enough, the stolen trinkets were found in the heap of dust.

During this visit, Loch explored most of Basra; walking alone through the crowded streets was impossible, 'without meeting with some insult', so he went on foot, escorted by a retainer from the factory. This impressive personage, a Turk with a large moustache, wore a scarlet turban, scarlet coat and trousers, trimmed with gold, a bright green, gold embroidered waistcoat, a white sash and yellow boots. He carried a pair of handsome pistols, a silver mounted dagger and a Mameluke sabre swung over one shoulder. The main bazaar was crowded with people shopping, gossiping and collecting round the doors of coffee houses listening to story-tellers. 'The Chaus was forced to apply his cane right and left to the shoulders of those who impeded us', which today, probably in Basra, most certainly in Bahrain, would cause an action for assault.

There being no more trouble up the river, Taylor decided to pay a visit to Bushire as the *Eden* was returning there. They reached Bushire on the last day of March, and Loch heard of the disaster which had befallen the Company's ship *Ariel*. She foundered at night off Bushire, so near to the coast that had it been daylight, many of the crew would probably have been saved. She met a strong shamaal – north-east wind – which increased into a gale. 'The vessel was put under easy and low sail, the top sails close reef'd, and her head laid to northward. In the middle of the night, the wind suddenly chopped round from N.E. taking the *Ariel* aback. Mountainous seas washed over the vessel's stern which immediate swamped her.' She carried a crew of about eighty officers and men, including Indian seamen. Only the Serang and two lascar sailors were saved; they had managed to cling to some spars and a hen coop, and were picked up by an Arab sailing boat.

During this visit Loch went for another expedition inland, over much of the country which he had seen before, but it presented a very different appearance. The whole area had been ravaged by locusts, and every green thing growing had been devoured. At Bushire it seemed to be the season for flies, and for birds which Loch calls swallows, but which from his description of them were fly-catchers. Flies were so bad that 'it became difficult to open your eyes or mouth without their being half filled by them'. Flies, dirt and dust were the cause of there being so many eye diseases among the Bushiris. It was unusual to see a man with two sound eyes, though the women, Loch says, were not so much affected as most of them wore veils, which kept away the flies. Eye diseases used to be very prevalent in the Persian Gulf towns; in Bahrain, a family of four brothers, wealthy merchants, had five eyes between them. Today in the states where there are hospitals and medical services, there are few signs of eye diseases among the younger Arabs.

One of Loch's difficulties in Bushire was to supply his ship with water, for the wells were several miles distant from the town. One morning, when he was riding along the coast near Bushire, he saw a villager planting young date trees in holes which he had made in the clay close to the shore. Loch noticed that as soon as the holes were dug, they filled with fresh water. He asked the man if he could dig deeper, to find out whether there would be sufficient water to supply the ship. The man agreed; next day, Loch sent a party ashore in a boat. Only four feet below the surface, they found 'as good water as could be produced anywhere in that part of the country'. So while the *Eden* was at Bushire, Loch sent a boat ashore every day to get fresh water. 'This man, beginning to cultivate a piece of ground, was one of the first good effects I had seen from the extinction of the piratical power. Previously, no property near the seashore was safe from their depredations.'

Before he sailed, on May 3rd, the Shaikh sent Loch 'a famous sword of valuable Persian workmanship as a mark of our friendship and long acquaintance'. Bruce, who was going on leave to Bombay, sailed in the *Eden* with Loch. They put in at Ras al Khaima, where they found Perronet Thompson 'in quiet possession of the garrison of the fortress, as well supplied with provisions as that miserable country could do, and most plenteously replenished with fish which was, for the native troops, a great luxury'. Hassan bin Rahmah and the other Joasmi Shaikhs were still living in the date groves near the town, the Arabs and the English had no communication with each other, each side regarding the other 'with watchfulness and distrust'.

The *Eden* spent the next four months in the Indian Ocean, visiting Bombay, Trincomalee, Madras and Pondicherry. In Bombay, she refitted, and took on some volunteers from two East Indiamen. At Madras, Loch accompanied the Commander-in-Chief when he called on the Nabob of Arrat. The naval officers were carried to the palace in palanquins, which Loch found 'uncomfortable, inconvenient, wretched things from which to observe anything, for the occupant had to lie on his back in what was like a long, closed box, with a small door in the centre of one side, through which it was impossible to see out. The palace was approached by a road 'as smooth as the smoothest Kensington gravel', through a magnificent park of stately trees. Loch says 'the Nabob is treated as to outward show, as a Prince, but without possessing any degree of power beyond his policy, which is about the extent of Hyde Park'.

'Near the palace were drawn up the Nabob's elephants, all caparisoned, and a park of artillery and his bodyguard.' The officers were received by the Nabob in the centre building of the large palace, necklaces of flowers were put round their necks, and they were handed arica nut and chanan, with betel nut rolled in plantain leaf, on silver trays. Near the palace, as in most of the big houses in Madras, was a 'tealery', a number of small buildings in a square, covered with wire, in which ducks were kept and bred.

At Pondicherry, Loch attended a ball at the house of a rich Armenian merchant. He describes it as 'une belle assemblee de belle filles'. He noticed that the ladies 'had not the pale, wan appearance which the English have, after being for a time in this climate, but whether it was so in fact, or whether a little assistance had been used at the toilette, I will not pretend to determine'. He remarked how 'the natives partake of the manner of the French, both in speech and gesture'.

In the middle of June, Loch was back in Trincomalee, where he got orders to return to the Gulf. He sailed on July 16th, in the Southwest Monsoon, by the southern route, as he says, 'the longest way round the shortest way home'. On this voyage, the *Eden's* best run was 217 miles in twenty-four hours, but she took thirty-nine days to reach Muscat. At Muscat, Loch learned, from the Commander of the *Mercury*, that the garrison of Ras al Khaima had been forced to evacuate the place owing to the impossibility of getting sufficient drinking water, and the ill effects of the unbearable heat on the men. They moved to Kishm Island where water supplies were good, and the climate was better than most places in the Gulf. Before leaving, Perronet Thompson had destroyed every building which might be used as a stronghold by the pirates. A few weeks later, Loch put in at Kishm and found the troops settled there in barastis, with plenty of good water, and even a certain amount of supplies provided by the inhabitants.

The weather at Muscat was at its worst, the temperature at sunrise being 101° so Loch only stayed there for the inside of a day. The south-east wind, known as the 'Ghoos' was blowing; it caused a 'distressingly suffocated feeling. Neither officers nor men could sleep in their beds, and the people lay down where they could find themselves most cool. I dressed in a thin white jacket and a pair of trousers, and lay on the deck of my cabin, for anything which was soft for one's bones, had such accumulated heat as to be unbearable. The wind was as if it had passed through an oven, causing inordinate thirst, and as the crew were on an allowance of water, it created a most uncomfortable situation.'

CHAPTER XV

'Once more upon the waters! Yet once more!
And the waves bound beneath me as a steed
That knows its rider.'
                    Childe Harold: Lord Byron – 1788-1824

ON September 5th, Loch was back at Bushire for the last
time. It had always been his favourite port in the Gulf,
mainly because he and Bruce, the Resident, were particularly good friends, and he enjoyed the hospitality of Bruce and
his family (though he scarcely ever mentions Mrs. Bruce). The
summer had been unusually severe – but then, almost every
summer is described by Europeans in the Gulf as being the worst
that there ever was – and many people 'had fallen a sacrifice to
coup de soleil'. When Rich was in Bushire, shortly afterwards,
his servants complained to him, saying: 'we can live in fire, as
in Baghdad, but not in an hamamm (Turkish bath)'. All who
had two-storied houses were living in their upper rooms, which
were cooler than those below. Many of the Bushire houses
had 'badgheers', tall, slender towers, with shafts through
which the wind entered and descended into the room below.
The wind towers were only in 'the dwellings of the affluent,
thereby pointing out the houses of rich men'. In some Gulf
towns, even the barastis had wind scoops, made of matting,
on the same principle as the masonry towers, and equally
effective. These graceful towers, usually painted white, were
a noticeable feature in the Persian Gulf, but since the days of
electric fans and air-conditioning, they are no longer being
built.

The heat was so great that Loch found it impossible to walk
through the streets when the sun was above the horizon, so he
excused himself from calling on the Shaikh, 'who was prosperous
in health and riches. The Shaikh, in a most civil manner, waited
on me at the Residency.'

Shaikh Abdul Rasool had evidently supposed that Loch was
not returning when, on his last visit, he presented him with a

sword, so he was curious to know why he had come again. Loch explained that he wanted to embark treasure for Bombay and Calcutta, when he sailed for India on the 15th, and would take as much as the Bushire merchants wished to send. There was, however, one point which he asked the Shaikh to explain to the merchants. A new regulation had been issued to the Navy, laying down that freight was to be charged according to the distance which the goods were carried, this would result in an increase of $\frac{1}{2}$% on treasure carried from Bushire to Bombay, and $\frac{3}{4}$% on goods carried to Calcutta. The change had been made 'in consequence of an Act of Parliament'. Loch says, 'I could not make him understand what an Act of Parliament was', which is not surprising! The Shaikh was convinced that the increases in freight rates were due to changes in the personnel of the Naval Command, probably suspecting that they would make something out of it, and not to the decision of a Parliament in England, of which he had never heard.

When Loch asked the Shaikh to do all that he could to encourage the merchants to ship their goods in the *Eden*, the Shaikh promised to do so, and said that he would summon them, and explain the matter to them. 'This assurance I, of course, depended on, it will be seen hereafter how well he kept it!' By this time, Loch ought to have known the Shaikh's shifty character, and it is surprising that he put such trust in him.

The fine new ship which the Shaikh had bought was in the harbour, ready to sail for India. The Shaikh sent for the merchants, and told them that the British had raised their shipping charges, saying at the same time that he was prepared to carry their treasure in his own ship at the old rate. He also warned them that if anyone consigned treasure to the *Eden*, he would suffer for it. The consequence was that when the *Eden* sailed, she carried no freight.

After Loch left, he heard what finally happened. Having induced the merchants to entrust their pearls and bullion to his ship, because they were anxious to send their treasure to India as soon as possible, the Shaikh told them that he now found it impossible to allow specie and pearls to be carried at the former rate. They would have to pay the same rate as Loch would have charged; this they were forced to agree to, so their goods were carried in the Shaikh's ship without security of being in a British man-of-war. The slippery Shaikh was an adept at turning everything to his own advantage.

One evening, before they sailed, 'Old Moffath' suggested that they should cool themselves by a bathe in the sea. This seems to have been quite an unusual thing, for throughout his diary Loch never mentions bathing in any of the places which he visited. At sundown, he and some of his officers went down to the shore, but the bathing expedition was not a success. 'Judge of our surprise when on immersing ourselves in the sea, we found the water much hotter than the atmosphere, but it had this good effect, we found ourselves cooler when we came out of the water, though the coolness almost immediately changed into heat, by the slight exertion of walking the short distance to the Residency.' In hot weather, the sea in the Gulf near the shore often reaches a temperature of 90°.

After bidding farewell to Bushire, Loch paid a final visit to Muscat. In return for the many kindnesses which he had received from the Sultan, he sent him a handsome chronometer by the hand of Moffath, who explained to the Sultan how it should be used. Moffath returned with a fine Arab sword for Loch, and a message from the Sultan asking him not to sail before sunset. The reason for this became apparent when, later, the Sultan sent on board a beautiful white Arab horse, which had been brought from his stables in the country behind Muscat. This second gift of a horse was rather difficult to deal with on board, so when Loch reached Bombay he presented it to Mountstuart Elphinstone.

Before leaving the Gulf, Loch summed up the position of the various Shaikhdoms. The most important and prosperous port was Muscat, whose ruler was now in possession of all his former dominions. Such was the state of peace at sea, that the Sultan was now using his ships of war for commercial purposes, carrying cargo between Muscat, India, Persia and Zanzibar. Loch mentions 'the selfish, tyrannical, misrule adopted by almost all' with the exception of the ruler of Muscat, of whom he says 'there was every appearance of his government lasting, unimpaired, during his existence'. This prophesy was to come true for Saiyid Said reigned until his death on October 19th 1856, 'when he passed quietly away when sailing in the sea of the Seychelles'. After Muscat came Bushire, where trade was flourishing in spite of the Shaikh's efforts to create a personal monopoly of all the trade in his port. The other places on the Persian coast were ruled by a number of almost independent Arab shaikhs, 'managing their own Sovereignties, both in respect of internal affairs, and external feuds as suited the whims and caprices of those who governed them'. In these states, lived some Armenians and a few Indians. The islands of Kishm and Hormuz and the town of Bundar Abbas, with its dependencies, on the Persian mainland, were held by the Sultan of Muscat 'under farm from the Persian Government'. On the Arabian coast, the Sultan's possessions extended from Masirah Island to Khor Fakhan, south of Ras Masandam.

Shaikh Sulman bin Ahmed, and his brother Shaikh Abdulla, were in possession of the Bahrain archipelago, and its numerous pearl banks, as well as Khor Hassan, and the Arabian coast as far as Katif, but the town of Katif was still in the hands of Jabr bin Rahmah. Bahrain was flourishing from the pearl industry, and from trade with other parts of the Gulf.

The Joasmi tribes occupied the Pirate Coast from Ras Masandam and the southern shore of the Gulf as far as Khor Hassan. Having lost their ships, and their fortifications having been demolished by the British, they were now at peace with their neighbours. Shaikh Hassan bin Rahmah had still not returned to Ras al Khaima, the once formidable pirate stronghold, Sharja, their second most important town, was under the rule of Shaikh Sultan bin Seggar.

Loch mentions that Taylor, the Resident at Basra, was not on good terms with the Turkish Governor. Soon after he left, Loch heard that the Residency had been temporarily removed from Basra to Grane, Kuwait. In all the ports, there was a revival of trade and ships were navigating the Gulf from coast to coast 'in perfect security, instead of creeping alongside during the day, afraid of being cut off if underweigh during the night'.

At midnight on September 30th, the *Eden* sailed out of Muscat harbour 'with a fine, light breeze off the shore'. Four days later, she passed one of the Sultan's ships on her way from Zanzibar to Muscat. On going on board her, Loch found that her cargo consisted of 'Elephants' Teeth, Gold dust and Ambergris'. Bombay was reached on October 13th, and here the *Eden* stayed for some time in dock, while repairs were carried out on the ship's bottom, which had been damaged when she grounded several times in the Gulf.

Loch took the opportunity of visiting Elephants' Island, which he had not seen before. He found the underground temples disappointing, and not as impressive as the much larger caves at Malta, or the galleries under the rock of Gibraltar. He did, however, admire 'the elaborate workmanship in the carving of figures and animals, which had withstood the rude hand of time, and the ruder hands of the Portuguese and the Mohammedans, which strike one with wonder and almost admiration for the forgotten people who constructed these temples'. He was, perhaps, more enthusiastic about the fish and the fruit in Bombay, particularly the mangoes, and the black and white pomphret, a fish which, he says, 'very much in taste resembles the John Dory, and in appearance not unlike the Bream of the Mediterranean'.

On October 27th, the *Eden* made sail out of Bombay harbour, bound for Trincomalee, carrying thirty-five tons of iron ballast to be landed at Cochin, where they anchored on November 6th. 'I here found my old acquaintances, Mr. and Mrs. Schuller, in good health, the former occupied with his contract of building two small frigates, for which the *Eden* had brought the ballast from Bombay.' Loch met another old friend at Cochin. Adey, 'the little Greek', who had been his interpreter in the Gulf, had by some means persuaded the Bombay Government to appoint him to supervise the building of the two frigates, though it seems unlikely that Adey knew anything about ship-building!

The *Eden* left Cochin on November 7th, but owing to contrary winds and currents, it was not until the 28th that she reached Ceylon. At Point de Galle 'the ship's company were occupied in receiving wood and water from the shore, by boats from the harbour, a most tiresome and tedious method, nor was it in my power to get them to bestir themselves, so it was December 2nd 1821 before the *Eden* sailed'. As they passed Dondra Head, a canoe came alongside with an enormous sword fish lashed to the craft. Loch bought it, and found that it measured eighteen feet six inches. 'I had part of the fish dressed for dinner, and found that it tasted exceedingly like Bonetta, the rest of the fish, I directed to be served out to the various messes, to the no small joy of the men.' Sailors in the ships in the Gulf, even in the hottest time of the year, lived mainly on salt beef, pork, plum pudding and pea soup, only very rarely were they given fresh vegetables, so fresh fish was a welcome change.

On January 6th 1821, the *Eden* anchored at Sangur Roads, the entrance to the Hooghly river. 'The roadstead,' said Loch, 'reminds me of lying at the Nore, so far as it has the appearance of an open anchorage, and the land, from which there is shelter, is very low. But there is no town such as Sheerness, and no even moderately high land. To the south-east, lies the island of Sangur covered with vegetation, the mangroves growing into the sea; to the east are the banks of the Hooghly, covered by jungle, which is the only thing to be seen.'

On the 7th, Loch boarded the pilot boat bound for Calcutta, taking with him Mr. Blackwood, one of his officers, the son of the Commander-in-Chief. The river was dangerous to navigate, and once the pilot boat was almost swamped, owing to the treacherous currents. 'I was surprised to see anxiety pictured in the manner and face of the pilot, as well as the people being more alive and active. The vessel was now making short bounds over the flood tide, against the north wind, when, all at once, the pilot called out "let go the anchor!" Down it went! The little brig touched the ground in a moment, and heeled over several streaks. Next moment, she swung with the velocity and strength of the tide, over the tail of the bank, and then righted in deep water.' The Pilot told Loch that 'many vessels, even large ones, had run on to the bank, and were rolled over by the strength of the tide, with all on board perishing'.

Higher up the river there were 'many elegant houses', and finally 'an expanse of water, more like a great lake than a portion of a river, the banks everywhere literally studded with palaces, the walls of which were covered by chanan, which takes a polish like marble. These buildings are in beautifully laid out grounds with magnificent trees. On the right bank are the delightful Botanic Gardens, near the walls of a Hindu college, now rising so as to show the extent of the building. The river then takes a gradual and beautiful turn to the left, where are placed Fort William, the Government House, and "the City of Palaces", as Calcutta is often called. Was it not for the unbearable heat of this climate, almost the whole year round, the enormous city with its magnificent white buildings, spires, cupolas and minarets under a clear blue sky, by the smooth great river with its splendid scenery of the Garden Reach, and its never-ending variety of vessels and craft passing and repassing with every tide, might be one of the most enjoyable places in the world.'

Loch landed at Garden Reach and went to the house of his cousin, John Adam, the son of William Adam of Blair Adam, whose sister, Mary, had married Loch's father. Loch was delighted to see John Adam, for whom he had a great regard. John Adam had a distinguished career in India, where his reputation for integrity, at variance with that of some of his contemporaries, who devoted their energies to enriching themselves, gained him the nickname of 'Honest John Adam'. He acted as Governor-General when Lord Hastings was on leave but, as Loch says, 'since the period I am writing, he fell a sacrifice to the baneful climate, yet not before he had raised himself to the highest pinnacle of honour, namely the succession to the Governor-generalship of India'. The rate of mortality among Europeans in Calcutta was higher than in most other parts of India. A writer says that it was not uncommon to have breakfast with a friend, apparently in good health, and to attend his funeral the same evening.

During the month that he spent at his cousin's house in Calcutta, Loch saw a good deal of the city and the neighbourhood. He was impressed by 'the comfort, neatness and appearance of wealth, and the enormous crowds of people flocking and bustling into Calcutta soon after daylight, and after sunset the same people returning, as if released from so many factories, all apparently happy, free and independent'. Having described the 'splendid and handsome buildings on the Grand Esplanade', he says, 'none of the streets in the part of the town where the natives live are to be compared with those which the European population inhabit, yet they are by no means mean, and though totally different in form and appearance, are very superior to the streets round Seven Dials, Wapping and St. Giles's, and various other parts of London. To be sure, there are no such streets and squares in Calcutta as there are in the West End, but again, there is nothing in London to equal the public buildings and those of the Europeans in the grounds of Charingo. The European population build themselves castles and palaces, keep enormous establishments, and live like princes. The Government House, and the Park and grounds of Barrackpore being the *ne plus ultra* of the whole of the human construction.' But another writer describes Barrackpore Park, which was 'created' by Lord Wellesley for 'rural privacy', as 'a specimen of architecture that has scarcely any claims to excellence'.

Soon after Loch's arrival, he and his cousin were invited to Barrackpore by the Governor-General, the Marquis of Hastings, who has been described as 'tall, upstanding, strong and athletic, with thick, black whiskers'. He was said to be 'the ugliest man in England, but this was balanced by his genial, affable manner'.

'It is impossible', said Loch, 'to give an adequate description of how much the park at Barrackpore struck me.' He describes 'the magnificent grandeur of the enormous, stately trees, the neatness with which the grounds were kept, the smooth roads and the sight of the great river sweeping past the grounds'. The house was not very large and Loch compared it, in size, to Lord Sidmouth's house in Richmond Park, 'though different in appearance and architecture'. Surrounding the main house were a number of bungalows for the accommodation of visitors, 'giving somewhat the appearance of a beautiful little village of neat thatched cottages. There is also a banquetting room, built in the form of a Grecian temple, which appears to have been done with remarkable taste. Not far distance from the house, is an extensive Menagerie and Aviary. It is an interesting sight to observe, each morning, the tamest of these animals and birds driven out before the sun becomes too hot for them.' The procession of beasts and birds, led by keepers, used to emerge in pairs. They included cheetahs, wild asses, storks, pelicans, cameleopards (giraffes), Adjutant birds and Secretary birds. 'It brought forcibly to my mind, Raphael's representation of the coming out from the Ark.'

On the morning after their arrival at Barrackpore the Governor-General with Admiral Sir Henry Blackwood the Naval Commander-in-Chief, drove up in a carriage and four a little before daylight. 'We had, the evening before, been informed by the Marquis of Hastings that he had ordered his elephants to be ready so that there might be a search for wild boar.' Loch and Adam drove in the carriage with Hastings and the Admiral through the park, and then out into the jungle till they reached the place where the elephants were drawn up in a line. 'I had never before in my life seen so many of these huge sagacious creatures collected together, caparisoned and ready for a hunt, but I was determined not to let the natives see my real feelings of wonder, from the dread of being ridiculed as "a Johnny Newcome".'

'Suppose the body of a chaise, fit only to contain two persons, to have the top cut off from it, then you have the Howdah which is placed on the back of the elephant. You ascend to it by a ladder, the Mahoot, at the same time, directing the animal to place his trunk so that he may put his foot on the curve made for its reception, is raised to the neck of the creature, across which he rides, straggle legged. His boathook shaped instrument is on the ear of the elephant, the hook being for this purpose, and the sharp point for pricking the elephant, when it does not obey the orders given to it.

'As soon as all were adjusted and ready the elephants moved on, abreast, in a line, from 15 to 20 yards apart. To me, it was the most uncomfortable motion that I could have conceived, between a walk and a hobble, and so irregular, that I could not in any way adapt myself to it. I was pressing with my foot and with my back, at the same time, to keep steady.

'We quickly got into the jungle country with long grass and reeds from which numbers of birds rose, among which the most beautiful was the Indian pheasant, but its beauty is all that it is worth. At last a bird, which I supposed to be a partridge, got up. I forgot that I was in the presence of the Governor-General, and I really did not know that if a bird flew across His Excellency I should not presume to fire until he did. So off went my gun, at the same instant as did the gun of the Marquis of Hastings. Down came the bird. Now I was so bad a shot that, had I been on my feet, instead of being tossed up and down in the Howdah, I could not have killed in one out of five shots. Yet it was thought necessary to exclaim "it was Your Excellency who shot it". I knew myself that I could not have done the bloody deed, and I felt ashamed of my want of good breeding and etiquette.

'Shortly after this, a herd of wild swine started rushing through between the legs of the elephants. What took place with the other elephants, I cannot state, but as soon as the boar rushed between the legs of the one on which I was mounted, it threw its trunk into the air, trumpeting, and at the same time, drawing its body together in a most disagreeable manner, so that I expected something like a tiger to spring out. However, my mind was not long left in suspense. The animals were goaded into a most rapid pace, in chase, and strange to say, if the walk was uncomfortable, the run was most rapid and easy. The herd was overtaken, and the Marquis shot one of them. Thus ended our morning's sport.'

On another day, Loch and Adam went to Serampore to visit the Missionary School, kept by a Mr. Carey, where they saw 'native children learning the Scriptures in various languages and the printing press, now worked by steam, where they were throwing off 23 different translations of the Scriptures in as many different languages'. They called on a rich Nabob, who lived near Calcutta, 'whose gardens were surrounded by dens, in which were wild beasts, lions, tigers, panthers, and other ferocious animals, which seemed to me finer than those at Barrackpore, though not so numerous'.

One evening, before dinner, Lord Hastings drew Loch aside, and 'with the best of feelings, not knowing the strong affection and intimacy between Mr. Adam's family and myself, acquainted me of the death of Mr. Adam's youngest brother'. Hastings asked Loch to break the news to his cousin John Adam.

'I will not attempt to describe the sudden, dreadful stun I felt. It was necessary to muster up every effort to restrain the grief which a man naturally suffers at the sudden intelligence of the demise of one whom he loves. What a time it appeared from the moment of our sitting down to dinner until withdrawing! How tiresome and irksome was the conversation, at least those scraps of it which I caught! Again, when in the drawing room, I thought I never would succeed in drawing Mr. Adam away. I made a thousand excuses to lead him to retire, which he thought a breach of good breeding. At last, I told him that a ship had arrived from England (which had been concealed from him) by which, I thought, we might have intelligence from home. This succeeded, and we started for Calcutta, but I would not wish my worst enemy to suffer what I did when I found myself seated by Mr. Adam in the chaise. I leave it to those who have feelings of affection to judge for themselves what we both suffered, nor do I think it unlike a man to be a human being.'

Loch paid two visits to Barrackpore, and then returned to Calcutta to prepare for his final departure from India. He describes the morning and evening scene on the Esplanade Road, 'which is as smooth as it is possible for art to make it, a really splendid carriage way. Mr. Elphinstone, the brother of the Governor of Bombay, kindly took me in his gig. It would have been supposed that all Calcutta turned out; as to the number of vehicles, it was like Hyde Park on a day when it was moderately crowded. The number of different kinds of vehicles was truly amusing, from the most splendid carriages, built after the most perfect in London, or imported from England, to the most miserable hackery or bullock carts, added to which, there were equestrians, and those born in palanquins, besides many natives walking or lounging. There were huddled together in a space of not more than a mile, many thousands of every religion, caste, country and dress, speaking most of the languages under the sun.'

Another place which roused Loch's admiration was the Botanical Garden opposite Adam's house. They crossed the river in a 'snake boat', a narrow sharp-pointed vessel rowed by eight men 'who made the boat, as sailors say, almost fly through the water'. The gardens were started by Colonel Kyd in 1786. At the time when Loch saw them, they contained almost 4,000 different species of trees, shrubs and plants. Among the features of the garden, were magnificent banyan trees covering vast areas of ground, and a Burmese Pagoda, somewhat reminiscent of the one at Kew Gardens. Visitors were asked not to pick the flowers, but when they arrived at one bush, which had magnificent flowers, 'not unlike the Cardinal Plant, only much larger', Loch was invited to pick some. He did so. 'No sooner had I plucked it, than I felt as if I had been stung by fifty wasps. The flower left my hand quicker than it had come into it, and in spite of shaking and jerking my arm, I found numbers of Great Black Ants settled and biting with all their might, and to no small purpose, as it was a real pain. This garden is different to the Garden of Eden. You are informed on entering that you are not to pluck the fruits, but when you reach this bush, you are allowed to do so; yet it is similar, for you are no sooner enticed to pluck the flower, that you are heartily punished for attempting to ravish the beauties of the shrub.'

Before he left Calcutta, Loch went over the dockyards. They, too, had been built by Colonel Kyd, who was at one time Chief Engineer of the East India Company. The docks were known as 'Kydapore'. They were now managed by Kyd's two sons, 'East Indiamen' who were famous ship-builders. In 1818, H.M.S. *Hastings*, named after Lord Hastings, a 74-gun ship, was built in these docks. The docks, according to Loch, were about the size of those at Deptford, affording employment to thousands of people. The dockyard was a private concern, owned by the Kyd family, whose founder occupied a large and handsome house on the bank of the river overlooking the yards.

On February 4th, Loch embarked on board one of the pilot boats, with Adam and Elphinstone, and proceeded to Kedgeree, going on board the *Eden* on the following day. On the 6th, Admiral Blackwood joined them, and Loch 'had now to bid farewell to Mr. Adam and Elphinstone, with whom I had lived for several weeks on the most intimate terms of friendship. It was a last farewell, the climate destroyed them both.' The *Eden* sailed at daylight on the 7th, and anchored at Madras on the 24th, 'a most tedious and tiresome passage', owing to contrary winds, which reduced the speed of the ship to not more than twenty to thirty miles a day, 'but the sea was without a ripple'. The *Eden* stayed one day at Madras, and then sailed for Trincomalee, which was reached on March 7th, 'thus we had been just four weeks in running a distance that would not have been more than ten days, had it been during the North-east Monsoon'. On March 13th 1821, the *Eden* weighed, in company with the *Leander* and the *Liverpool*, and ran out of Trincomalee Harbour on her homeward voyage to England.

At the end of his diary, Loch mentions the number of men whom he lost during the time that the *Eden* was in the East. The ship carried one hundred and twenty-five men and nineteen officers when she sailed from Plymouth. Of these, seventeen seamen and four officers died, and two seamen lost their lives in accidents. As Loch says, the number of casualties was 'a large proportion for so small a complement'. But the number of deaths was probably no higher than the average proportion in other ships which were engaged in similar duties in the East.

Some time after leaving the Gulf, Loch was given command of H.M.S. *Victory* and, in 1841, he was Superintendent of the Quarantine of Stangate Creek, in the Medway. In 1847, he became Naval A.D.C. to Queen Victoria, three years later, he was promoted to Rear-Admiral of the Blue, and in 1862, he was put on the Reserved Half-Pay List, as an Admiral.

Loch was a personal friend of Queen Adelaide, who left with him the copy of a memorandum intimating her wishes regarding her funeral arrangements. He took Princess Amelia in his ship for a voyage to Mauritius, when she was suffering from consumption, from which she subsequently died; the sea trip was probably regarded as being beneficial to her health.   On another occasion, he took the Duke of Cumberland in his ship to Canada.   He lived in Edinburgh until his wife died in 1859.   After her death, he retired to Cheltenham, where 'he followed a retired mode of life' until he died in 1863, at the age of seventy-five.

A portrait of Francis Loch, after he retired, shows him a very typical Victorian old gentleman, seated by a small table, on which his top hat is deposited, with a book in his hand.   He has white hair, white whiskers and a chin beard and a slightly petulant expression on his full, round face.

In 1908, Percy Gordon Loch, who was then in the Indian Army, was employed as an Attaché to the Resident at Bushire, and in 1916 was appointed Political Agent in Bahrain and again in 1932.   Gordon Loch was the great-great-nephew of Francis Loch, who almost a century before, had played such an active part in the affairs of Bahrain; one of his great interests was genealogy, and it was while he was in Bahrain, that he completed his book *The Family of Loch*.   He used often to talk to me, in the old Political Agency at Bahrain, about his naval ancestor who had been there so many years before, but it seems that he had then no knowledge of the diary kept by Francis Loch, during the expedition against the Pirate Coast.

CONCLUSION

LIFE in the Persian Gulf today depends on oil; 150 years ago, it was centred on piracy. The smoke which now rises in the daytime, and the flares which light the night sky above the oil fields, which are visible for many miles, are caused by burning off gas. At one time, conflagrations such as these, would have signified the destruction of villages by pirate hordes.

There have been more changes in the Persian Gulf in the last forty years than during the last century and a half. Oil, air travel and wireless have changed the Gulf Arabs more than any other developments. Wealth from oil has provided schools, hospitals and many social services for the people of the oil states, and has given well paid employment to Arabs from the Shaikhdoms where no oil has been found. Air travel, wireless and television have enabled the Gulf Arabs to realise how the rest of the world lives, and to mingle with people of other races and religions.

The degree of change in different parts of the Gulf has depended upon whether or not oil is being produced in the state. Kuwait, in Loch's time, was a small Arab settlement, which he only mentions once in his diary. Forty years ago, it was a quiet, pleasant little Arab coast town, whose people were comfortably prosperous from pearl diving, boat building and trade. Today, it is a metropolis, the El Dorado of the Middle East. It looks more like a flamboyant American city than a Persian Gulf port, with a population enormously swollen by immigrants from all over the Middle East.

Bahrain has always been a comparatively thriving country. From earliest times it was a commercial entrepot, for centuries it was the centre of the pearl industry, and it had the great advantage of having plenty of fresh water for agriculture. Loch describes it as a flourishing place, and that description fits it today. It was the first state in the Gulf in which oil was found, but it has the smallest oil field in the Middle East. Its income has risen from £90,000 in 1926 to about £6,000,000 in 1965. But this cannot be compared to the enormous revenue of Kuwait, which is more than £200,000,000, or Qatar, with over £20,000,000, or Abu Dhabi which, it is believed, may one day rival Kuwait.

Some of the buildings which Loch mentions in Bahrain are still standing, and forty years ago, the bazaars were much the same as when he saw them. Today, there are big shops, with plate glass windows, displaying goods from all parts of the world; the number of cars is causing traffic problems, and there are more Arabs wearing European clothes than Arab dress. New western-style buildings, dual carriage ways, electric pylons and hundreds of modern bungalows detract somewhat from its former pictur-esque appearance. But the changes in Bahrain have not been as sudden and dramatic as those in Kuwait and Qatar. Because it always enjoyed moderate prosperity, though to a greater degree after oil was found in 1932, it has developed gradually, which was all for the best.

Qatar is not mentioned in Loch's diary. It used to be an appendage of Bahrain, a barren, primitive country inhabited by a few Bedouin tribes. It is the newest of the Gulf Shaikhdoms having been established for less than a century. Since oil was found, in 1939, its one town, Doha, has become a flourishing city, with all the attributes of newly acquired wealth, and a vastly increased population of foreign immigrants, as in Kuwait.

If Loch were to see the Shaikhdoms of the Pirate Coast today, he would find less to surprise him. The people themselves look much the same as when he saw them, their dress has scarcely altered, and their way of life has not noticeably changed. In most of the Shaikhdoms, the rulers are descended from the pirate chiefs and, forty years ago, their appearance and outlook did not differ greatly from that of their ancestors. Today, however, it is not unusual to meet descendants of the pirate chiefs, dressed by London tailors, staying at West End hotels, when they come to London to discuss political matters or oil affairs, though at home they wear Arab dress.

Some of the forts which existed in his day are still standing, but there are now schools and dispensaries in Ras al Khaima, once the pirate capital, Sharja and Dubai. Dubai is now a thriving port, producing a sufficient income from trade, not from oil, to enable the Shaikh to carry out modern developments. Abu Dhabi, the most recent oil state, is regarded as a problem child by the British authorities. The Shaikh is unwilling to see his country suddenly swung into the maelstrom of modernisation so his determination to move slowly is viewed with disapproval.

Today, the Sultanate of Muscat and Oman, the largest, and for many years the most important state in the Gulf, no longer retains the position which it held in the 19th century, when its ruler was the central figure in Gulf affairs. It has an area of over 82,000 square miles, and a population of more than half a million Arabs but it now has little commerce and lower revenues than some of the smaller Gulf States. But in spite of its comparative poverty, Muscat retains much of the dignity which it enjoyed in the past. It has none of the brash 'nouveau riche' atmosphere of Kuwait, it is not full of Europeans and crowded with American cars like Bahrain – it would be difficult to use cars in Muscat – and there are no ostentatious palaces like those in Qatar.

Arabs in the rich oil states are critical of the lack of progress in Muscat, but it is difficult for a ruler to develop and modernise a large country without adequate funds. Forty years ago, Muscat had a larger budget than Bahrain, today it has less than one-fifth of Bahrain's income.

The Sultan, who is the thirteenth of his dynasty to reign, is a man of learning, having been educated at a college in India. Having seen the difficulties, caused in some of the other states by an influx of foreigners from the Middle East, he is reluctant to encourage them to come to Oman, which is still a territory little known to Europeans. It has such a variety of climate and terrain that it offers great possibilities for agricultural and mineral development. A search for oil is being carried out and the prospects of finding oil appear to be encouraging. Muscat has scarcely changed since Loch first saw it on New Year's Eve, 1818. It is not a place which could change. It owes its almost dramatic appearance to natural surroundings, to the towering black mountains, which hem in the little white town, and the still, deep water in the bay which reflects the steep craggy cliffs surmounted by fortifications.

The change in the mentality of the Gulf Arabs has accelerated since the coming of the oil era. Forty years ago, they hardly concerned themselves with the affairs of the outside world. Not more than a dozen men from the Gulf had ever been in Europe. The Gulf Arabs had closer connections with India than with the countries of the Middle East, for most of the Gulf trade was with

Bombay. The few young men who were sent abroad for education, went to schools or colleges in India. Today, many young men are receiving higher education in the universities of the Middle East, and they are keenly interested in Middle East politics as well as in those of the West.

Today, there is much talk here about 'the haves and the have-nots' in the Gulf which, in general, means the people in the oil Shaikhdoms and those of the Shaikhdoms where there is no oil. In the Gulf there has never been acute want, and the inhabitants of the Shaikhdoms appear to be healthier than those of other Middle East countries. The sea provides unlimited quantities of varied and most excellent fish, dates are grown in Hasa, Bahrain and Oman, and there has always been enough money in the Shaikhdoms to import rice, sugar, tea and coffee, and other goods from India. The fact that many of the poorer Arabs live in barastis is often mentioned by Europeans as a proof of their poverty, but in a damp, hot climate where the rainfall is only two or three inches a year, a barasti is a better habitation than a house, unless the latter is provided with electric fans or air-conditioning. The Gulf is not one of those places where there are immense differences between 'the haves and the have-nots!'

It is only in recent years that the younger generation of Gulf Arabs have become politically minded, which is the inevitable result of education, foreign travel and broadcasting. In the oil states the sense of values has changed. The possession of a date garden, a fish trap, a pearling dhow or some camels is no longer an indication that a man is well to do. Television sets, radios and cars have now become status symbols. But it is open to doubt whether the people are more happy and contented today, than they were forty years ago, or even when Loch was in the Gulf.

Loch's diary makes the reader realise how many British lives were sacrificed in suppressing piracy. Later, the British succeeded in putting an end to the slave trade – but that is another story. Britain achieved these objects, not with any ambitions towards territorial conquests, but in order to make the seas safe for the ships of all nations and to put an end to the people of the Gulf carrying off their fellow creatures into slavery. Unfortunately very few of the present generation of Gulf Arabs realise the part which Britain played in the past.

BIBLIOGRAPHY

Aitchison, C. W., *A Collection of Treaties, Engagements and Sannads relating to India and Neighbouring Countries.* Vol. XI. 1919.

Albuquerque, Affonso de, *Commentaries.* Hakl Soc. 1875.

Alexander, C., *Baghdad in Bygone Days.* 1928.

Arnold-Foster, F. D., *The Madagascar Pirates.* 1957.

Astley, T., *Voyages and Travels.* 1745.

Badger, G. P., *History of the Imams and Seyyids of Oman*, by Salil ibn Razik. Hakl Soc. 1871.

Belgrave, C. D., *Personal Column.* 1960.

Bent, J. T., *Southern Arabia.* 1900.

Bibby, T. G., *Four Thousand Years Ago.* 1961.

Bibby, T. G., *The Testimony of the Spade.* 1956.

Blunt, Lady A., *A Pilgrimage to Nejd.* 1879.

Bruce, J., *Annals of the Honorable East India Company.* 1810.

Buckingham, J. S., *Travels in Syria, Media and Persia.* 1830.

Burckhart, J. L., *Notes on the Bedouins and Wahabys.* 1831.

Carre, Abbé, *Travels.*

Chardin, J., *Travels into Persia and the East Indies.* 1692.

Chesney, F. R., *Narrative of the Euphrates Expedition.* 1868.

Curzon, Hon. G. N., *Persia and the Persian Question.* 1892.

Danvers, E. C., *The Portuguese in India.* 1894.

Della Valle, P., *Fameux Voyages de Pietro della Valle.* 1664.

Downton, N., *Voyage to the East Indies.* 1681.

Faria Y Sousa, M. de, *The Portuguese in Asia.* Trans. J. Stevens. 1695.

Fontanier, V., *Voyage dans l'Inde et dans le Golfe Persique.* 1844.

Foster, W., *Letters received by the East India Company from its servants in the East.* 1898.

Francklin, W., *Observations made on a tour from Bengal to Persia.* 1790.

Fryer, J., *A New Account of the East Indies.* 1727.

Gibbon, E., *The History of the Decline and Fall of the Roman Empire.* 1828.

Graves, P., *The Life of Sir Percy Cox.* 1942.

Hamilton, A., *A New Account of the East Indies.* 1727.

Harrison, P. W., *The Arab at Home.* 1923.

Johnson, C., *Lives of the most Notorious Pirates.* Folio Soc. 1962.

Johnson, W. G., *General Perronet Thompson.* 1957.

Keppel, G., *Personal Narrative of a Journey from India to England.* 1827.

Le Strange, G., *The Lands of the Eastern Caliphate.* 1905.

Loch, G., *The Family of Loch*. 1934.

Longrigg, S. H., *Four Centuries of Iraq History*. 1925.

Low, C. R., *History of the Indian Navy*. 1877.

Malcolm, J., *History of Persia*. 1829.

Marco Polo. *The Book of Ser Marco Polo the Venetian*. Ed. by Sir Henry Yule. 1921.

Maurizi, V., *History of Seyd Said*. 1819.

Miles, S. B., *The Country and Tribes of the Persian Gulf*. 1919.

Mir Khwand, *History of Persia*. Trans. J. Stevens. 1715.

Nebhan, M. K., *History of Bahrain*. Not published. About 1915.

Niebuhr, C., *Description de l'Arabie*. 1771.

O'Leary, de L., *Arabia before Mohammed*. 1927.

Ouseley, W., *Travels in various countries of the East*. 1819.

Palgrave, W. G., *Narrative of a year's journey through Central and Eastern Arabia*. 1865.

Philby, H. St. J. B., *Arabia of the Wahabis*. 1928.

Philby, H. St. J. B., *Saudi Arabia*. 1955.

Ruete, R. S., *Said bin Sultan*. 1929.

Sadlier, G. F., *Diary of a Journey across Arabia*.

Saldanha, J. A., *Selections from State Papers*. 1908.

Stevens, J., *The History of Persia*. 1715.

Sykes, P. M., *A History of Persia*. 1922.

Tavanier, J. B., *Voyages*. 1678.

Teixeira, P., *Travels and Kings of Harmuz*. Hakl Soc. 1902.

Van Linschoten, J. H., *Discours of voyage into ye Easte and West Indies*. 1598.

Villiers, A. T., *The Indian Ocean*. 1952.

Vincent, W., *Voyage of Nearchus*. 1809.

Waring, E. S., *A Tour to Shiraz and History of Persia*. 1809.

Wellsted, J. R., *Travels to the City of the Caliphs*. 1840.

Wilson, A. T., *The Persian Gulf*. 1924.

Woodruff, P., *The Founders*. 1954.

Reports of the Danish Archaeological Expedition to Bahrain.

INDEX

French East India Company, 17
— Embassy to Persia, 17
Fryer, Dr. John, 13, 16, 39, 64
Fury, 31
Funchal, 39
Funeral at Rio, 44

Gama, Vasco da, 6
Gazelle, 99-100
Gerrha, 2
Ghatrusha, 131
Gibraltar, 138, 170, 180
Gift Horses, 156, 178
Gil Blas, 69
Gipsies, 170
Goa, 6, 15, 50-52
Gombroon, 13
Governor General of India, 32, 103
Graham, Captain, 32
Grane, 123, 179
Granis, 86
Gufa, 90
Gujarat, 53

Haffar Cut, 169
Hajar, 3
Hall, Lieutenant, 34
Hamilton, Captain A., 14
Hasa, 3
Hastings, Lord, 103, 182-5
Hastings, H.M.S., 186
Hassan bin Rahmah, Joasmi Chief, 95, 121, 141, 143, 173
Hawala Tribe, 19, 20, 115, 153
Hawks, 100
Hejaz, 27, 105
Herbert, Sir Thomas, 13
Hippalus, 3
Hormuz, straits of, 1; island, 5, 6, 7, 9; taken by Anglo Persian force, 10-12; 13, 179
Hooghly River, 181
Horse, riding, 39, 68; trade, 89
'Honest Ali', 84, 101
Husayn, Shah, 18, 19
Hyde Park, 186

Ibn Taymiya, 25
Ibrahaim Pasha, 103, 105, 121
India, 10, 49, 191, 192
Indian Navy, 28
Indus, 2
Iraq, 4
Isa bin Ali, Shaikh of Bahrain, 79
Isfahan, 17, 18
Islam, established in the Gulf, 4
Itinerant singer, 98

Jalahamah Tribe, 75, 122
Jamaica, 33
James I, King, 11, 13

James, 10
Jask, 10
Jebel Dukhan, 153
Jerun, 5
Jews, 50
Jhelum, 2
Joasmi tribe, 22, 36; prisoners, 73; 80, 105; women, 140
Jones, Felix, 85
— Sir Harford, 32
Juvenile Drama, the, 61-62

Kais, 5, 19
Kalb Ali, 21
Karim Khan, 85
Katif, 2, 8, 103, 104, 130, 179
Kawari, 156
Kazaroon, 114
Kenn Island, 29; Cape, 74
Kerbala, 27
Kharak Island, 86, 116, 150
Khalifah Tribe, 26, 75, 115
Khalifah bin Mohammed, Shaikh, 124
Khalifah bin Sulman, Shaikh, 159
Kier, General Sir W. G., 136, 145, 170
King, Admiral Sir Richard, 46, 109, 169
Kishm Island, 8, 10, 11, 28, 31, 32, 34, 37, 71, 72, 73, 111, 143, 145, 174, 179
Koran, 25
Kung, 13, 15
Kutch, 53
Kuwait, 24, 31, 107, 123, 179, 189
Kyd, Colonel, 186
Kydapore, 186

Lacu, original name of Loch, ix
Lamu, 22
Latif Khan, 19, 20
Leander, 187
Linga, 28, 130, 133
Littlefield, Major, 96
Liverpool, H.M.S., 66, 134, 135-7, 140-1, 187
Loch, F. E., Captain R.N.: ancestry and diary, ix; sails in command of H.M.S. *Eden* June 9th 1818, 38; at Funchal June 18th, 39; leaves Madeira June 21st, accompanied by *Tees*, 41; arrives Rio de Janeiro July 26th and leaves Aug. 6th, 43; arrives Trincomalee Oct. 6th, 46; sails for Bombay Nov. 6th, 48; anchors at Cochin Nov. 11th, 49; arrives at Goa Nov. 20th, 50; arrives at Bombay Nov. 22nd, 52; leaves Bombay Dec. 4th, 53; sights two dhows off Ambah Dec. 18th, 53; anchors at Astola and meets *Psyche*, 55; encounters pirates Dec.

Loch, F. E., Captain R.N.—*cont.*
25th, 56; anchors off Makran coast,
57; sights seven pirate ships Dec.
28th, 57; captures one pirate ship,
58; anchors in Muscat Cove Dec.
31st, 1818, 60; lands at Muscat Jan.
1st, 1819, 62; stays three days in
Muscat then cruises for a week
along Persian coast, 71; sights seven
large pirate ships Jan. 10th, one
escapes, 71-73; crosses Gulf to Ras
al Khaima, 73; arrives at Bushire
Jan. 23rd, 74; in command of
squadron for rescue of European
lady at Bahrain, 78; abandons
search for her, and goes to Bushire,
81; returns to Bushire and stays
with the Resident, Bruce, 84; sails
from Bushire Feb. 28th and arrives
Basra March 7th, 86-87; starts for
Bushire March 16th, with Bruce
and Colquhoun, 94; arrives Bushire
March 21st, 95; goes for tour in
Persia with Bruce and Major Littlefield, 96; returns to Bushire
April 11th, and meets Shaikh, 100-
1; leaves Bushire for Bombay May
2nd, 101; sights six large dhows
near Quorns, 101; pursues them to
Ras al Khaima, 102; reaches Muscat
May 15th, 103; meets Captain G.
Foster Sadlier, 103; sails from Mus-
cat May 16th, 107; arrives Bombay
May 24th, 108; arrives Trincomalee,
109; lands at Madras, 109; meets
Colonel Mansel, 109; refits at Trin-
comalee July 2nd, 110; sails for
Muscat Aug. 20th, 111; arrives at
Muscat Sept. 30th, 111; chases
pirate vessels near Barka, 111;
meets Wakil for negotiations about
Truce, 112; visits Shaikh Abdul
Rasool in his caravanserai, 113; in
Bushire during Ramadhan, 119;
meets Rahmah bin Jabr, 122, 129,
130; with Bruce seizes pirate ships
at Linga, 133; leaves Bushire Oct.
20th, awaiting expedition from
Bombay, 133; meets Company's
Tormati Oct. 24th, 134; arrives Ras
al Khaima Dec. 1st, 136; with
Liverpool takes part in attack on
Ras al Khaima Dec. 3rd, 137; sails
for Kishm Dec. 13th, 143; sails for
Ras al Khaima Dec. 26th, 143; at
meeting of General Kier with Hassan bin Rahmah, 143; with Bruce
leaves Ras al Khaima Jan. 3rd,
1820, for expedition against Joasmi
pirates at Bahrain, 150; they interview the Shaikh of Asaloo, 151;
destroys two pirate ships, 151;
with Bruce dines with Shaikh Abdulla at Muharraq, 157; destroys
two pirate ships at Bahrain and
captures three, 157; and pearl-
diving, 163; leaves Bahrain Jan.
27th and deposits pearls with
Bruce, 167; leaves Bushire for
Basra, Feb. 5th, 168; returns from
Bushire March 10th and stays with
Taylor, 170; and Necromancer, 171;
visits Bushire March 31st, 172; sails
May 3rd, and spends four weeks in
Indian Ocean, 173; at Muscat, 174;
at Bushire for the last time, 176;
final visit to Muscat, 178; sums up
positions of Shaikhdoms, 178; leaves
Muscat Sept. 30th and arrives
Bombay Oct. 13th, 179; to Cochin
Oct. 27th with iron ballast, 180;
arrives Ceylon Nov. 28th, 180;
anchors at Sangur Roads Jan. 6th,
1821, 181; in pilot boat with Blackwood to Calcutta on 7th, 181; stays
with his cousin John Adam, 182;
both stay with Lord Hastings at
Government House, 183; boar hunt
on elephants, 183; visits Missionary
School at Serampore, 185; visits
Botanical Gardens, 186; visits dockyard, 186; embarks on *Eden* Feb.
5th, 187; anchors at Madras Feb.
24th, 187; starts for home March
13th 1821, 187; subsequent career,
187-8
— David Henry, ix
— George of Drylaw, ix
— Mary Freda, ix
— Percy Gordon, 188
Locusts, 172
Lousa, Count, coat of arms, 8
Luft, 34

Macaulay, Lord, 24
Madagascar, 28
Madeira, 39; garden at, 40; wines, 40
Madras, 39, 41, 109, 173-4
Makan, 2
Makran, 22, 57
Malabar Coast, 49
Malcolm, of Poltalloch, 99
— Sir John, 21, 32, 98, 99
Maldive Islands, 51
Malta, 180
Manama, 76, 77
Manesty, Mr. Samuel, 30, 88, 89, 91
Mangoes, 46-47
Mansel, Colonel John, 38, 43, 47, 109
Marco Polo, 5